MATERNAL THINKING
Gifts, Mothers' Bodies, and Earth

PROCEEDINGS OF THE ASSOCIATION
FOR THE STUDY OF WOMEN AND MYTHOLOGY
VOLUME 4

Edited by
Sid Reger, Mary Jo Neitz,
Denise Mitten, and Simone Clunie

Printed in the United States of America
ISBN: 978-1-960922-99-1

Published by

Women and Myth Press
PO Box 150018, Van Brunt Station, Brooklyn, NY 11215
www.womenandmyth.org

Interior and cover designed by Rebekkah Dreskin ~ www.blameitonrebekkah.com
Front cover art "Bee Goddess of Rhodes Banner" by Lydia Ruyle
Bee goddess logo by Sid Reger

DEDICATION

All women and their kin and kith benefit from the deep wisdom of Indigenous women. Indigenous women are leaders in modelling reciprocal relationships with the more than human worlds—those who fly, swim, walk, and remain in place. Also, we must never forget the missing, murdered, and incarcerated Indigenous women worldwide. This volume is dedicated to Indigenous women everywhere.

CONTENTS

FOREWORD

This volume, which focuses on the theme of motherhood and maternal relations, contains a range of papers that shed light on this topic from a variety of perspectives. Various academics have contributed a wealth of insights from different cultures: the Near East, European, American, Indigenous, and also from different times, such as the past of the Bronze Age and the present of our own epoch.

The common "thread" throughout these contributions is the centrality of motherhood. They exhibit a profound awareness of motherhood, be it human motherhood, the key to creating and maintaining a caring and healthy society, or the motherhood of the great Mother Earth, with which it is necessary to develop a loving relationship, not only in order to survive but also to be a nurturing member in the web of all beings. This motherhood-oriented approach was lost with the development of patriarchy around a few thousand years ago, a development which deeply debased motherhood and exploited women, and whose devastating effects have now reached their peak, endangering life itself on Earth.

During the longest periods of time, humans respected motherhood as the most important function in society, and they venerated Mother Earth as the all-embracing primordial goddess with many faces. This is the core value in matriarchal societies of the past and in some Indigenous ones that still are with us today. They are all mother-centered and motherhood forms the basis of their cultural model, as has been shown by the new discipline of Modern Matriarchal Studies. Matriarchies take their values from the prototypical behavior of the mother: nurturing, caring, gift giving, peace keeping, and with perfect reciprocity, thereby creating a peaceful, egalitarian society. They lived, and still live, in harmony with Mother Nature, whom they regard as their teacher. For thousands of millennia, this was the common way of life for humanity, and it can still be found today, repeated in how each individual mother cares for a child. Humanity must return to a mother-centered, matriarchal future, or we will have no future at all.

This maternal attitude and approach are wonderfully reflected in each of the contributions to this volume, but the papers also act as a warning, underlining the need to put a stop to the lethal compulsion in which humans seem to be lost today. In principle, they bring matriarchal values into the fore again. This can take the form of Indigenous women elders and maternal gift-giving in material and linguistic terms, or as a total change of perspective for a history that had been totally obscured by male interpretations, thereby regaining pieces of the matriarchal worldview. Or it can take the form of the sacredness of healing powers in myths and the female body, including the sacredness of grief, which can transform, as well as a practical undertaking to invent and develop new forms of a mother-centered, integrative lifestyles through art and rituals.

It is to the great credit of the women who founded the "Association for the Study of Women and Mythology" that they have dedicated this volume to the central importance of motherhood, a motherhood that is free from patriarchal fetters, thereby helping to reclaim motherhood as the basis of life and the power of healing. It is absolutely necessary to bring the origins of our existence back into the fore, in all ways possible, and this particularly holds true for our shared home, Mother Earth.

~ Heide Goettner-Abendroth

INTRODUCTION

MATERNAL THINKING:
Gifts, Mothers' Bodies, and Earth

*Volume 4, Proceedings of the Association
for the Study of Women and Mythology*

We are living in a time of crisis. Humans are destroying Earth, our home, and thus, humankind and other than human inhabitants. Individuals who control important resources have created structures that benefit themselves and exploit others and the environments we inhabit together. In her recent book, *Oneness vs the 1%*,[1] ecofeminist, scholar, and agricultural activist Vandana Shiva provides powerful examples of the effects and dangers of First World, single-model agricultural development, and the harmfulness of "philanthrocapitalism" as practiced by Bill Gates, Warren Buffet, Mark Zuckerberg, and other wealthy individuals. In a panel presentation organized by the Maternal Gift Economy Movement organization in November 2021, Shiva cites 2011 global estimates from a paper by Robert Costanza and colleagues[2] of Nature's monetary value at \$125 trillion per year versus GDP (exchange economy total) at \$75 trillion. These two figures, in Shiva's words, represent a process in which the exchange economy "floats on a sea of gifts" from the Earth, from women, and from the ancestors."[3] Shiva has campaigned against globalization, monoculture, and genetically engineered seeds. She is an advocate for native seeds, organic farming, and fair trade, and she calls for local, diverse, and democratic approaches to growing food and living with care on Mother Earth where no one owns the seeds or the land. When so many people experience fear, social chaos, and threats to planetary ecosystems, this is a vital message, one that resonates with the work of the Association for the Study of Women and Mythology (ASWM).

The ASWM is dedicated to a vision of another way of being with the Earth, living in relations of respect and mutuality with all beings. Our mission supports scholarship that presents the stories and values of cultures that honor our mother the Earth and reciprocal and gift-giving relationships among all who dwell here. We continue to learn from the pathbreaking work of archaeologist and folklorist Maria Gimbutas,[4] whose excavation of Neolithic sites in southern and eastern Europe provided evidence of early egalitarian cultures where women shared power with men in peaceful societies. The archaeological record indicates that these peaceful societies were conquered by warriors on horses who came from the Northern Steppes (the Kurgan hypothesis). ASWM appreciates the research of the many scholars who continue to bring forward knowledge of these egalitarian Bronze Age cultures. We look to Indigenous scholars who bring a practiced understanding of reciprocity through their local Indigenous and traditional ecological knowledges (ITEK) to ASWM's collective archive, adding those stories and ways of being to the reflections of the ASWM community of scholars. ASWM also seeks other scholars who trace specific rituals and artifacts honoring mother/goddess energies and generative powers tied to particular places, and scholarship that demonstrates how the stories and rituals are retained in place memory (see Volume 3). Finally, ASWM appreciates the work of critics, those who deconstruct the process through which patriarchal cultures appropriated, covered over, or eradicated the ancient wisdom of egalitarian societies. The scholarship in this volume elucidates this alternative vision of egalitarian societies in varied ways. It is our hope that the work collected here—a whole that is more than the sum of its parts—strengthens the vision and moves the conversation ahead.

This volume focuses on the theme of motherhood and maternal relations as practice and models of and for understanding human relations based on care and gift giving. Papers presented at ASWM conferences constitute the core of the volume. As we editors considered the papers submitted to us for this, ASWM's fourth proceedings volume, we began to see ways that, through the format of a published book, we could place these papers in relationship to one another within an interpretive frame that would further a conversation about the centrality of maternal thinking to ASWM's vision. As we editors worked to construct the interpretive frame, we sought additional contributions that would give added depth and breadth to this volume.

Mothering is used here to describe a type of caring relation similar to and more spacious than a biological relation between a woman and the child she bore. As you read the through the volume you can see that the idea of "mother" across these essays is an expansive one. Thus, mothering can be carried out by "other mothers" and "motherers"—people who practice such care giving. Many Indigenous cultures honor ways in which care-giving practices are taught to humans by other-than-humans, including the Earth, elemental forces of nature, and various animals and other living creatures. In their stories and myths, animals and spirits teach humans how to live in ways that all life is respected and preserved. Mothering entails giving of gifts, receiving, and reciprocity.

At first glance, "maternal thinking" may appear oxymoronic. For some scholars, the word "maternal" calls up embodied, affective processes and ways of being, the opposite of "thinking," which suggests disembodied rational processes. Some feminist writers, however, challenged this separation between thinking and action. They asked how practices of mothering and other forms of care work produce patterns of thinking that can become integral to our ideas about how to live on the planet in ways that are cooperative and reciprocal. Across many disciplines these scholars have surmised that the activities of caring could influence how those who perform the activities think. Hence, "maternal thinking" offers a radical rejection of mind–body dualisms. While the language they use and the specific questions they ask vary according to training and background, many researchers have brought their minds and hearts to this project, such as Carol Gilligan in psychology and moral development, Joan Tronto and Sara Ruddick in political theory, and Nel Noddings in philosophy of education.[5] All were inspired to think about mothering in new ways and worked to articulate an ethics of care.

Robin Wall Kimmerer and Genevieve Vaughan have inspired our thinking about this volume, as both scholars view life as fundamentally relational and provide a generous frame within which to think about the essays herein. Although emerging from very different scholarly disciplines and biographical/geophysical locations, the two offer approaches that propose relational ways of life counter to the settler colonialism and capitalist hetero-patriarchy that dominate the world today.

Robin Wall Kimmerer—botanist, professor, and member of the Citizen Potawatomi Nation—is author of the well-known *Braiding Sweetgrass*,[6] as well as many scholarly and other popular works. Kimmerer brings together both Western science and Indigenous traditional ecological knowledge, along with stories of raising her daughters, teaching her students, and learning from her elders. Evocative stories of her early experiences with her family in nature provide lessons about the gifts we get from the Earth. She shares her experiences of learning the Potawatomi language as an adult, and how the language itself provides way of thinking about the relationships among beings that are very different from the underlying assumptions of English. In Potawatomi, the personhood of animals, plants, and landscapes is recognized in the language, which reconfigures the boundaries between humans and nonhumans. In a 2017 essay published in *Orion Magazine*, Kimmerer wrote, "Those whom my ancestors called relatives were renamed natural resources. In contrast to verb-based Potawatomi, the English language is made up primarily of nouns, somehow appropriate for a culture so obsessed with things."[7] Kimmerer's work expands our thinking and reminds us of the gifts from our mother the Earth, and of the necessity of human participation in this web of reciprocity.

Genevieve Vaughan is a peace activist and founder of the Sekhmet Temple in Nevada. Built to honor this goddess, the temple exemplifies the principles of the gift economy, reciprocity, and reparation, as the land around the site has been returned to the Western Shoshone after many years of colonial encroachment. Vaughan's intellectual work began in semiotics, and her thinking about language and how humans learn to communicate is the genesis for her thinking about maternal relations as an observed practice and guide for human relations. Vaughan's work in some ways runs parallel with that of North America feminist scholars in the 1980s and 1990s, mentioned above, who began to theorize about mothering as a practice and thus maternal thinking. Although Vaughan's work shares many concerns with these authors, she conceived of mothering and the gift relationship in a somewhat different way, in that she focuses on *economies* based on gift giving rather than the individualistic, profit-maximizing model of economic man. Vaughan's theory about how economies are organized addresses Western thought in ways that are critical of both capitalism and standard Marxist approaches.

Genevieve Vaughan's work has been foundational for the Association for the Study of Women and Mythology because she connects her ideas about language, economy, and scholarship on mothering with research from the modern matriarchal studies movement. Like Vaughan's work, the central focus of matriarchal studies is egalitarian forms of society based on maternal values of care. Matriarchal studies researchers argue that these values exist in real communities, not an imagined alternative to patriarchal capitalism and exchange-based economies. Such values are found in current matrilineal, matrifocal cultures around the world as presented in a comparative analysis by Heide Gottner-Abendroth[8]; some Indigenous traditions experienced in existing communities (e.g., Thomas, Echeverria, and Colby in this volume); and the matrilinear societies of Old Europe documented by Maria Gimbutas and many subsequent researchers. Social scientists J.K. Gibson-Graham[9] and K. Dombroski[10] have also documented pockets of alternative systems developing in response to the failures of capitalist economic exchange to work for certain segments of the population. They present diverse cases of communities experimenting with alternative ways to sustain themselves.

Although the source of their inspiration may not the same—for Vaughan it is the relationship between those who mother and a child who has needs and for Kimmerer it is the Earth as giver—, their understandings of the significance of the gift economy have much in common. For both, gift economies are relational. Vaughan has focused on particular qualities in the relation between motherers and children. Material gifts from the motherer are not reciprocated; Vaughan presents language as "verbal gift giving, verbal nurturing: satisfying others' communicative and cognitive needs with word-gifts." In her essay in this volume, Vaughan's feminist eye explores a theory of language as verbal gift giving. For Vaughan, language is an originary location, from which we can build a caring society with communities based on trust and mutuality. Although Vaughan notes that "it can be extended to include other-than-human things in several ways: by attending to and caring for them, by recognizing them as gifts and by receiving them," these have not been major directions of her own writing. At this point in time, however, we editors feel the urgency of that extension to the vision of a caring society toward imagining nonexploitative and commensal relations between humans and other than humans. We are grateful to have several contributions from Indigenous women in this volume who can help us with this work. Indeed, we are grateful to all our authors for the pieces that they add to this important work of envisioning a world in which maternal thinking and practice can flourish.

Following this introduction, we are fortunate to have Lynne Thomas's artwork, *The Land Is Our Home*, to open our minds with its visual storytelling. Thomas created the original artwork for an interpretive sign in Nunnock Swamp in the Southeast Forest National Park in New South Wales to show visitors how to understand the landscape from an Indigenous perspective. The image presents to the viewer a creation story. The viewer sees humans and their dreaming, traversing the song lines, camping. Everything in the drawing is intentional—the animals, the birds, the frogs, the plants, the rocks, the mountains are part of the life of that place. Everything exists in balance. In the center of the image, the hands of Mother Earth hold up a wooden vessel, a *Coolamon*, full of water, which depicts the gift of life that Mother Earth offers her people. In an interview with Denise Mitten, Thomas commented on the imagery, emphasizing how the Earth and all beings live in relation to each other. Along with the images, we have reproduced parts of the interview. Thomas's piece reinforces the themes of maternal gift giving, relationship to the land and each other, and the value of Indigenous traditional ecological knowledge in responding to the threat to our planet posed by capitalist models of extraction and wealth accumulation by the few.

Part One: Grounding

The first chapter is a theoretical piece. It explicates the idea of the gift economy and how a society based on it would be different from the market economy that dominates our world. It offers a mode of expression essential for the work of envisioning that this volume strives to accomplish, and speaks to the importance of relational ways of being, and to the deep connections between mind and embodied practice. We hope that this first section provides readers with tools for making connections between the works collected here and sparks a deep engagement with our project in this volume.

In her chapter, "The Gift Economy Inside and Outside Patriarchal Capitalism," Genevieve Vaughan helps us understand her perspective of the gift economy and how it is different from accepted Western economic thinking: maternal thinking is alter-centric not ego-centric; gift giving as an alternative to the exchange relations of patriarchal capitalism; the gift economy predates heteropatriarchy and capitalism, and it still exists. She asks us to question the necessity, the "naturalness" of the market economy. Vaughan frames mothering as a mode of distribution—an economy. She focuses on direct need—satisfying gifting as opposed to *quid pro quo* exchange. She presents the gift economy as rooted in values of care as opposed to market-based values of competition and domination.

Part Two:
New Questions and Interpretations about Old Stories

ASWM scholarship incorporates many disciplines and methodologies. A significant body of work has returned to evidence from earlier times with different questions and perspectives from those of standard scholarship. This research has been fundamental to goddess scholarship, producing new insights and nourishing thinking about alternatives to the heteropatriarchal capitalism that so many people take for granted.

In "A Working Hypothesis for the Study of Religion in a Minoan Village: The Theories of Harriet Boyd Hawes, Marija Gimbutas, Heide Goettner-Abendroth, and Jan Driessen," Carol P. Christ incorporates a number of ideas that are key to our framework for this volume, and then moves to question how we understand artifacts from ancient Crete. Since excavations in the early twentieth century by Arthur Evans, many people have viewed the structures at Knossos as the "palace" of a king. Based on insights from key scholars in the maternal thinking tradition, Christ questions this assumption. While her interpretations are tentative, the theoretical re-orientation is ground-breaking. Christ gathers into her theoretical frame Maria Gimbutas's ideas about the existence of matrifocal, matrilinear societies without war that were destroyed by patriarchal warriors who came out of the north. She adds Heide Goettner-Abendroth's conceptualizations of matriarchy, a cultural rather than biological model of mothering in societies in which the value of love, care, and generosity are at the center. Another essential idea comes from Sherri Mitchell from the Penobscot Indian Island Reservation, for whom this cultural model of motherhood is regarded as a reflection our living cosmos with Earth as a generous mother. These writers understand the goddess less as a transcendent deity and more of a unifying force. These ideas provide Christ with a novel perspective that opens the way to asking different questions about the "evidence" and the nature of religion practiced in Gournia in ancient Crete.

In her chapter, "Women, Snakes, Water, and Healing: Hygieia and Her Bronze Age Roots," Lisa Lubarr takes us to Bronze Age Greece as she recounts the stories of Asklepios, a mortal hero and healer who was later promoted to god status. As a god, she notes, he was ever present at his holy shrines throughout Greece. Of greater interest to Lubarr, however, is that he is accompanied by his "daughter," Hygieia, with her snake. This daughter does not figure in the stories about Asklepios the mortal, but Lubarr argues that the female divinities were necessary to support claims about healing that occurred at the shrines. Lubarr argues that Hygieia and the snake both represent older mythologies that predate the Classic Age. Lubarr shares evidence of Bronze Age goddesses linked with healing, snakes, and water, and she argues that even later in the Classical and Hellenistic periods, the inclusion of these elements contributed to the success of pilgrimage sites. Lubarr thus links the presence of Hygieia in later times to recognition by at least some seekers that health and healing are connected to maternal nurturing and the life-sustaining gifts of Mother Earth.

In "A Midrashic Look at Queen Michal: The Tragic Lover-Hero of the Davidic Narrative," Hannah Irish asks us to reconsider the Biblical story of Queen Michal, the daughter of Saul, and the first wife of King David. Irish takes up the Jewish midrash tradition (scriptural exegesis) to tell a story about Michal that includes her agency, portraying her as the hero in her own story. The Biblical story emphasizes Michal's roles as daughter of Saul, the old king, and as wife of David, the new king. In the Biblical account, Michal loves David, and saves him from Saul's plot to kill him. David flees Saul, leaving Michal behind. He marries six additional wives. Michal is married to another man. When David emerges as the victorious warrior in a battle for the kingdom he demands the return of Michal his bride (after having no contact with her for many years). The usual interpretations describe Michal as a victim or pawn in David's power games. The text makes six different references to Michal, and in three of them Michal is the object of her father or her husband's actions, but in two of them Michal initiates the action. The first is saving David from Saul, and the second is calling him to account when she thinks he has behaved shamefully. Michal's story ends with an observation that she bore David no children. The meaning of this coda to Michal's story is unclear, in part because a previous passage refers to five children, possibly Michal and her husband's. It is also possible that she adopted (cared for) her sister's children after her sister died. Irish is explicit about all that we do not know about Michal and her relationship to David. But Irish disputes the interpretation that Michal's presumed lack of children is her fault, and she wrests a complicated story about Michal's agency from a grand patriarchal narrative of a "tragic lover hero."

Dilşa Deniz's chapter, "Shaymaran: The Lost Goddess of Kurdistan," also shows how the interests of researchers inform their interpretations. Deniz sees her work as a decolonizing project on behalf of stateless Kurdish people whose lands have been colonized by monotheistic Muslims. Her discussion of both the myth and the image of Shaymaran, the snake goddess, draws on Kurdish (mainly Alevi) sources. Deniz's work reaches back to an ancient story that has continuing significance for Kurdish people. For decades the Kurdish language was prohibited in Turkey, and Islam forbade the production of images. State gatekeepers ensured that their views were the ones represented in academic journals and museums. Yet Kurds continued to transmit the myth of a strong androgynous goddess, half female and half male, who represented in her form the powers of life and death. Kurdish people called on her powers of protection, transformation, and reproduction, and valued her connection to a past in which women had equal status. Deniz argues for the persistence of an old Kurdish religion and resistance to the prevailing monotheism.

Part Three:
Myth and Grief: Rewriting the Stories, Healing Our Wounds

The chapters in this section continue to excavate, reclaim, and reimagine the ancient stories. In addition, the authors center their own experience as they reflect on the meaning of the received wisdom. Jaffa Frank describes her work as "embodied mythopoesis." For her, and the other authors in this section, our understanding of reality is based on our embodied experiences, as interpreted by our story-telling mind. The authors share experiences of suffering that is incongruent with the ideal model of reciprocal relations and mothering gifts, and the stories they narrate describe processes of actively working with the mythic materials to achieve a realignment.

In her contribution, "The Creation of Kunsikeya Tamakoce," Lushanya Echeverria first shares her painful story about her and her mother's exclusion in Indigenous ritual settings, when first her mother, and then Lushanya herself, came out as two-spirit women. Echeverria describes a process in which she comes to understand how the stories of a matriarchal past that she learned in her mother's womb had been masked and hidden from her as she grew up in a "modern" (post-colonial) Indigenous context in which patriarchal elements are embedded. Her own memory and attunement to what she had first learned in her mother's womb becomes the basis of the creation story she calls back from the matriarchal past for her own healing, and shares with us here.

For Frank, creative reflection on myth can transform and heal, without denying the reality of suffering. She argues that "by relating to embodied experience as archetypal visitation, pathology can be rendered sacred and approached compassionately to reveal meaning." In her chapter, "Loving Medusa, Redeeming Athene: Restorying Female Blood, Sovereignty, and Agency," Frank presents an account of her disabling experience of endometriosis, and the way she came to understand that condition through the stories of Athena and Medusa. She argues that her early identification with a patriarchal version of Athena (and estrangement and identification with her father) allowed her to succeed in a male world. Yet it was contradicted by her bleeding body and her experience of endometriosis. Frank takes us through her reflections on Medusa that led her to also reimagine Athena, ultimately as united with the Gorgon. Leaving behind the misogynistic accounts, Frank relates a story of transformation.

In her chapter, "Grief and the Mother/s Odyssey: Personal Reckoning and Collective Responsibility," Angelina Avedano turns to the myths of four grieving women—Innana, Demeter, Anticlea (mother of Odysseus), and Mary (mother of Jesus)—to craft a method for surviving devastating loss. Avedano's work comes out of her personal experiences with her own son and her scholarship in goddess mythology. She describes her transformation through a process of shamanic scholarship and suggests a model for others to follow. The mother's odyssey does not imply a biological relationship to the object of grief, but rather a disruption of the practices of caring and reciprocity that are so important for sustaining life. Avedano describes it as "a loss of something or someone of supreme value" and as "the loss of some aspect of oneself." Important for our purposes is that

Avedano explicitly connects the deep feeling of the mother–child bond to the relationship of humans to our Mother Earth, and the collective grief that many feel about the degradation the environment and the catastrophic losses we are facing. In the healing process of the grief passage, one can move through endurance, emergence, embrace, and ultimate integration or ensoulment characteristic of the mother/s odyssey. In her conclusion, Avedano turns to Julia Kristeva's insistence on the crucial significance of maternal passion, which for her is the prototype of the love relation. Avedano argues that healing that "love relation" within ourselves, with one another, and with the world, is necessary for dealing with our collective trauma and grief and taking up the transformational work that is necessary for the survival of the planet.

Karen Nelson Villanueva's chapter, "The Mother of the Buddhas," takes us to the Tibetan Buddhist tradition to tell the mother–daughter story of Yeshe, who, in the myth, is first the mother and then the daughter. Nelson Villanueva uses the story to explicate the foundational values of compassion and empathy rooted in the experience of recognizing and repaying the kindness of the mother. Nelson Villanueva reflects on the concept of "emptiness," showing how it is a way of expressing the interdependence of all beings, within which there is one mother, the mother of all sentient beings. In her conclusion, Nelson Villanueva states, "Ultimately, this is the message of Buddhism—to love one another as a mother loves her favorite child." Resonating with other authors in this volume, she also states that one does not have to give birth to love others with empathy, care, and compassion.

Part Four:
Contemporary Engagement: Critique and Reclamation

In this final section, we move to chapters highlighting contemporary critiques and engagement. Throughout this book we have included, in addition to scholarship, storytelling and works of art. This work speaks to us on many levels. Art has been especially important to the study of women and mythology as we reclaim the past and imagine the future. The last chapter describes a local project involving the creation of mandalas—temporary works of art—to tell an alternative story of a community. This closing chapter brings together scholarship, art, ceremony, and community engagement, a reminder that our scholarship is connected to concrete practices in pursuit of our vision.

"The Goddess Dandelion: First of the Weed Women," a work by Australian artist Ceardai Demelza, begins this section. As an ecofeminist artist, Demelza's artwork presents new goddesses for our time. In conversation with goddess scholarship, she has imagined images of our time. Her work offers a critique of patriarchal capitalism and the domination of nature as well as playful images that speak to those of us living in postindustrial urban landscapes.

In "Deconstructing Patriarchal Motherhood," Austrian-American scholar, Miriam Irene Tazi-Preve brings us to contemporary Euro-American societies and explores the many ways that motherhood is under threat, as mothers do not get the support they need to nurture and to model norms and practices of maternal thinking. Tazi-Preve offers a critique of the patriarchy that dominates contemporary Europe and the United States. She brings to the table a conceptualization of patriarchy developed by Claudia von Werlhof[10] in conversation with the work of Heide Goettner-Abendroth on matriarchy.[11] In this scholarly tradition, patriarchy can best be understood in relation to matriarchy—it is the repudiation of matriarchy. Tazi-Preve argues that what we have today is "patriarchal motherhood," with women's power cancelled and replaced by that of fathers, while women continue to bear the burdens and do the work. Drawing on many examples from Austria, Germany, and the United States, Tazi-Preve shows how women have lost power, and are increasingly dependent on the state, and, for some, on men with higher incomes. The conclusion of her chapter takes us back to the principles of matriarchal motherhood, renewing the call for a system of living together where everyone lives in an "atmosphere of interdependence, solidarity, and responsibility."

In the closing chapter, "San Juan Baptista, California: Reclaiming 'Truth in History' through the Arts," Jennifer Colby shares the story of a 2019 art project in her community of San Juan Baptista that worked to undo the settler colonialist narrative and reclaim Indigenous knowledge and a matrifocal, gender-balanced history. San Juan Baptista is the site of one of the twenty-one Franciscan missions established by Spanish conquerors on the California coast. In the project, Colby worked with a collective of Indigenous, Latina, African American, and Anglo women to create four mandalas, linking the mandala making with ceremonies for the four seasons. The mandalas, described as temporary public art pieces, served to remind viewers that the history of this place predates the founding of the mission in 1797. The mandalas emphasize the continuous presence of the Amah Mutsun (Indigenous people of the area), as well as "the people of the corn," Mexican peoples of mixed Indigenous, European, and African inheritance who arrived in California with the Spanish expedition of 1775–1776. Colby's chapter not only describes the art works, but also the process of working together across differences to tell the stories in a respectful way, attentive to issues of appropriation. Ceremonies, some closed and others open to the entire community, created spaces in which Indigenous knowledge was honored through an ecofeminist, matrifocal, decolonizing art form.

With this volume we have continued ASWM's practice of publishing work presented at our biennial conferences in a thematic proceedings volume. The works included come from many academic disciplines, and use various forms of expression, spanning prehistoric times to the present, and representing many places and traditions. Each article and work of art is grounded in a specific conversation. Yet the perspective of maternal thinking offers a way of seeing connections between these conversations. It offers tools for critiquing the settler colonialist heteropatriarchy in which we live. It also articulates a way of thinking about the gift economy, reciprocity, and a balance that recognizes the ways that we are all related and points to other ways of being together on this Earth, our mother, Pachamama.

Endnotes

1 Vandana Shiva with Kartikey Shiva, *Oneness vs the 1%: Shattering Illusions, Seeding Freedom* (White River Junction, VT: Chelsea Green Publishing, 2020).

2 Robert Costanza, et al., "Changes in the global value of ecosystem services," *Global Environmental Change* (2014), 152–158.

3 Vandana Shiva, Panel Presentation Virtual Conference, Maternal Gift Economy: Breaking Through, November 26, 2021 (https://www.maternal-gifteconomymovement.org/2021-conference/, accessed January 12, 2022).

4 Marija Gimbutas, *The Goddesses and Gods of Old Europe, 7000 to 3500 BC: Myths, Legends and Cult Images* (London: Thames and Hudson, 1974); *The Language of the Goddess: Unearthing the Hidden Symbols of Western Civilization* (San Francisco: Harper & Row, 1989); *The Civilization of the Goddess: The World of Old Europe* (San Francisco: Harper, 1991).

5 Carol Gilligan, *In a Different Voice: Psychological Theory and Women's Development* (Cambridge, MA: Harvard University Press, 1982); Joan Tronto,

"Beyond gender difference to a theory of care," *Signs* 12 (summer 1987): 644–663, and *Moral Boundaries: A Political Argument for an Ethic of Care* (New York: Routledge, 1993); Sara Ruddick, *Maternal Thinking: Towards a Politics of Peace* (Boston: Beacon Press, 1989; Nel Noddings, *Caring: A Feminine Approach to Ethics and Moral Education* (Berkeley: University of California Press, 1984), and Suzanne Gordon, Patricia E. Benner, and Nel Noddings, eds., *Caregiving: Readings in Knowledge, Practice, Ethics, and Politics*, Studies in Health, Illness, and Caregiving in America (Philadelphia: University of Pennsylvania Press, 1996).

6 Robin Kimmerer, *Braiding Sweetgrass: Indigenous Wisdom, Scientific Knowledge and the Teachings of Plants* (Minneapolis, MN: Milkweed Editions, 2013).

7 Robin Wall Kimmerer, "Speaking of Nature," *Orion Magazine*, March/April 2017, https://orionmagazine.org/article/speaking-of-nature/.

8 Heide Goettner-Abendroth, *Matriarchal Societies: Studies on Indigenous Cultures across the Globe* (New York: Peter Lang, 2013).

9 See J. K. Gibson-Graham, *A Postcapitalist Politics* (Minneapolis: University of Minnesota Press, 2006), and J.K. Gibson-Graham and K. Dombroski, *The Handbook of Diverse Economies* (Cheltenham, UK: Edgar Elgar, 2020).

10 Claudia von Werlhof, "Capitalist Patriarchy and the Negation of Matriarchy: The Struggle for a'Deep' Alternative," in *Women and the Gift Economy: A Radically Different Worldview Is Possible*, edited by Genevieve Vaughan, 139–153 (Toronto: Inanna Publications, 2009).

11 Goettner-Abendroth, *Matriarchal Societies*.

"THE LAND IS OUR HOME": INTERVIEW WITH LYNNE THOMAS[1]

LYNNE THOMAS

Fig. 1. Land Is Our Home. Drawing by Lynne Thomas, 2013.

The Project

This is a project (see Fig.1) I've been working on with the National Parks, doing interpretations for them. The parks service asked me to express how to understand the landscape from an Indigenous perspective, so I created this artwork in 2013, to honor my father. I did this artwork with a small felt pen. The words and stories are mine as well. I also used some of my dad's sayings.[2] The display sits on Brown Mountain that runs up to the highlands of Cooma. You can get to it in the national park called Nunnock Swamp.

This image depicts the Great Spirit creating the landscape that has evolved through time, weather, and space. The swamp was once an ancient bog from the glaciers millions of years ago. We get an amazing effect from shifting glaciers. Down near the border, Eden's magnificent shoreline has hidden dinosaur imprints through the rock formations that are slowly being

covered by sand. This beautiful water we have in Nunnock Swamp is an ancient bog. Now it's home to a lot of threatened species, mainly frogs, birds, amazing flora, and fauna. It was at once a song line and traveling route by Aboriginal people, as they have been here for over 60,000 years.

This dreaming story is a living place that can take you back in time. It is a place connected closely to our hearts and minds. You know when people look at these drawings, there's so much to see and the beauty of it is that if you put little things around, then those who are really looking just look at every little thing. And that's the learning. So, I put little frogs there and birds in the trees because when we look at a beautiful environment like this, sometimes we don't see these species that look after it or need these landscapes. So, when you put little things like this in the drawing, it gets people thinking, "Oh wow, yeah, these tiny little lives are all important parts of the ecosystem."

Song Lines from the Mountains (Fig. 2)

Everything we see in this artwork is a part of all creation—the dreaming story, the snake, the song lines, where people camped, and where children were born. Not only do our song lines go on the land, but out under the water there are big mountains, and following that song line goes right

Fig. 1. Land Is Our Home. Drawing by Lynne Thomas, 2013.

Fig. 2. Land Is Our Home (Panel 1). Drawing by Lynne Thomas, 2013.

around the world. My father used to always say, "The trees and the rocks belong together and so do we, because we come from the Earth and we're going to go back to the Earth." The reason why I added the people walking was because it is a song line. It's the Indigenous people just, you know, going on a Sunday stroll, but they're also learning, using the natural vegetation and everything, and teaching too.

There's the little possum, it's one of the threatened species. There's a kookaburra there too. He's going to make a little sing-a-long there when the people come along. And there are all the bushes and tussocks of grass. When Aboriginal people planted certain plants like this specific *waratah* bush, in certain places, they made their own traffic lights, traffic signs. They're the bushes that they planted and when you follow them the path goes all the way down to Eden. And up on the highlands you follow these trees that bloom, and that's where my ancestors, my grandfather and my uncles, went down through the mountains.

Fig. 3. Land Is Our Home (Panel 2). Drawing by Lynne Thomas, 2013.

And those big boulders are important to us. In the summer they can be nice and warm or cool. And in the cold, when it's really cold, they're part of shelters as well. They're important because it's the balance of the tree and the rock. And that's why it's important that we understand the balance of everything that we see.

The Moon and the *Coolamon* (Fig. 3)

That's the moon in the sky. I created the drawing when that moon was actually happening on that day. And you see that little dark spot on the moon, the planet there, Venus, was happening then too. I added it to show the timeline of when I'd actually done the artwork. The aboriginal people understood stories about the moon and stars and walked on the landscape to get to certain places for ceremony. They knew when they had to be at a certain place for ceremonies when the sun or moon or constellation comes up from behind and is in the right place.

And in the middle, you've got the bog there, or the river, the creek. You can see the hands holding it up because water is life. Everything that evolves in this earth needs water. The hands are like a *coolamon*.[3] So Mother Earth is handing water out to us and saying, "This is a gift from the Creator," and we need to respect and look after it and to understand it, so we can sustain all the living things that once we came from. That's why Indigenous people have been looking after the landscape for such a long time. We need all those species of plants and animals, and we need to work together to look after these places.

Everything that we need, that we depend on, sits in that *coolamon*. That's what Mother Earth is offering—the knowledge. Every Aboriginal person in every place, a long time ago, was given the gift by the Creator, to look after the landscape, to take care and nurture the landscape. So, they might have knowledge of different areas, like down in the desert or down on the coast. Their kinship was made up of knowledge handed down through the dreaming stories, and artworks, and dances, and sitting down and learning about the stars. All that education, everything they learned, is so important now because that is how kinship is passed on.

When you put the animals in, like owls and possums and frogs, it gets people thinking, "Oh wow, these tiny little lives all matter!" There are so many different types of frogs in the highlands, sustaining and looking after

Fig. 4. Land Is Our Home (Panel 3). Drawing by Lynne Thomas, 2013.

that water for us. And for women especially. We know that frogs can be frozen in the glaciers, and they can survive and start again. And then we go across from the frog, there's a black cockatoo. That's in the highlands up there. The special ones are the yellow- and the red-tailed ones that are now threatened, and that's a part of my father's skin totems.[4]

The Track to the Coast (Fig. 4)

So this side goes right down the coastline. This is up high, along what they call Brown's Mountain. If you ever go there, on the way up to this place, this river and this bog, there are massive big rocks that sit up on the top of the mountain range. That's a creation snake that meanders up along the mountain. It's a big snake and you can just see it from below. And so the dreaming snake of course makes the song lines and makes these connections. And so this track meanders around and down to where the aboriginal people danced down on the coast and had big ceremonies.

We have a place down there on the coast called Tathra, which is where you see the "wild cat," the *quoll*.[5] Here it is. See that little white spot? They glow in the dark and they're like our native "cats." We also have the [spotted] owl that's part of the threatened species up there in the highlands.

On the far right side there's another little frog and he's part of that gift of water as well. Certain frogs were used by women, because what they did was to wee on the frog and if that frog swelled up, they knew that they were pregnant. Anyway, the frogs represent the female, for birthing, and the women knew a lot of those special things.

See this big boulder sticking up. When everything sort of settles, and you know, there's erosion, you get rocks that have always been there and are a part of the creation. These rocks are very special too because not only do they look after our insects and our animals like our frogs and shelter them, but they're markers too. This boulder is there to show the measurements, the idea of closeness and then going in the distance. So the boulder shows how to measure the distance.

Everything we see in this artwork is a part of all creation—the dreaming story, the snake, the song lines, where people camped, and where children were born. It's part of the waterfall for women as well, and for men. It's all the balance that we need in life. It's been a part of our past, our present, and, you know, hoping for the future.

Endnotes

1 Lynne Thomas, interview by Denise Mitten, PhD, January 24, 2022

2 Lynne says: "My dad's name that he used in this life is Guboo Ted Thomas. He was one of the last Yuin Tribal lore men of this era. 'Guboo,' his most well-known name, was his tribal name meaning 'good friend.' He was a prominent spiritual leader and an advocate for land and people's rights." Through his work with the Australian Institute of Aboriginal Studies, an invaluable record was made of sacred sites along the New South Wales coast. He was recognized for his tireless work in developing mutual respect and understanding and in the renewal of the Spirit and the Dreaming.

3 "*Coolamon*" is an anglicized Aboriginal word used to describe an Australian Aboriginal carrying vessel. It is a multi-purpose shallow vessel, or dish with curved sides, ranging in length from 30 to 70 cm, similar in shape to a canoe. See https://www.aboriginal-bark-paintings.com/aboriginal-coolamon/

4 Similar to a surname, a skin name indicates a person's blood line and language group. It also conveys information about how generations are linked and how they should interact. Unlike surnames, husbands and wives don't share the same skin name, and children don't necessarily share their parents' names

5 "*Quoll*" is the Aboriginal name for several carnivorous, nocturnal marsupials with long noses and distinct white spots in a dark coat. The spotted-tail or tiger *quoll* is native to this area of New South Wales. All *quolls* are endangered in Australia and threatened in Tasmania due to predators and urban development

SECTION 1

GROUNDINGS

THE GIFT ECONOMY INSIDE AND OUTSIDE PATRIARCHAL CAPITALISM

GENEVIEVE VAUGHAN

The gift economy provides an alternative point of view from which to analyze the market economy and patriarchy. It is an alternative that has always existed and still exists today at a time when patriarchal capitalism is demonstrating its devastating effects on humanity and the environment. I believe that gift-giving is the original human economy of which the exchange economy is an elaboration and a distortion. The reasons for choosing to access and practice this original economy are psychological as well as material. That is because the way we procure our sustenance influences what we think both at the level of daily life and at the more theoretical level of Marxian structure–superstructure. By making the distinction between direct gifting to satisfy needs and quid-pro-quo exchange, we can see the gift economy as the source of the values of care and connection as opposed to market-based values of competition and domination. These two kinds of values then feed back into the market economy where the practice of quid-pro-quo exchange dominates free gift-giving. Indeed, profit, the motivator of the market, is formed by the taking of the gifts of the many by the few.

Understanding this perspective requires some re-framing and some new ways of connecting the dots in old discourses. By framing mothering as economic, a mode of distribution in contrast to market exchange, we can understand its commonality with the gift economies of Indigenous peoples.

Since the 1960's I have thought that the market with its logic of exchange is the source of our many problems and that it is not by assimilating more people into it that we can create a peaceful and abundant society. Hidden behind the market, though, is the other economy, a free economy that has its own unrecognized and functional logic. In the market, where everything is valued and defined in monetary terms, gift-giving seems to be nothing. "Free" is at most a gimmick used to sell more commodities.

Instead, on closer inspection we can see that free giving-and-receiving has a basic logic of its own: very briefly, *A gives to B* implies that B is valuable for A or s/he would not have given to h/er. On the other hand, A is valuable to B as the source of the gift. The gift itself is valuable in that it is used to satisfy a need. In passing the gift on, *A gives to B* and *B gives to C*, which implies that A gives to C. Continuing this gifting from A to B, C, D, E, and F creates a gift circle of shared value and solidarity. Starting from different points weaves the implications in different ways. Giving and receiving different kinds of gifts and services has different kinds of qualitative implications as does giving and receiving with different partners. These are relational implications and the logic of the gift is primarily relational. It can be extended to include non-human relations in several ways: by attending to and caring for them, by recognizing them as gifts and by receiving them. We can project our gift relations onto Nature and receive from Nature as well, encompassing perceptions, synchronicities, and all the infinite variety of material gifts that Nature provides, although many of these are not widely accessible in a regime of private property. *The human free economy is aligned with the "economy" of Nature, which is also free. Only human property and the market are artificial and dysfunctional.*

In 1493 Columbus wrote of the people he encountered in the "New World" that they were "artless and generous with what they have, to such a degree as no one would believe but him who had seen it. Of anything they have, if it be asked for, they never say no, but do rather invite the person to accept it, and show as much lovingness as though they would give their hearts."[1] The free gift economy is always vulnerable to the economy that dominates and takes. It was not only the Europeans' horses and military technology that allowed the conquest but the ego-oriented (non- or anti-gift) motivation of acquisition and domination, typical of the market economy. As time went on and Europe's destructive hold on the Americas and other colonies became solidified, the contact with "pre"-capitalist[2] economies sustained the developing capitalist economies materially because the Indigenous people were forced to direct their gifts toward the foreign conquerors.[3]

It is important to take the long view in order to understand the two logics of gift and exchange. They have coexisted for centuries but the market is not ubiquitous, "natural," or necessary. Gift-giving and receiving are more fundamental. They are first encountered in socialization through the basic and free need-satisfying care that is essential for infants' survival. The care of small children can be performed by biological mothers, other family members, entire villages, or paid child-care workers, but for the child the care is free.[4] This is demonstrated by the fact that children do not begin to understand exchange and money until they are around four years old.[5] While early childhood has often been seen in Freudian terms as pre-Oedipal, it should also be seen in even more socially relevant terms as "pre"-market. In this sense everyone is born into a gift economy and practices it during the period in which s/he is learning language and basic life skills. It is only later that the child even begins to understand exchange and starts to adapt to a market economy based on quid pro quo interactions. Children are protected by their lack of development from embracing market logic in their earliest years. If adults are to succeed in bringing them "up," children also have to adapt to the economy of direct giving.

A New Understanding of Intersubjectivity

"Freud, Piaget, and Skinner contributed to the 'myth of the asocial child,' a myth which is now being overturned by research on preverbal intersubjectivity, neonatal imitation, and mirror neurons. Neonatal imitation depends on a close coupling between perception and action that undergirds intersubjective engagement with others.... [S]elf–other connectedness is functional at birth."[6] Children are born pro-social. At the age of twenty minutes they are already able to imitate facial expressions and tongue protrusion. Gaze following and understanding goals and intentions soon develop. "Intersubjectivity is a precondition for culture not the outcome of it," say Meltzoff and Brooks.[7]

Caring for infants is thus consciously interactive from the beginning, not the care of a passive ego-centric being. In fact, children are already carrying on "proto conversations"[8] with their mothers as early as the age of two months. They respond positively to the motherer's satisfaction of their needs and also provide her/him with cues that satisfy her/his own psychological, communicative, and cognitive needs regarding the child's needs. Although in a sense there is reciprocity, because each satisfies the other's needs at different levels, this interaction is not exchange in the sense of *do ut des* constraint. It is not an exchange, although motherer and child are keyed to each other and intricately time their turn-taking initiatives.[9] The interactions are both turned toward the other; they are, as Stein Braten says, "altercentric."[10] The interactions between motherers and small children necessarily have giving and receiving material care and sustenance as their main theme and context. In fact, communication *is* at first this material care along with all the accompanying multisensory experiences of touch, taste, smell, and so on. The child's body and mind are the product of that material care work.

This early economy of giving and receiving is a mode of distribution and a life-enhancing one.

The relations it creates are the mutuality and trust that form the basis of community. These are relations of bonding prior to the relations of debt and obligation that are typical of exchange. The interactions involved are mutually attuned turn-taking at giving and receiving and are not quid pro quo exchange. The motherer provides unilateral material gifts for the child. Her gifts do not depend on the child's equivalent return gifts. The child provides communicative gifts for the motherer. S/he does not make them contingent on an equal exchange.

Two Logics

Exchange follows a contrary logic. Giving in order to receive an equivalent cancels the other-oriented implications of the gift and transforms them to ego-orientated implications. The purpose of the gift is to satisfy the need of the other. The purpose of exchange is to satisfy one's own need, using the satisfaction of the need of the other as means. Gift and exchange constitute two logics, which contradict but are also intertwined with each other.

The decoupling of gift-giving from needs via exchange disempowers our idea of gift-giving and alters our conception of needs. Mainstream economics uses the concept of "effective demand," which restricts our understanding of needs by making relevant only the needs for which the buyers can pay. "Supply" and "demand" are translations of gift and need into economic terms that take for granted "effective demand." *Unmonetizeable needs, and people who have needs but not money, are irrelevant.* Instead, in maternal gift-giving, the motherer actually "mind-reads" the child, focusing on the child and trying to understand by guessing even when the child cannot tell the motherer (much less pay her/him).

In gift economies, needs are not monetarily expressed, nor do all needs have to be verbally expressed. People use their intuition to focus on others and they are sensitive to their feelings and circumstances. They recognize other minds in their variety and not only according to the limited though mutually or equally adversarial perspective of a point of profit and loss/ benefit and cost in exchange. Direct interpersonal giving is qualitative and thus more informative for both giver and receiver, than merely quantitative exchange. The gift carries something of the personality or spirit of the giver. Not just material but psychological needs are important, including the need for reciprocal respect

The gift economy thus has relational consequences (heightened intuition and deep connectedness) that are different from those of the exchange economy, which are typically more adversarial: competition for domination and control, striving for accumulation and autonomy, reciprocal ego orientation,[11] lack of emotion—values and motivations similar to the patriarchal bag of tricks.

The Archaeology of the Present

Young children everywhere have to begin life in a gift economy and there are pockets of the gift economy in the market economy, namely in the "domestic sphere." These are rendered difficult by the social focus on, and self-validating credibility of, the market. In fact, the gift economy requires and creates abundance, while the market requires and creates scarcity in order to maintain control of the flow of gifts. If too much abundance accrues, the "excess" is eliminated by wasting it in endeavors such as patriarchal wars.

The context of scarcity created by the market makes gift-giving difficult. Not only gender roles but the lack of access to independent sources of the gifts of Nature and the community penalize anyone who does not do monetized work and especially those who are responsible for the lives of their children. *It is isolation in the context of exchange that makes the free labor of motherers difficult and sometimes self-sacrificial, not the gift economy itself.* In fact, it is the market system, merged with patriarchy, that is the problem. Although it may help a few for a time, and thus seem like a gift to them, assimilation into the system is only an individualistic and partial solution. It is the gift-exploiting system that needs to be changed.

The encounter between exchange and gift economies within capitalism is similar to the conquest and encroachment by the European market economy and culture on Indigenous peoples wherever they have found them. Indigenous gift economies, many of which existed in the past and still exist in surviving matrilinear, matrilocal, and/or matriarchal societies,[12] pose an alternative model that threatens the market. Gift practices were considered barbaric and much was done by the colonizers to eliminate them. On the other hand, the values of the market insinuated themselves and transformed the Indigenous ways from within with the help of drugs, alcohol, missionaries, and violence. Either way the encroachment of the market privatized and enclosed Native lands and allowed the gifts of resources and territories to be seized by the colonizers.

By making the comparison between childcare in patriarchal capitalism and Indigenous gift economies, I do not mean to somehow infantilize the "pre"-capitalist societies. Instead I argue that they have developed the logic of direct giving/receiving, elaborating it in ways other than the market to distribute goods and services and create culture (gifting in festivals, spiritual gifts, and symbolic gift exchange). In fact, the market itself is also a way of using gifting—doubling it back and forcing it to be contingent, thereby transforming it into its opposite: giving in order not to give.

In capitalist patriarchy, we consider the market the province of adult behavior. For Indigenous gift economies, the market is extraneous, the province of no one. Of course, the encounter between the market and Indigenous peoples has brought about many hybrids; for example, the market of Juchitàn that is traditionally controlled by women. Gifting continues, however, through almost daily festivals offered to the community by one woman or another.[13]

I propose that we understand the gift economy as primary and the exchange economy as secondary, that is, derivative. Isolated in the domestic sphere, ontogenesis is "pre"-patriarchal even inside patriarchy and "pre"-capitalist even inside capitalism. In the traditional patriarchal heterosexual model, the practice of the gift economy becomes the responsibility of one woman, the mother, while the husband is supposed to work in the market economy and provide the means of giving. As women have joined the paid labor force, it is also the woman herself who works in the market economy in order to sustain her own practice of the gift economy with her children.

Capitalist patriarchy controls the means of giving and takes gifts from the gift economy in the same way that at another level it takes from "pre"-capitalist societies and at still another level that it takes gifts from Nature. It creates scarcity and makes independent gift-giving almost impossible.

Patriarchal Capitalism Plunders the Gift Economy

The altercentric processes and values that we learn as mothered children provide the structure of human communication and must be made visible in order to generalize them. They have not been generalized until now because the foreground of our thinking (and doing) has been occupied by the combined system of the market and patriarchy. This system isolates women in the role of mothers practicing the gift economy alone, depriving them of the extended families or villages that they would have had in "pre"-patriarchal–"pre"-capitalist societies.

In many matriarchal societies the father is nurturing while the mother's brother provides authority.[14] In others the mother's brother provides support for the biological mother in satisfying the physical and psychological needs of the child.[15] Males, fathers or uncles—mothers' brothers—therefore also do the kind of detailed nurturing that females, especially biological mothers are expected to do in patriarchy. Moreover, because the mother's brother's relation with the mother is not sexualized, there is no stimulus for the Oedipus complex in such societies and there is little or no violence against women.[16]

The values of direct, need–satisfying gifting are practiced by both males and females in matrifocal and matriarchal societies, and they extend to the society as a whole. In patriarchal capitalism where men and money are in power and women are assigned the entire responsibility of gift-giving and care work in isolation with their children, the processes and values of the gift economy are not generalized. Indeed they are particularized, individualized as morality, and/or essentialized as common to one biologically identified sex.

The values comprising the superstructure of the gift economy seem to be "women's values." Instead they are the birthright of everyone as "pre"-patriarchal–"pre"-market values, the superstructure of an economy that has been interrupted, splintered into little pieces, and located inside each isolated home.

The role of motherer in patriarchy is usually gender specific, and despite many individual variations, biological sex is identified with mothering (female) or not-mothering (male). As boys grow up in our society, they are usually educated not to embrace the values of the gift economy, and they are given a gender ideal that is more functional to the social reproduction of the market and patriarchy.

Aggression is a kind of variation on the gift, where one person touches another as in giving but with force, and establishes a relation with the other, not of mutuality but of dominance. The socialization of males into a role opposite that of the gift-giving motherer makes aggressiveness seem to be a specific masculine characteristic. This violence is integrated with exchange, in fighting as the exchange of blows, war as military "exchanges," and justice as punishment for crime. The war against Afghanistan is "justified" by the attempt to "pay back" Al Qaeda for its attack on the World Trade Center.

It is not the biological necessity of mothering that is the basis of the gift economy, but rather the biological necessity for children to be mothered. The fact that because of our upright stance women's pelvic opening is narrow requires children's brain size to be small at birth and increase later and their craniums to be undeveloped, which results in a long post-natal period of dependency on someone's care. This care is called forth by the social responsiveness of the child, and societies assign the role of care giver to the biological mother because they socially interpret the biological fact of giving birth to mean that women must take on this intense and time-consuming job, a job that is actually the practice of a "pre"-market economy. This economy is kept in a rudimentary stage and never allowed to develop as a system. The market economy takes its gifts and creates the scarcity that keeps the gift economy disempowered. At the same time it monopolizes the attention of all, hiding the importance of gift-giving and making it difficult for people to recognize the existence of the gift economy. Downplayed, disempowered, and devalued, gift-giving becomes subservient to the exchange economy.

In patriarchal capitalist society, the gift economy is gendered female because women do most of the mothering. In Indigenous matriarchal societies this is not necessarily the case because gift economy and mothering are not restricted to one sex or gender. This has the result that Indigenous women sometimes do not identify with feminism. Euro-American patriarchy and the opposition to it are extraneous to those "pre"-patriarchal societies. At the same time though, patriarchal capitalism plunders their gifts and marginalizes and dominates them as it marginalizes, dominates, and plunders its own "pockets" of the gift economy as well as the gifts of Nature.

Language and Communication

I have been trying to map the gift economy onto language for many years because I believe it is a key to the paradigm shift we so badly need in order to access the gift economy and to re-elaborate a mode of distribution beyond the market, one that will satisfy the needs of all. I can only briefly mention it here to outline the fundamental idea.

The altercentric interaction between motherers and children is pre-linguistic communication, and giving/receiving, nurturing/being nurtured is material pre-linguistic communication. At around 18 months, when this material communication is already well established, children typically begin to say their first words. They learn to speak in the "pre"-market period of life. It is my hypothesis that language is not just triggered by but actually modeled on gift giving-and-receiving material communication, the nurturing satisfaction of needs.

The generalization of gift-giving that is not allowed by the market is already present in language but unrecognized. In fact, language is verbal gift-giving, verbal nurturing: satisfying others' communicative and cognitive needs with word-gifts.

The many and various schools of linguistic investigation leave the need of the other out of their concept of language. For example, Chomskian linguistics asserts the infinite creativity of the speaker but does not mention satisfying the *listener's* communicative needs. The philosophy of language revolves around the speaker's "intention" that the listener is supposed to pick up or grasp. Neuro-linguistic investigators think children do "statistical sampling" to learn the meanings of words.[17] In my experience, relevance theorists Sperber and Wilson[18] have come the closest to mentioning need satisfaction by talking about the "positive cognitive effect" of communication. However, they do not actually address a receiver's need for this positive effect. Rather they see the entire communicative interaction in terms of calculated cost/benefit.

Patriarchal capitalism is an economy of not-giving and the taking and control of gifts. It seems neutral and neutered because both men and women can participate in it. It is not neutral and it is only neutered because it puts both (or all) genders in an anti-gift mode. The interaction of not-giving becomes the deep source of neutral and neutered scientific ideology, which leaves aside the maternal model of the free satisfaction of needs. Mothering seems to have nothing to do with life processes. In reality, giving and receiving form the communicative lens through which we (and scientists too) understand the world.

Now "neutral" psychology and neuroscience are making headway in conceiving language without gift-giving. They are successfully construct-ing explanations for how the human acquires language that ignore the fundamental importance of the altercentric mother/child model. (This is like explaining walking by describing the actions of the muscles, positions of the limbs, blood rate, etc., rather than the means to get somewhere.) A recent study of child altruism showed that fourteen-month-old children would spontaneously help an experimenter with a task.[19] The explanation offered for this capacity of altruistic action is that it is a genetic predis-position. The alternative seemed to be that adults "train" children to be altruistic. Appealing to training or to heredity here puts instructional or genetic "transmission" in the place of the maternal gifting model as an explanation. It would seem more reasonable to say that children have participated in and been the focus of other-centered initiatives—gift work—from the beginning. Through their "innate intersubjective sym-pathy,"[20] children learn to be helpful because their motherers have been helpful to them. What we are born with is a pro-social capacity, which develops into helpfulness through the social interaction of material com-munication: mothering/being mothered.

Researchers realize that social interaction is necessary for language learning but "the mechanism that controls the interface between language and social cognition remains a mystery."[21] However, it is only by including the human maternal model that this interface for language can be under-stood *and* that the positive economic and political aspects of a non-neutral, non-neutered economy beyond the market can come forward.

The altercentric mother–child model is not itself biological or neuro-logical, but interpersonal, whatever its neurological underpinnings may be. It is relevant at the level at which models are propagated—the level of consciousness, imitation, and metaphor. Indeed heredity itself is a metaphorical projection of giving and receiving, handing down (economic) gifts between generations.

Gift-giving is the basis of material communication; in giving and receiving material gifts we establish human relations with each other. The same thing happens in language. We establish human relations with each other when we give and receive verbal gifts satisfying each other's cognitive and communicative needs.

Presently patriarchy in its phallic domination version of the symbolic order of the father[22] and its neuter version in physical science has eliminated the model of the maternal human. The concept of language is one important place in which to restore it.

George Lakoff and Mark Johnson launched the field of cognitive linguistics over thirty years ago via recognizing metaphor as one of the main structural forms of language.[22] They suggested that "image schemas" coming from bodily experience are projected into language from a source to a target area. For example, the schema *path to goal* comes from the bodily experience of moving along a path. It underlies such linguistic expressions as "Life is a journey" and such ideas as the passage of time from point to point. *Up is good* is projected into such expressions as "feeling high" or "feeling low." Going into and out of *containers* is mapped onto categorization. There are numerous other schemas that have been studied extensively.

I believe the image schema that underlies both material and verbal communication is the interactive, interpersonal sensory–motor schema of giving and receiving, first located not in the body of the child alone but intercorporeally, beginning in a moment in which the child has recently been part of the body of the mother, in the womb and proceeding through the long period during which s/he is completely dependent on the need-satisfying gifts and services of the motherer for h/er body's very existence. This is a complementary intercorporality embodied in the individual and implies the body/mind of the other. The motherer takes the initiative to give to the child in many ways and the child receives the gifts not passively but creatively. In fact, the passive receiver is an invention of patriarchy, as it derives from a false idea of women as passive. Gifts must be accepted and actively used if they are to achieve their completion. Food must be actively consumed and digested. Maternal gifts and services must actually satisfy the need of the child; otherwise the motherer just has to repeat them.

The child is first embedded in the mother's body and then in the material care accomplished by the motherer's body (and mind). Later, as s/he grows older, s/he continues to be embedded in the perceptual and material gifts of the environment and of society at large—that is, if they have not been made scarce by a plundering economy.

The roles of the dependent child necessarily imply the roles of the motherer. The role of giver of cries implies a receiver, and also the role of being the gift given from hand to hand. Meanwhile the role of infant receiver implies an actively engaged, attentive, and repeated giver who is always doing "mind reading," inferring the child's needs and is successful in satisfying them. The child can play these three complementary roles him/herself, and quite early can understand the other's part in the interaction because s/he also takes turns and plays that part in another moment. S/he knows it by doing it.

These are the roles of the gift image schema that underlie the transitivity of language as a verbal gift economy. In fact the transitive sentence is formed in that schema with the subject as giver, the predicate as gift or service and the object as receiver. A simple example is "The girl hit the ball." Here "girl" is the giver; "hit," the gift or service; and "ball," the receiver. At the same time the speaker (or writer) gives the gift of the sentence to the listener (or reader). Words themselves can be considered as verbal gifts, given to satisfy the cognitive and communicative needs of others regarding the world. This aspect of language is "altercentric" in that it is the need of the other that we satisfy with words. We have to use the language of the other, the word-gifts she knows, in order to create a relation for her regarding some part of the world. Once his/her need for the word-gift has been satisfied, our own relation to that part of the world has an equivalent in his/hers and becomes aligned with his/hers. If language is framed as self-expression, it is not clear how the listener or reader understands. Considering language to be altercentric makes connection with the other the basis and the possibility of linguistic communication about many things, including the expression of the self. As I mentioned above, language is also not simply infinitely creative as Chomsky suggests but infinitely creative in satisfying the communicative and cognitive needs of others.

Even intransitive sentences are given by one person to another and thus remain in the gift frame. Linguists talk about words modifying each other because they have slots and fillers, ways they fit into each other. However, the gift can be projected into this metaphor also and words can be seen as having needs that other words satisfy. The word "ball" cannot on its own express the red quality of the ball and so we give it the gift of the word "red" to satisfy that need.

These few indications can give an idea of the how we can see language as an ongoing construction of human relation—creating verbal gifts. It is an ideal gift economy, where we give and receive in abundance because giving verbal gifts does not mean that we don't have them anymore.[24]

If as philosophers tell us, language is our species-specific trait and if gift-giving is its internal structure, humans are basically gift-giving maternal animals. We have been alienated from this human capability by the economy based on exchange.

Patriarchal capitalist interactions are not very satisfactory for those engaged in them. Our uncompassionate system takes a heavy toll even on those who are materially benefitted by it, creating loneliness, meaninglessness, and depravity. In fact, much research is being done at present on the neurological and health benefits of generosity. Many new initiatives such as www.charityfocus.org encourage gift-giving at the level of kind acts in daily life, and this group has started a free restaurant, the Karma Cafe in San Francisco, where clients pay only for the clients who come after them. There are widespread initiatives in the USA and other countries for reclaiming and sharing the commons, community experiments, "free stores," gifting circles, and giveaways like the Really Really Free Market, and others like www.couchsurfing.org, bikes not bombs, food not bombs, and freecycling, which provide free resources, while still in the context of exchange. None of these initiatives recognize the connection with motherers, altercentric childhood, or women, though some do refer to Indigenous gift economies, usually in Maussian anthropologists' terms of "gift exchange."[25]

The free software movement has been an attempt to practice a kind of gift economy interpreted as competitive "gift exchange." In fact the Internet has much potential for practicing the gift economy because of the abundance of knowledge gifts it provides. However, like other gift sources it is vulnerable to capitalist appropriation. Globalization has shown how the privatization and commodification of previously free gifts like water, seeds, Indigenous knowledges, and even genes, can feed capitalist patriarchy. In fact, commodification of the Internet and now even of the needs, interests, and desires of users through data collection is only one more new way to plunder gifts. To me perhaps one of the most troubling of these developments is the commodification of language through advertising. We have commodified language before ever realizing it was a gift.

It is time for a matriarchal[25] gift economy to replace the market economy. Perhaps this can be achieved by uniting across categories as gift-giving-and-receiving people—Indigenous people and motherers of all nations and genders, providers of solutions and satisfiers of needs of all kinds, speakers and listeners, writers and readers. Actually this human multitude potentially includes everyone who was mothered in childhood and everyone who can speak, even those who are still deeply entangled in the paradigm of exchange.

References

Amadiume, Ifi. *Re-Inventing Africa: Matriarchy, Religion and Culture.* Zed Books, 1997.

Bateson, M. C. "The Epigenesis of Conversational Interaction: A Personal Account of Research Development." In *Before Speech: The Beginning of Interpersonal Communication,* 63–78. Cambridge, UK: Cambridge University Press.

Bennholdt-Thomsen, C. ["The Child's Position in Civilization"]. *Munch Med Wochenschr* 99, no. 15 (April 12, 1957): 505–10

Bourne, Edward Gaylord, and Julius E. Olson, eds. *The Voyages of Columbus and of John Cabot.* New York: Charles Scribner's Sons, 1906.

Braten, Stein, ed. *Intersubjective Communication and Emotion in Early Ontogeny.* Cambridge: Cambridge University Press, 1998.

Derrida, Jacques. *Spectres of Marx: The State of Debt, the Work of Mourning, and the New International.* New York: Routledge, 1994.

Goettner-Abendroth, Heide. *Matriarchal Societies: Studies on Indigenous Cultures across the Globe.* Peter Lang Inc., 2012.Goettner-Abendroth, Heide, ed. *Societies of Peace.* Toronto: Inanna Publications, 2009.

Gopnik, Alison. "How Babies Think." *Scientific American* (July 2010): 76–81.

Kuhl, Patricia K. "Early Language Acquisition: Cracking the Speech Code." *Nature Reviews* 5 (November 2004): 831–35.

Lakoff, George, and Mark Johnson. *Metaphors We Live By.* University of Chicago Press, 1980.

Malinowsky, Bronislaw. *Sex and Repression in Savage Society*. Routledge: [1927] 2001.

Meltzoff, A. N., and R. Brooks. "Eyes Wide Shut: The Importance of Eyes in Infant Gaze Following and Understanding Other Minds. In *Gaze Following: Its Development and Significance*, edited by R. Flom, K. Lee, and D. Muir, 217–41. Mahwah, NJ: Erlbaum, 2007.

Muraro, Luisa. Translated by Francesca Novello. *The Symbolic Order of the Mother*. Albany: SUNY Press, [1992] 2018.

Reddy, Michael. "The Conduit Metaphor: A Case of Frame Conflict in Our Language about Language." In *Metaphor and Thought*, edited by A. Ortony, 284–310. Cambridge: Cambridge University Press, 1979.

Sperber, Dan, and Dierdre Wilson. *Relevance: Communication and Cognition*. 2nd ed. Oxford: Blackwell, 1995.

Trevarthen, Colwyn. "Communication and Cooperation in Early Infancy: A Description of Primary Intersubjectivity." In *Before Speech: The Beginning of Human Communication*, edited by M. Bullowa, 321–47. Cambridge: Cambridge University Press, 1979.

Trevarthen, Colwyn. "The Concept and Foundations of Infant Intersubjectivity." In *Intersubjective Communication and Emotion in Early Ontogeny*, edited by Stein Braten, 15–46. Cambridge: Cambridge University Press, 1998.

Trevarthen, Colwyn. "What Is It Like to Be a Person Who Knows Nothing? Defining the Active Intersubjective Mind of a Newborn Human Being." *Infant and Child Development* (January 2011). doi.org/10.1002/icd.689

Vaughan, Genevieve. *Women and the Gift Economy: A Radically Different Worldview Is Possible*. Toronto: Inanna Publications, 2007.

Waihong, Choo. *The Kingdom of Women*. I.B. Tauris, 2017.

Warneken, Felix, and Michael Tomasello. "Varieties of Altruism in Chimpanzees and Children." *Trends in Cognitive Science* 13, no. 9 (2009): 397–402.

Watson-Franke, M.-B. "A World in Which Women Move Freely without Fear of Men: An Anthropological Perspective on Rape." *Women's Studies International Forum* 25, no. 6 (2002): 599–606.

Weatherford, Jack McIver. *Indian Givers: How the Indians of the Americas Transformed the World*. New York: Fawcett Columbine, 1988.

Webley, Paul. "Children's Understanding of Economics." In *Children's Understanding of Society*, edited by M. Barrett and E. Buchanan-Barrow, 44–50 (online 43–67). Hove, East Sussex: Psychology Press, 2005.

Endnotes

1 Edward Gaylord Bourne and Julius E. Olson, eds., *The Voyages of Columbus and of John Cabot* (New York: Charles Scribner's Sons, 1906).

2 I use quotation marks here because saying "pre" may suggest that that what comes later is more developed or advanced. Patriarchy is not an improvement on pre-patriarchy, and capitalism is not an improvement on the gift economy.

3 Jack McIver Weatherford, *Indian Givers: How the Indians of the Americas Transformed the World* (New York: Fawcett Columbine, 1988), Chapter 1.

4 I call all of them "motherers" in order to show that I am talking about a social practice in which anyone can be engaged. This practice is carried out more often by birth mothers because societies interpret the biological fact as an indication that the role of motherer should be assigned to them.

5 Paul Webley, "Children's Understanding of Economics," in *Children's Understanding of Society*, ed. M. Barrett and E. Buchanan-Barrow, 44–50; online 43–67 (Hove, East Sussex: Psychology Press, 2005). The market is now also encroaching on the childhood gift economy through advertising to infants.

6 Meltzoff, A. N. Meltzoff and R. Brooks, "Eyes Wide Shut: The Importance of Eyes in Infant Gaze Following and Understanding Other Minds," in *Gaze Following: Its Development and Significance*, ed. R. Flom, K. Lee, and D. Muir, 217–41 (Mahwah, NJ: Erlbaum, 2007), 153–54.

7 Ibid., 163.

8 M. C. Bateson, "The Epigenesis of Conversational Interaction: A Personal Account of Research Development," in *Before Speech: The Beginning of Interpersonal Communication*, 63–78 (Cambridge: Cambridge University Press, 1979), 651; Colwyn Trevarthen, "Communication and Cooperation in Early Infancy: A Description of Primary Intersubjectivity," in *Before Speech: The Beginning of Human Communication*, ed. M. Bullowa, 321–47 (Cambridge: Cambridge University Press, 1979), 321; Colwyn Trevarthen, "The Concept and Foundations of Infant Intersubjectivity," in *Intersubjective Communication and Emotion in Early Ontogeny*, ed. Stein Braten, 15–46 (Cambridge: Cambridge University Press, 1998).

9 Trevarthen, "Concept and Foundations of Infant Intersubjectivity."

10 Stein Braten, ed., *Intersubjective Communication and Emotion in Early Ontogeny* (Cambridge: Cambridge University Press, 1998), 105.

11 For decades there has been a discussion among philosophers exploring the possibility of the unilateral gift. In *Spectres of Marx: The State of Debt, the Work of Mourning, and the New International* (New York: Routledge, 1994), 13–14, Jacques Derrida questioned the very existence of free giving. He said that being

recognized as having given a gift necessarily brings an ego boost for the giver that pays him/her for the gift, thus turning the transaction into an exchange. However, if everyone is doing it (as motherers are), there would be no ego boost, so the gift would indeed be free.

12 See Heide Goettner-Abendroth's *Matriarchal Societies: Studies on Indigenous Cultures across the Globe* (Peter Lang Inc., 2012), for a discussion of a number of these societies. Her edited book, *Societies of Peace* (Toronto: Inanna Publications, 2009), brings the voices of many Indigenous women together. My own edited book, *Women and the Gift Economy: A Radically Different Worldview Is Possible* (Toronto: Inanna Publications, 2007), is a collection of essays by Indigenous and non-Indigenous women.

13 C. Bennholdt-Thomsen, ["The Child's Position in Civilization,"], *Munch Med Wochenschr* 99, no. 15 (April 12, 1957): 505–10.

14 M.-B. Watson-Franke, "A World in Which Women Move Freely without Fear of Men: An Anthropological Perspective on Rape," *Women's Studies International Forum* 25, no. 6 (2002): 605.

15 The Mosuo in China are a good example. They have "visiting marriages" and matrilocality. Goettner-Abendroth, *Matriarchal Societies*, Chapter 5.2.

16 This idea was broached by Bronislaw Malinowsky in *Sex and Repression in Savage Society* (Routledge: [1927] 2001), Chapter 5, and was widely discussed and contested. More recently, in *Re-Inventing Africa: Matriarchy, Religion and Culture* (Zed Books, 1997), 40, Ifi Amadiume discussed the lack of Oedipus complex among African groups like the Jeljobe. She says, "The presence of these fundamental matriarchal systems generating love and compassion also means that we cannot take the classical Greek Oedipal principle of violence as a basic paradigm or given in the African context."

17 Alison Gopnik, "How Babies Think," *Scientific American* (July 2010): 81.

18 Dan Sperber and Dierdre Wilson, *Relevance: Communication and Cognition*, 2nd ed. (Oxford: Blackwell, 1995), 3.1–2.

19 Felix Warneken and Michael Tomasello, "Varieties of Altruism in Chimpanzees and Children," *Trends in Cognitive Science* 13, no. 9 (2009): 397–402. In a phylogenetic investigation, the authors showed that chimpanzees also have a kind of rudimentary altruism. I would just comment that chimpanzees have mothers, too!

20 Colwyn Trevarthen, "What Is It Like to Be a Person Who Knows Nothing? Defining the Active Intersubjective Mind of a Newborn Human Being," *Infant and Child Development* (January 2011): 119. Trevarthen says, "[I]t seems that cultural intelligence itself is motivated at every stage by the kind of powers of innate intersubjective sympathy that an alert infant can show shortly after birth. We are born to generate shifting states of self-awareness, to show them to other

persons, and to provoke interest and affectionate responses from them. Thus starts a new psychology of the creativity and cooperative knowing and meaning in human communities."

21 Patricia K. Kuhl, "Early Language Acquisition: Cracking the Speech Code," *Nature Reviews* 5 (November 2004): 838.

22 Italian philosopher Luisa Muraro opposed Lacan's "symbolic order of the father" in her book, *L'Ordine Simbolico della Madre*: *The Symbolic Order of the Mother*, trans. Francesca Novello (Albany: SUNY [1992] 2018).

23 George Lakoff and Mark Johnson, *Metaphors We Live By* (University of Chicago Press, 1980).

24 Cognitive linguists might object that gift-giving is too similar to the "conduit metaphor" studied by Michael J. Reddy in "The Conduit Metaphor: A Case of Frame Conflict in Our Language about Language," in *Metaphor and Thought*, ed. A. Ortony, 284–310 Cambridge: Cambridge University Press, 1979). Reddy found hundreds of metaphors in English that had to do with transmission, such as "I can't get my idea across." Reddy thought that tool use was a more appropriate metaphor. Because it is necessary for the child's survival, gift-giving/receiving (GGR) is a more fundamental interaction than transmission through a conduit, the use of tools, packaging and unpacking, and coding and decoding, and it is more likely that GGR is projected into language.

25 See the French journal MAUSS (*www.revuedumauss.com*), founded in 1981.

26 I use the term "matriarchy" in consonance with the modern matriarchal studies movement, not to connote a mirror image of patriarchy but as a name for an egalitarian form of society based on maternal values of care.

SECTION 2

NEW QUESTIONS AND INTERPRETATIONS OF OLD STORIES

A WORKING HYPOTHESIS FOR THE STUDY OF RELIGION IN A MINOAN VILLAGE: THE THEORIES OF HARRIET BOYD HAWES, MARIJA GIMBUTAS, HEIDE GOETTNER-ABENDROTH, AND JAN DRIESSEN

CAROL P. CHRIST

Gournia, excavated by Harriet Boyd Hawes[1] at the beginning of the twentieth century, is the only Minoan village to be excavated fully. Much of Minoan archaeology focuses on the so-called "palaces," such as Knossos. According to archaeologist Jan Driessen, the excavator of Knossos, Arthur Evans concluded on the basis of very little evidence that he had discovered a palace at Knossos ruled by a king and a queen. Later archaeologists have generally followed Evans in assuming that a king or a ruling elite presided over ancient Crete. It may be easier to assume that prehistoric cultures were hierarchical, warlike, and male dominant like our own, than to challenge established authorities and conventional wisdom.[2] Reacting to this, Driessen penned an essay titled "The King Must Die," arguing that because there is no convincing evidence that a king ruled in ancient Crete, scholars should consider alternative social structures.[3]

With the publication of *Gournia* in 1908, the work of Boyd Hawes became foundational for the understanding of Minoan Crete. Though her work as an excavator is respected, her theories about Minoan religion and culture have been ignored. Boyd Hawes stated that Minoan culture was very different from the Mycenean and classical Greek cultures that came after it. She wrote that Crete "long retained traces of the matriarchal system,"[4] defined as *matriliny* or the mother family in which the status of

Fig. 5. Gournia. Photo by Laura Shannon, 2021.

women was "strong and independent."[5] She spoke of "the pre-eminence of a goddess, almost to the exclusion of male divinities, and the prominent place held by women in ancient Crete ... evidenced by many representations of their daily life in the wall-paintings."[6] Boyd Hawes distinguished the ancient Cretans from the patriarchal and warlike Indo-Europeans or "Aryans"[7] who entered Greece at the end of the third millennium BCE[8] and their descendants, the Achaeans or Myceneans who later conquered Crete, as well as from the cultures of the Nile and Euphrates Valleys whose art she described as "monumental and sacerdotal" in contrast to the "emotional character" of Cretan art, which "in its aesthetic aims ... surpasses both."[9] "Monumental and sacerdotal" refer to the sacralizing of hierarchical kingship in larger-than-life–size friezes, frescoes, and statues in Egypt and Mesopotamia, while "emotional" describes the feeling of connection of all life in the small-scale art of ancient Crete. Citing evidence of pre–Indo-European words in the Greek language, Boyd Hawes argued that the languages of the earlier inhabitants of Greece known as the Pelasgians and of ancient Cretans cannot have been "Aryan."[10] Her colleague Blanche E. Williams wrote of a "Great Goddess" with many aspects of the prominent deity of ancient Crete.[11] She disputed the idea that the bull represents a male god[12] and Evans' contention that the pillar is a "representation of a *male* divinity."[13] She noted further that "[t]he presence of priestesses in Minoan cult scenes is noteworthy."[14] Boyd Hawes and Williams presented the first, and for a long time, the only, woman-centered view of Minoan Crete.[15] They anticipated the more fully developed ideas of archaeologist Marija Gimbutas,[16] including her understanding of a "clash of cultures" between the Old Europeans and Indo-Europeans and her theory of Kurgan[17] or Indo-European invasions of Old Europe.[18]

Marija Gimbutas coined the term "Old Europe" to refer to the peaceful Neolithic cultures ca. 6500–3500 BCE[19] that preceded invasions of Europe by Indo-European–speaking peoples ca. 4400–2500 BCE. The Indo-European invaders were semi-nomadic, had domesticated the horse, and came from north of the Black and Caspian seas. They were patriarchal, patrilineal, warlike horse riders who worshipped the shining Gods of the sky as reflected in their shining bronze weapons; they were indifferent to art.[20] In contrast, the Old Europeans were peaceful, settled and agricultural, highly artistic, worshipped the Goddess as the powers of birth, death, and regeneration in all of life, and were matrilineal and probably matrilocal. Recent DNA research has confirmed Gimbutas's theory of Indo-European invasions. The Y (male) DNA (R1a and R1b) of the Yamnaya people who invaded Europe ca. 2500 BCE is the most common in Europe.[21]

Although Gimbutas's theories about religion and Goddesses in Old Europe have been dismissed by many archaeologists as nothing more than romantic fantasy,[22] I agree with Paul Wheatley who said, "[a] theory is not to be rejected on the basis of lack of evidence. A theory is not even to be rejected on the basis of adverse evidence. A theory is only to be rejected in favor of a better theory."[23] I find that Gimbutas's theories help to interpret the meaning of ancient Cretan artifacts. Her insight that the Goddess symbolized the cycles of birth, death, and regeneration in all of life in Old European religion can be seen in the recurring image of the spiral spiraling into another spiral on Minoan artifacts, while triangles denote the female triangle as the Source of Life, dots represent seeds, and wavy lines water. Her theory that Old European cultures were matrilineal and matrifocal

Fig. 6. Gournia. Photo by Laura Shannon, 2021.

better explains the artistic record of ancient Crete than the theory that it was ruled by kings or male elites.

Boyd Hawes describes the culture of ancient Crete as matriarchal and matrilineal, while Gimbutas calls it matrilineal, matrifocal, and probably matrilocal. A matrilineal society traces descent through the mother. In a matrilocal society, females stay in their family homes and males either visit or move in with their female partners. In matrilocal societies, land, often held communally, is passed down in female lines. Philosopher Heide Goettner-Abendroth[24] provides a structural definition of matriarchy based on her research on living matriarchies that can help us to understand how matriarchy, matriliny, and matrilocality might have functioned in ancient Crete.

Goettner-Abendroth insists that matriarchy is not the opposite of patriarchy; matriarchies are egalitarian because women share power with men.[25] She defines matriarchy as "mothers at the beginning."[26] Motherhood does not refer solely or primarily to the capacity or act of giving birth. Instead, it refers to the fact that the values associated with motherhood—care, love, and generosity—are considered to be the highest values. As Goettner-Abendroth explains, the biological fact of motherhood is transformed into a cultural model.[27] In matriarchal societies a woman does not have to have given birth in order to be considered a mother, for she will love and care for the children of her sisters and cousins. The values of love, care, and generosity are not limited to child care. Matriarchal peoples believe they should apply everywhere, from the nurturing of young plants to the nurturing of the vulnerable in general. Boys and men care for children, and they are expected to embody the values of love and care in all of the activities they undertake.[28] The gender binaries of modern Western culture—male active and aggressive, female passive and receptive—would make no sense to members of matriarchal cultures; they understand mothering values to be active, do not limit them to women and the home, and would not tolerate aggressive behavior from anyone.

Goettner-Abendroth finds that matriarchies have four common structural characteristics:

- They generally practice agriculture and maintain relative equality through well-established practices of gift-giving.

- They are matrilineal, with family identity being passed through the mother line, and matrilocal, with the primary residences and agricultural land being held by the maternal clan.

- They have well-developed systems of participatory democracy and consensus.

- They tend to view the earth as a great and giving mother.[29]

Matriarchal societies usually practice small-scale agriculture, often called horticulture, with the majority of the farm labor being done by hand using simple tools. Women are generally responsible for planting, nurturing small plants, and weeding, with men contributing heavy labor. Matrilineal groups usually live in large extended family households consisting of a grandmother, her daughters and their daughters, as well as male and female children. The brothers, sons, and grandsons of the grandmother and her descendants live in the matrilineal home and are the role models for male children; biological fatherhood may be known, but is not relevant to lineage, on-going care and support of children, or inheritance. Decisions about the internal life of the clan are made by the grandmothers, who have been taught to take account of the needs of all of their children and grandchildren, as expressed in daily interactions and in clan meetings. The internal life of the clan includes family, agriculture, production of pottery, cloth, and other goods, as well as intra-clan politics and economics. Decisions about trade and relations with other groups—the external life of the clan—are often made by elder men or great-uncles; their leaders are usually appointed, approved, or subject to removal by the women's councils in order to ensure that the best interests of everyone in the clan or society is taken into account.[30]

In matriarchal societies the "cultural ideal" of motherhood as love and generosity is understood to reflect the cosmic principle: the earth is viewed as a loving and generous mother who provides for her children, inspiring them to live in emulation of her. Sherri Mitchell, who grew up on the Penobscot Indian Island Reservation in Maine, expresses this idea:

> We have been born into a natural gifting economy through our natural healthy relationship, balanced relationship, with mother earth that is based on reciprocity—that there is this constant give-and-take; and we have ceremonies that acknowledge that beginning at birth and going all the way through our lives until our death. So, when we are carrying our children, when our children are in our wombs, that is the first ecosystem of the child, this holding place where they are nourished and nurtured and cultivated with what they need in order to be born into the second ecosystem, which is, of course, our mother earth, *nicoscitemis* [the Penobscot word for mother earth], and then mother earth nurtures, cultivates, and cares for the bodies of our children from that point forward until the time of their death. And then when we die our bodies return to mother earth, and we become the nourishment in the soil for the future generations. And so, we have ceremonies that recognize this, that take place connected to birth—where the placenta is buried underneath a tree in order to recognize the continuation of our connection to th[e] tree of life, but also the umbilical cord is buried to represent the transition [of the child] from birth mother to earth mother.[31]

Gratitude to Mother Earth for the gift of life is at the center of ritual and religion and is expressed through ceremonies of "giving back" to the earth what she has given, through offerings and libations. Food offerings to Mother Earth connected with the harvest are consumed in communal feasts. In this way, community is created and sustained, and individuals learn that the gifts provided by Mother Earth are not the property of individuals or clans, but are to be shared by all.

Anthropologist Ruby Rohrlich-Leavitt stated that her colleagues will generally "concede" that women invented agriculture, but do not draw any conclusions from this important fact.[32] This silence may be the reason women's invention of agriculture has not been at the center of theories about female power in the Neolithic. As the primary gatherers of plants and the primary preparers of plant foods, women would have been the ones to notice that seeds dropped after the harvest sometimes sprouted up around the campsites. Over a long process of observation and experimentation, women would have learned when and how to plant, how to nurture young plants, how to water and weed, and when and how to harvest and preserve seeds. This information, understood as an aspect of the mysteries of birth, death, and regeneration, would have been passed down the female line through story, song, dance, and ritual. Pottery-making and weaving would also have been seen as mysteries of transformation rooted in the processes of birth, death, and regeneration, and the secrets of their production would have been passed down in rituals. Women would have been the ones to lead these rituals. Female power in Neolithic matrilineal and matrilocal cultures had a material and economic base—it was not just about "birthing babies." It was spiritual as well, because the power to nurture children and plants was understood to be a reflection of the life-giving power of Mother Earth.

DNA evidence suggests that the Neolithic culture of Crete was the basis of the more technologically developed and highly artistic culture of Bronze Age Crete. Although many archaeologists have insisted that the Bronze Age culture of Minoan Crete must have been brought in by migrants from the Near East or elsewhere, there is no DNA evidence suggesting that a new cultural group or groups settled in Crete in the early Bronze Age.[33] As there was no population change, Bronze Age technology would have been integrated into the existing culture. The new bronze technology may have enhanced the roles of men as traders and workers in bronze, but as long as agriculture, pottery, and weaving retained their importance in the culture as a whole, women would not have lost status or independence.

Belgian archaeologist Jan Driessen, an expert on Minoan architecture, has been exploring the hypothesis that ancient Crete is best understood as a matrilocal and matrilineal culture. He finds evidence that grandmothers, mothers, and their children lived in large or great houses rather than in smaller nuclear family dwellings. Driessen refers to these large houses as the Established House or simply as the House. He notes that large Houses are usually connected to matrilineal social structures, while smaller nuclear family homes reflect the tendency of patriarchal families to divide into smaller units.[34] He re-examined excavated houses and villas in ancient Crete to see if he could find great House structures. The hypothesis of the House provides an answer to the question of whether the so-called villas, such as those at Tylissos—which have distinct ritual features such as lustral basins and altars—are a rich person's home or local shrines. Driessen argues that they are extended family Houses and suggests that rituals concerning birth, death, and the inheritance of ancestral wisdom would have taken place in them. Driessen reconfigured the outer walls of attached houses in Minoan villages. In Gournia, he found that there were walls of different thicknesses: counting only the thickest walls as the outer walls of house structures, he reinterpreted what had been viewed as a series of nuclear family dwellings into a smaller number of Houses or neighborhood complexes consisting of related families sharing common areas.[35] In Malia, Driessen found ritual spaces near the kitchens, suggesting that rituals in the House took place in women's spaces and would have been led by women.[36]

Taking all of this into account, we can formulate a working hypothesis for reinterpreting the archaeological records, based on the assumption that the religion of ancient Crete arose within a matrilineal mother-centered culture in the Neolithic that continued into the Bronze Age. We should expect to find evidence that women had leadership roles in religion. Numerous seal rings show women as the leading participants in rituals. The miniature frescoes from Knossos show a group of older women sitting in the place of honor and a group of women performing a ritual dance.[37] Where evidence concerning gender is lacking, it should not be assumed that leadership must have been in the hands of men.

We should not be surprised to find the Goddess or Mother Earth to be at the center of rituals and ceremonies. However, to say that the Goddess is central begs the question of what we mean when we say "Goddess." In the West, the deity is understood to be transcendent of the world, a dominant male other and judge of the living and the dead. Citing the *Shorter Oxford Dictionary*, archaeologist Colin Renfrew based his discussion of Minoan religion on the idea of divine transcendence.[38] But if we accept Marija Gimbutas's insight that the Goddess represents the powers of birth, death, and regeneration in all of life, the Goddess is immanent in, rather than transcendent of, the world. She is the enlivening force in human beings and all of nature. She is not the judge of the living and the dead, for the dead are returned to her body.[39] Unlike later Greek deities, the goddesses of Old Europe and ancient Crete are not generally portrayed as idealized human beings. Though they often have eyes, breasts, and sacred triangles, they also have beaks and wings, are shaped like mountains, and decorated with flowing lines symbolizing rivers or streams. These hybrid forms suggest that all life is in the image of divinity and that humans are not higher, better, or separate from other life forms. They call human beings to participate in and enjoy this world, not to escape or rise above it. Jacquetta Hawkes's insight that the religion of ancient Crete celebrated "the grace of life"[40] is exactly right.

Is the Old European or Minoan Goddess one or many? Gimbutas and other Goddess scholars have been criticized for imposing monotheism on ancient religions. Theologian and liturgist Marcia Falk's distinction between exclusive and inclusive monotheism is helpful here.[41] Inclusive monotheism is an intuition of the unity of being within the diversity of the world: celebrating the unity of being, it welcomes a plurality of images to represent diversity and difference. When Gimbutas spoke of the powers of birth, death, and regeneration in all of life, she was referring to the unity of being underlying the diversity of life forms, including plants, animals, and human beings. Similarly, when Indigenous peoples speak of Mother Earth as the giver of all and all beings as relatives, they recognize that all life is sustained by a single source. The fact that ancient Cretans imaged divinity in different ways and with different characteristics does not require the conclusion that they worshipped many discrete deities.[42] I suggest that they intuited a unity of being while celebrating the diversity of life.

If matrilineal, matrifocal, and matriarchal cultures tend to view the earth as a great and giving mother, we can expect this insight to be expressed in rituals and ceremonies. Gratitude is the appropriate response to gifts freely given. Gratitude for the gift and gifts of life was not only a focus, but, I believe, the central focus, of religion in ancient Crete. We might expect to find evidence of rituals celebrating the gift of life in the birth of babies, the coming-of-age of girls, for the ancestors. Many of these rituals would have taken place in the matrilineal House. Rituals for the ancestors might also have taken place in cemeteries. We should also expect to find rituals expressing gratitude for the food that sustains life, for example, in offerings of first fruits to Mother Earth and in the pouring of libations that are absorbed back into her body. We should find rituals focused on planting, harvesting, and storing seeds. Some of these rituals might have taken place in the matrilineal Houses, while others surely took place in the fields. We should look for evidence of rituals associated with pottery and weaving in the Houses or in workshops. It is known that rites in ancient Crete involved trees, mountains, and caves, as well as water sources. We must ask if and how such ceremonies expressed gratitude to Mother Earth, the source of life, and the cycles of birth, death, and regeneration. The results of every inquiry are shaped by the standpoint from which we ask questions. I hope that this new perspective will help us to overcome patriarchal assumptions as we strive to understand the nature of religion at Gournia and in ancient Crete.

References

Boyd Hawes, Harriet, with Blanche E. Williams, Richard B. Seager, and Edith Hall. *Gournia: Vasiliki and Other Prehistoric Sites on the Isthmus of Hierapetra Crete*, 2nd ed. Philadelphia: INSTAP Academic Press, [1908] 2014.

Christ, Carol P. "A Different World: The Challenge of the Work of Marija Gimbutas to the Dominant Worldview of Western Culture." In *From the Realm of the Ancestors*, edited by Joan Marler, 406–15. Manchester, CT: Knowledge, Ideas & Trends, 1997.

Cichon, Joan M. *Matriarchy in Bronze Age Crete: A Perspective from Archaeomythology and Modern Matriarchal Studies.* Oxford: Archaeopress, 2021.

Conkey, Margaret, and Ruth Tringham. "Archaeology and the Goddess: Exploring the Contours of Feminist Archaeology." In *Feminisms in the Academy*, edited by D. C. Stanton and A. J. Stewart, 199–247. Ann Arbor: University of Michigan Press, 1995.

Dexter, Miriam Robbins. "The Roots of Indo-European Patriarchy: Indo-European Female Figures and the Principles of Energy." In *The Rule of Mars*, edited by Cristina Biaggi, 143-154. Manchester, CT: Knowledge Ideas and Trends, 2006.

Driessen, Jan. "The King Must Die." In *Monuments of Minos: Rethinking the Minoan Palaces*, Proceedings of an International Workshop Held in Louvain-la-Neuve, 2001, edited by J. Driessen, I. Schoep, and R. Laffineur, 1–15. Liège: Aegaeum 23, 2002.

Driessen, Jan. "Spirit of Place: Minoan Houses as Major Actors." In *Political Economies of the Aegean Bronze Age*, edited by Daniel J. Pullen, 35–65. Oxford: Oxbow Press, 2010.

Driessen, Jan. "A Matrilocal House Society in Pre- and Protopalatial Crete?" In *Back to the Beginning: Proceedings of the Leuven Workshop*, edited by I. Schoep, P. Tomkins, and J. Driessen, 358–383. Oxford: Oxbow Press, 2011.

Driessen, Jan. "Understanding Minoan In-House Relationships on Late Bronze Age Crete." In *Minoan Architecture and Urbanism: New Perspectives on Ancient Built Environment*, edited by Quentin Letesson and Carl Knappett, 80–106. Oxford: Oxford University Press, 2017.

Fitton, J. Lesley. *Minoans*. London: British Museum Press, 2002.

Gimbutas, Marija. *Goddesses and Gods of Old Europe.* Los Angeles: University of California Press, [1974] 1987.

Gimbutas, Marija. *The Language of the Goddess*. San Francisco: Harper & Row, 1989.

Gimbutas, Marija. *The Civilization of the Goddess*. Edited by Joan Marler. San Francisco: HarperCollins, 1991.

Gimbutas, Marija. *The Living Goddesses*. Edited by Miriam Robbins Dexter. Berkeley: University of California Press, 1999, 2001.

Goettner-Abendroth, Heide. "Introduction: Matriarchy and Modern Matriarchal Society." In *Societies of Peace*, edited by Goettner-Abendroth. Toronto: Inanna Publications, 2009.

Goettner-Abendroth, Heide. "The Deep Structure of Matriarchal Society." In *Societies of Peace*, edited by Goettner-Abendroth, 17-28. Toronto: Inanna Publications, 2009.

Haak, Wolfgang, Iosif Lazaridis, Nick Patterson, et al. "Massive Migration from the Steppe Was a Source for Indo-European Languages in Europe." *Nature* 52 (June 11, 2015). doi: 10.1038/nature14317.

Hawkes, Jacquetta. *Dawn of the Gods*. Random House, 1968.

Hodder, Ian. "Women and Men at Catalhöyük." *Scientific American* 290/1 (January 2004): 77–83.

Hughey, Jeffrey, Peristera Paschou, Petros Drineas, et al. "A European Population in Minoan Bronze Age Crete." *Nat Commun* 4, no. 1861 (2013). https://doi.org/10.1038/ncomms2871

Mann, Barbara Alice. *Iroquoian Women: The Gantowisas*. American Indian Studies, vol. 4. Peter Lang Inc., International Academic Publishers, 2006.

Marinatos, Nanno. *Minoan Kingship and the Solar Goddess*. Urbana Champaign: Illinois University Press, 2010.

Meskell, Lynn. "Goddesses, Gimbutas, and the 'New Age' Archaeology." *Antiquity* 69 (1995): 74–86.

Moss, Marina L., *The Minoan Pantheon: Towards an Understanding of Its Nature and Extent*. International Series 1343. Oxford: British Archaeological Reports, 2005.

Redfield, James M. *The Locrian Maidens: Love and Death in Greek Italy*. Princeton, NJ: Princeton University Press, 2003.

Rohrlich-Leavitt, Ruby. "State Formation in Sumer and the Subjugation of Women." *Feminist Studies* 6, no. 1 (1980): 76–102.

Sanday, Peggy Reeves. *Female Power and Male Dominance: On the Origins of Sexual Inequality*. New York: Cambridge University Press, 1981.

Sanday, Peggy Reeves. *Women at the Center: Life in a Modern Matriarchy*. Ithaca, NY: Cornell University Press, 2003.

Spretnak, Charlene. "Anatomy of a Backlash: Concerning the Work of Maria Gimbutas." In *The Journal of Archaeomythology* 7 (2011): 25–51. Spretnak-Journal-7.pdf (archaeomythology.org), accessed February 2, 2021.

Waihong, Choo. *The Kingdom of Women*. I.B. Tauris, 2017.

Endnotes

1 Harriet Boyd married shortly after completing the excavations at Gournia and published her major work on Gournia and related sites under her married name, Harriet Boyd Hawes. I will refer to her as Boyd Hawes because that is the name she used after her marriage. Blanche E. Wheeler contributed to the Gournia volume under her married name, Blanche E. Williams.

2 Carol P. Christ, "A Different World: The Challenge of the Work of Marija Gimbutas to the Dominant Worldview of Western Culture," in *From the Realm of the Ancestors*, ed. Joan Marler, 406–15 (Manchester, CT: Knowledge, Ideas & Trends, 1997).

3 In J. Driessen, I. Schoep, and R. Laffineur, eds., *Monuments of Minos: Rethinking the Minoan Palaces*, Proceedings of an international workshop held in Louvain-la-Neuve, 2001, 1–15 (Liège: Aegaeum 23, 2002).

4 Harriet Boyd Hawes, with Blanche E. Williams, Richard B. Seager, and Edith

Hall, *Gournia: Vasiliki and Other Prehistoric Sites on the Isthmus of Hierapetra Crete*, 2nd ed., (Philadelphia: INSTAP Academic Press, [1908] 2014), 9b.

5 Ibid., 9b, n. 47.

6 Ibid., 9b.

7 The term "Aryan" was used in the nineteenth and early twentieth centuries to refer to early speakers of Indo-European languages. The term fell out of favor after having been used in Nazi racial propaganda.

8 Boyd Hawes, *Gournia*, 8b.

9 Ibid., 9b. Boyd Hawes would have been critical of recent trends in archaeology that interpret the religion and culture of ancient Crete using models from the ancient Near East and Egypt, such as Nanno Marinatos, *Minoan Kingship and the Solar Goddess* (Urbana Champaign: University of Illinois Press, 2010). She also did not and would not find comparisons to classical Greece helpful.

10 Boyd Hawes, *Gournia*, 8b.

11 Ibid., 51b–52a.

12 Ibid., 52b.

13 Ibid., 53a.

14 Ibid.

15 The theories of Boyd Hawes and Williams are not explicitly named as woman-centered or feminist, nor are the two scholars consistently critical of androcentric assumptions. For example, in discussing the makers of pottery, Boyd Hawes refers to "craftsmen" and uses the generic "he." Today, in the village of Thrapsano in Crete, men throw the pots on the wheel, but women paint them. This could also have been the case in Minoan Crete. And it may be that women made pots as well, especially since many were for domestic use. For a recent woman-centered view, see Joan M. Cichon, *Matriarchy in Bronze Age Crete: A Perspective from Archaeomythology and Modern Matriarchal Studies* (Oxford: Archaeopress, 2021).

16 Gimbutas did not seem to have been familiar with the theories of Boyd Hawes and Williams; I have not been able to find a citation in her work to them. Crete was not one of her areas of specialization.

17 "Kurgan" is a term used by Gimbutas to refer to the Indo-European invaders of Europe. The term is derived from the name of their characteristic "big man" warrior graves which were constructed with a mound of earth over them.

18 See Marija Gimbutas, *Goddesses and Gods of Old Europe* (Los Angeles: University of California Press, [1974] 1987); *The Language of the Goddess* (San Francisco: Harper & Row, 1989); *The Civilization of the Goddess*, ed. Joan Marler (San Francisco: HarperCollins, 1991); and *The Living Goddesses*, ed.

Miriam Robbins Dexter (Berkeley: University of California Press, 1999, 2001). The theories mentioned below are discussed in these books.

19 The end date of 3500 BCE cited by Gimbutas reflects the fact that the Indo-Europeans came in waves. The second wave, which began about 3500 BCE, destroyed many of the Old European cultures. See Miriam Robbins Dexter, "The Roots of Indo-European Patriarchy: Indo-European Female Figures and the Principles of Energy," in *The Rule of Mars*, ed. Cristina Biaggi (Manchester, CT: Knowledge Ideas and Trends, 2006), 148. The third wave, ca. 2500 BCE, was the largest and most destructive.

20 Gimbutas is referring to plastic art. Boyd Hawes notes that the Indo-Europeans were talented storytellers.

21 Wolfgang Haak, Iosif Lazaridis, Nick Patterson, et al., "Massive Migration from the Steppe Was a Source for Indo-European Languages in Europe," *Nature* 52 (June 11, 2015): 208; doi: 10.1038/nature14317, accessed October 16, 2020.

22 Among others, Margaret Conkey and Ruth Tringham, "Archaeology and the Goddess: Exploring the Contours of Feminist Archaeology," in *Feminisms in the Academy*, ed. D. C. Stanton and A. J. Stewart, 199–247 (Ann Arbor: University of Michigan Press, 1995)–; Lynn Meskell, "Goddesses, Gimbutas, and the 'New Age' Archaeology," *Antiquity* 69 (1995): 74–86; Ian Hodder, "Women and Men at Catalhöyük," *Scientific American* 290/1 (January 2004): 77–83. Charlene Spretnak documents the controversy and defends Gimbutas against her detractors in "Anatomy of a Backlash: Concerning the Work of Maria Gimbutas," *The Journal of Archaeomythology* 7 (2011): 25–51; Spretnak-Journal-7.pdf (archaeomythology.org), accessed February 2, 2021.

23 Reconstructed quote in James M. Redfield, *The Locrian Maidens: Love and Death in Greek Italy* (Princeton, NJ: Princeton University Press, 2003), xii.

24 See International Academy Hagia for Modern Matriarchal Studies, https://www.hagia.de/en, accessed January 26, 2021.

25 In *Female Power and Male Dominance: On the Origins of Sexual Inequality* (New York: Cambridge University Press, 1981), Peggy Reeves Sanday reviewed the archaeological record, and did not find one example of a female-dominant society, nor any trace of male-power societies that were egalitarian.

26 Heide Goettner-Abendroth, "Introduction: Matriarchy and Modern Matriarchal Society," *Societies of Peace*, ed. Goettner-Abendroth (Toronto: Inanna Publications, 2009), 1. The Greek word "arche" can also be translated as "first principle," that which is expressed in everything.

27 See Angela Dolmetsch and Alessandra Piccoli, with Giovanna Berber, "Maternal Gift Economy Movement: Break Through, Virtual Salon #4," January 16, 2021, 4:34–43, Videos—Maternal Gift Economy (maternalgifteconomymovement.org), accessed and transcribed January 20, 2021.

28 Choo Waihong describes her surprise when, arriving on time for an appointment with a Mosuo elder man, he asks her to wait while he bathes and changes the diapers of a set of twins, in *The Kingdom of Women* (I.B. Tauris, 2017), 139.

29 Heidi Goettner-Abendroth, "The Deep Structure of Matriarchal Society," in *Societies of Peace*, (Toronto: Inanna Publications, 2009), 21–24.

30 See Peggy Reeves Sanday, *Women at the Center: Life in a Modern Matriarchy* (Ithaca, NY: Cornell University Press, 2003), and Barbara Alice Mann, *Iroquoian Women: The Gantowisas*, American Indian Studies, vol. 4 (Peter Lang Inc., International Academic Publishers, 2006).

31 Sherri Mitchell, quoted in Angela Dolmetsch and Alessandra Piccoli, "Maternal Gift Economy Movement, Salon #2," December 19, 2020, 1:40–42, Videos—Maternal Gift Economy (maternalgifteconomymovement.org), accessed and transcribed January 20, 2021.

32 Ruby Rohrlich-Leavitt, "State Formation in Sumer and the Subjugation of Women," *Feminist Studies* 6, no. 1 (1980), 76–102; https://www.jstor.org/stable/3177651?seq=1#page_scan_tab_contents, accessed February 1, 2021.

33 As stated by J. Hughey, P. Paschou, P. Drineas, et al., in "A European Population in Minoan Bronze Age Crete, *Nat Commun* 4, 1861 (2013) https://doi.org/10.1038/ncomms2871, "Our data are compatible with the hypothesis of an autochthonous development of the Minoan civilization by the descendants of the Neolithic settlers of the island."

34 "A Matrilocal House Society in Pre- and Protopalatial Crete?" Proceedings of the Leuven Conference, Back to the Beginning [2007], accessed on ResearchGate, https://www.researchgate.net/publication/285768820_J_Driessen_A_Prepalatial_Matrilinear_Society_in_I_Schoep_P_Tomkins_J_Driessen_Back_to_the_Beginning_Proceedings_of_the_Leuven_Conference, 11; published as "A Matrilocal House Society in Pre- and Protopalatial Crete?", in *Back to the Beginning: Proceedings of the Leuven Workshop*, ed. I. Schoep, P. Tomkins, and J. Driessen (Oxford: Oxbow Press, 2011).

35 "Spirit of Place: Minoan Houses as Major Actors," in *Political Economies of the Aegean Bronze Age*, ed. Daniel J. Pullen (Oxford: Oxbow Press, 2010), 36–38.

36 Jan Driessen, "Understanding Minoan In-House Relationships on Late Bronze Age Crete," on *Minoan Architecture and Urbanism: New Perspectives on Ancient Built Environment*, ed. Quentin Letesson and Carl Knappett, 80–106 (Oxford: Oxford University Press, 2017), pp. 81–82, 94–95.

37 Castleden, Rodney, *Minoans: Life in Bronze Age Crete* (London: Routledge, 1990), 28, 140.

38 See J. Lesley Fitton, *Minoans* (London: British Museum Press, 2002), 172.

39 This contrast is portrayed in two frescoes in the Byzantine church of the Panagia Kera outside Kritsa in Crete. In them, Mother Earth and Mother Sea are required to give up the dead they have accepted back into their bodies for judgment by the Christian God. See Christ, Carol P., *A Serpentine Path* (Cleveland, Ohio: The FAR Press, 2016), 136.

40 Hawkes, Jacquetta, *Dawn of the Gods* (London: Chatto and Windus, 1968), 52. Hawkes credits this phrase to Dutch archaeologist Henriette Groenewegen-Frankfort.

41 See Falk, Marcia "Notes on Composing New Blessings: Toward a Feminist-Jewish Reconstruction of Prayer" in Plaskow, Judith, and Carol P. Christ (eds), *Weaving The Visions* (San Francisco: Harper & Row, 1989), 128-138. According to Falk the term "exclusive monotheism" should be used for forms of monotheism that exclude and demonize the plurality of images. See also Christ, Carol P., *Rebirth of the Goddess: Finding Meaning In Feminist Spirituality* (New York, N.Y: Routledge, 2004), 109-112

42 For example, Marina L. Moss argues for distinct divinities with different attributes and powers in *The Minoan Pantheon: Towards an Understanding of Its Nature and Extent*, International Series 1343 (Oxford: British Archaeological Reports, 2005).

WOMEN, SNAKES, WATER, AND HEALING: HYGIEIA AND HER BRONZE AGE ROOTS

LISA LUBARR

Introduction

The ancient Greek goddess Hygieia, considered one of the daughters of the healing god Asklepios, remained an important figure for the millennium that pilgrims traveled to the many renowned sanctuaries throughout Magna Graecia dedicated to this healing family, as they sought help for chronic and debilitating illnesses that could not otherwise be cured. Yet, from all available evidence, Hygieia and her sisters were not originally connected to Asklepios. Instead, they were part of a notable transformation: they were—in essence—principles of healing and health that were included in the divine "family" of Asklepios only when he transitioned from mortal to hero to god sometime after the Bronze Age. I wish to highlight this change as it signals that the god alone was considered insufficient for the healing process. Why was this so? In classical Greece, including divine female healers as an essential aspect of any return to health and well-being was imperative. Not only did this provide a greater balance of male and female agency, but it appealed to a population of seekers that was still attuned to far more ancient practices when the healing function was most potently in the hands of a mother goddess and then spread to further generations and layers of female deities devoted to nurturing and care-taking those in need. Nurturing is indeed a primary matriarchal function, from pregnancy to childbirth to breastfeeding to sustaining life, and as the earth was always seen as mother, erasure of the mother's function was impossible without dire consequences. Somewhere in the transition from

Fig. 7. **Hygieia** and Snake. Painting by author, 2022.

Gaia's hegemony to the Olympian male leader gods, the memory of what had been was never entirely lost.

Thus, I would like to highlight here that the Aegean Bronze Age bears various types of evidence of healing and regenerative goddess figures in a pantheon of deities with a diversity of roles—already filling out the many different functions of sustaining life. And, the study of Minoan and Mycenaean iconography provides telling material for an early linking of female divinity, snakes, sacred water, and healing that was so potent that later healing sanctuaries (*asklepieia*) in the Classical and Hellenistic periods were aided enormously by their inclusion. In fact, the success and fame of these curative pilgrimage sites as they spread throughout Greece and its many colonies were due in great part to Hygieia's presence, as the latest incarnation in a long line of nurturing female deities. Certainly within Archaic and Classical Greece, the ancient association of women, serpents, and healing waters perpetuated in the form of nymphs, and the asklepieia were often situated at springs already considered sacred to these female divine entities. At Skoteino Cave in Crete, I also describe devotion to a later female, Christian healing saint as a way to infer the nature of the far earlier, Bronze Age goddess who may have been venerated at the site in a continuity of practice spanning perhaps four thousand years or more. Here, I suggest the unending devotion to a healing female deity whose name may have morphed over the centuries—perhaps many times—but whose function remained constant. Indeed, the precedents for Hygieia and her magnificent serpent—with their attendant nurturing, regenerative powers—run quite deep in the history of the ancient Aegean and persist to this day. Restoring the balance of female and male agency by illuminating this oft-obscured through-line feels paramount for the precarious health of our planet and our stricken human community—we are at a crossroads now, to say the least.

Hygieia, Asklepios, and the "Divine Family"

The story I tell can help to tease out threads of this larger history, and I begin with the surge of Asklepios's influence and why this was so notable. The legends of Asklepios describe a mortal man, a truly gifted physician thought to have lived during the Late Bronze Age and most likely born in Tricca, who became honored as a hero and ultimately divinized as a god.

His healing was considered physical and miraculous, and his powers oracular. As a man, he fathered (and presumably trained) the famed Trojan War physicians Machaon and Podalirius, and gave rise ultimately to a "genealogy" of Ascleipiades who, as honorary or perhaps even actual descendants of Asklepios, studied and promoted healing throughout Magna Graecia. As a hero, he was assigned a new father (Apollo), a birth by miraculous divine surgery from Koronis as she blazed in a pyre (life from death), and a journey to the Underworld to round out his own powers to raise the dead. Stories of this half-human, half-divine hero depict "all his being ... integrated into one function, that of healing and helping mankind."[1] Sent by his father Apollo to be trained in medicine by the centaur Chiron, the hero "was indeed well qualified to become the patron of human healers even long before he became venerated as a god."[2] Killed by Zeus's thunderbolt for reducing Hades' population through his miraculous healing, he was nonetheless given a place "as the constellation *Ophiocus* (which depicts a man holding a snake, the god's sacred animal), where people could see Asklepios every night if they looked up to the heavens."[3] Finally, as an immortal god, Asklepios was "ever-present in the holy shrines at Epidauros, Tricca, Athens, Cos, Pergamon," where he would—unremittingly—reveal his compassionate, salvific presence to all comers praying in their distress for divine help and succor.[4] But he was not alone.

By his side, for the millennium[5] that the god's healing sanctuaries flourished, appeared his "daughter" Hygieia, whose name means "health." She is most often depicted with a snake wrapped around her body, and is attendant in the abata with Asklepios in the famed nocturnal healing rituals, when the supplicant would purify, sacrifice, and finally sleep in this special chamber on the ground, in hopes that the god would visit via dreams, either as the gentle, bearded physician or as a snake, to heal or to suggest the means to a cure. Hygieia's presence both amplifies and supports the god's healing power and was clearly essential to the healing process. While her divine sisters (Aceso, Aegle, Iaso, and Panacea) are mentioned with some frequency during the early period of the cult but then seem to recede, Hygieia's name and image remain firmly affiliated with Asklepios, and the two were most often worshipped as a pair. Pausanias even records eleven sanctuaries where their cult statues stood side by side.[6] At Epidauros, Asklepios's newly designated wife Epione was also prominent.[7] Yet the earliest written evidence for Asklepios, pointing to his mortal life and family, mentions only his two mortal sons and their extraordinary healing ability; there are no named wife or daughters, healing or otherwise,[8] nor any description of a tomb, *heroon* (hero's shrine), or *hieron* (temple) for any heroic female family members.[9]

From the 4th century BCE on, when they are included in the hymns, the god's daughters and wife, along with their brothers Machaon and Podalirius, "constituted the divine family of Asklepios and were recognized everywhere."[10] While the sons had most likely lived as mortal Bronze Age physicians, the female family members are considered "personifications of abstract concepts, of medical functions" and "represent the healing power itself."[11] Little is known of Aceso beyond her possible origins in Epidauros.[12] Aegle's name implies that she is a goddess of light, and was perhaps included "because of the importance of the sun for the healing of disease"[13] or "may personify the light of day which the Asklepios worshippers asked him to let them see forever when invoking him as the giver of health in solemn prayer."[14] Iaso had been known in the 5th century BCE as a child of Amphiaraus, and was "a healing spirit in her own right, originally associated with various gods, but finally fixed in the Asklepios family. The same is true of Panacea, the 'universal remedy.' She too originally was an independent goddess and was linked together with the god of medicine only later."[15] Epione's name derives from the Greek word for "soothing," and she was most likely a personification of the care needed for recovery.

Edelstein and Edelstein note that "the close cooperation between Asklepios and his iatric daughters in the beginning of his career" reveals that possession of the divine "healing power" and "universal remedy" were a necessary enlargement and intensification once the hero became god.[16] Still, as the cult of Asklepios gained momentum, "his descendants were gradually forgotten," with the exception of his daughter Hygieia.[17] Seemingly connected with Asklepios in approximately 400 BCE, "she is the one daughter who is 'worth as much as all the others'" and later "precedes all her brothers and sisters."[18] There are key features of Hygieia's unique presence highlighting her maternal and nurturing abilities that come through vividly in her many sculpted images and help to illuminate why she in particular was so necessary to the cult that she could not be erased as were the other family members in an increasingly male-dominated society that had primarily (but not entirely) shifted the healing function to a male deity.[19]

Snakes

Apollodorus ascribes the power of Asklepios, who "not only prevented some from dying, but even raised up the dead," to the goddess Athena, "for he received from Athena the blood that flowed from the veins of the Gorgon [Medusa], and while he used the blood that flowed from her left side for the bane of mankind, he used the blood that flowed from her right side for salvation, and by that means he raised the dead."[20] The snake is one of the primary chthonic elements assigned to the god Asklepios. While it is true that the serpent is "an iconographic sign of heroization,"[21] and so would not be unusual to be applied to the hero-become-god, the healing snake was most likely added to the legend of Asklepios once he became divinized, for "in the old heroic myth ... no mention was made of the serpent at all."[22] The serpent, which is shown in countless images wound around the staff of the god, is an ancient symbol with various meanings, both "propitious" and "ominous" for Mediterranean cultures; "its meaning depends on the quality of the god or hero to whom the snake is attributed or whom it represents."[23] There are numerous gods, goddesses, and heroes associated with snakes, and it can connote fertility, oracular ability, and protection on the beneficial side, as well as embodying terror or punishment in other fearsome cases. According to Joan Bretton Connelly, at the Athenian Acropolis "the Serpent still keeps vigil over a sanctuary that in antiquity teemed with the imagery of snakes, sea monsters, and serpent-tailed human composite figures.... Since the second quarter of the 6th century BCE, limestone sculptures filling the pediments of the Archaic sanctuary buildings would depict coiled serpents ready to strike, a triple-viper–bodied monster pleading for mercy, and Herakles battling both the fish-tailed Triton and the snake-headed Hydra." Marija Gimbutas considers the "energy exuded by this spiralling or coiling creature" as representing the life force itself.[25]

In the cult of Asklepios the serpent appears with potent healing properties: the holy domestic snake was "thought to personify the gentle god of healing, because its qualities of watchfulness, fidelity and protection so aptly fitted the medical work of the divine physician."[26] The harmless Elaphe longissimi, which was intentionally and abundantly bred in the ancient asklepieia and even sent from Epidauros to Athens and Rome to found new healing sanctuaries, belongs to the family Colubridae; "smooth, glossy, and slender, the snake has a uniformly brown back with a streak of darker color behind the eyes. The snake's belly is yellowish or whitish and has ridged scales that catch easily on rough surfaces, making it especially adapted for climbing trees."[27] I find it fascinating that Asklepios would come to his patients in their incubation within the abaton, not with a serpent, but at times *as* a serpent, to heal[28] and Aristophanes in his Plutus describes "two great enormous serpents" who "issued from the holy shrine" of the god and licked the eyelids of a blind petitioner, restoring sight.[29] Macrobius in Saturnalia explains that "images of serpents are attached to the statues of these gods [Asklepios and Hygieia], because they symbolize that human bodies, shedding the skin of infirmity, as it were, return to their original vigor, just as serpents grow young again every year by shedding the skin of old age."[30]

In relationship to women, I find it notable that Hygieia is nearly always depicted in statuary with a snake across her body or wrapped around her arm, and she holds as well a phiale with water to feed it[31]; this is distinct from Asklepios whose sacred snake is more apt to wrap around his staff or appear at his side. As the snake helped to preserve the life of men and women, the goddess nurtured and cared for the snake, preserving its life. This nursing and maternal function—with a kourotrophic appeal—must have been a key part of Hygieia's symbolic potency; there are, in fact, precedents for a tradition of women and protective, life-preserving snakes. At the Athenian Acropolis, the snake had a crucial safeguarding role. According to Herodotus, a real snake (ophis) was kept on the Acropolis to guard the Sacred Rock, and was fed honey-cakes by the priestess of Athena[32] just as, later, Hygieia is depicted feeding the sacred snake of Asklepios. This nourishment of that which safeguards life in Athens, would be a powerful function to apply to the new goddess Hygieia, preserver-of-health. Interestingly, Erechtheus, "the first Athenian king to be mentioned in Greek literature,"[33] is born from the earth, and (according to the Iliad) nursed by Athena on the Acropolis; he is "often shown with snakes"[34] and Pausanias considered the great golden snake coiled inside the shield of Phidias's massive chryselephantine statue of Athena inside the Parthenon to be this "progenitor" of all Athenians.[35] Yet the connection between Athena and snakes transcends Athens and is essential to her very nature. Nilsson cites a cup depicting a huge snake behind the goddess, where "it is very noteworthy that this vase painting is Boeotian and not Athenian, for it shows that not only at Athens was the snake the sacred animal of Athena."[36]

Further, "Herodotus tells us that Erechtheus and Athena were worshipped jointly at Athens. The people of Epidauros made an annual sacrifice to the divine pair, according to an old agreement by which the Epidaurians gained, in return, permission to cut Athenian olive trees for the carving of sacred statues."[37] This fascinating connection between Epidauros (the seat of the most legendary asklepieion, from which all others followed suit) and Athens supports the syncretism of Hygieia/serpent and Athena/serpent. There is also attested in the 6th–5th century BCE a cult of Athena Hygieia, which fades at the arrival of the cult of Asklepios in Athens in approximately 420 BCE; while she receives state sacrifices at the annual Panathenaia as late as the 4th century BCE, no private dedications to her are found after the Asclepieion is built on the south slope of the Acropolis.[38] So for a span of time Athena Hygieia had provided for the health of her people; Plutarch and Pliny record a tale that Athena appeared to Perikles in a dream, instructing him as to what medicine to use to cure an injured workman during the construction of the Propylaia, after which he dedicated a bronze statue to the healing goddess, near an earlier altar.[39] Pausanias saw a statue of Hygieia commemorating Asklepios's daughter very near that of Athena Hygieia.[40] Thus "Health" becomes affixed to the god Asklepios in the person of his "daughter" in the late 5th century BCE, and the frequent images of the new goddess "Hygieia" with a snake make perfect sense given this evolution—particularly here in Athens where a clear transferal of healing power from Athena to the male god Asklepios would have been received even more seamlessly with the inclusion of a similar function in a female deity.

Women, Water, and Healing

There is yet another connection in ancient Greece I would like to highlight: in Greek legend women were closely allied with healing in the form of nymphs, who "are described with great frequency as the daughters of Zeus, of Ge, or of various river gods."[41] In fact, "in the Homeric epics, our earliest literary sources, the nymphs already have most of their defining characteristics."[42] They "regularly personify and inhabit springs, rivers, and lakes. ...Nymphs, because of their association with springs, are often healing deities. Healing gods as a rule are close to a water source, preferably one that is heated or has interesting mineral properties."[43] While sacred springs well up from the earth in numerous places (notable is the Kastalian spring at Delphi where the Pythia, her priests, and those seeking an oracle would all stop to purify before ascending to the temple),[44] and mountains as a source for these springs have many connotations, such as places "where societal norms undergo temporary reversal, as in Dionysiac revels,"[45] nymphs ultimately become associated in cave sanctuaries with the male healing god Apollo and the goat-god Pan—just as Hygieia and her sisters become linked in the abaton with Asklepios (Apollo's son) and therefore (somewhat analogously) with his teacher, the centaur Chiron. We even find in Thessaly a cave near Pharsalos where Pantalkes (or his followers) inscribed in the 4th century BCE a listing of the deities honored there, which begins, "Welcome visitors, every male and female ... to a place holy to the Nymphs and Pan and Hermes, Lord Apollo and Herakles and his companions, the cave of Chiron, and of Asklepios and Hygieia. Theirs is the place, and all the sacred things in it, growing things and tablets and dedications and many gifts."[46] It is attested that "Greece is riddled with caves created by the action of water. Caves large and small are likely to contain springs, and in fact the cave is the most common cult site of the nymphs, although by no means belonging exclusively to them."[47] I want to emphasize that this early linking of chthonic cave, sacred spring, healing, and female deity was so powerful that it had to find expression even beyond the Olympian conquest of Gaia. On Crete, the Asclepieion at Lebena (dedicated in the 4th century BCE at the arrival of the god from Epidauros) is located at the site of "the old shrine of the nymphs and Acheloös. Despite the new god's advent, the Lebenians were required to continue their sacrifices of a piglet to Acheloös and a kid to the nymphs. This superimposition of Asklepios'[s] cult onto that of the nymphs must have been fairly commonplace, as both were concerned with healing, and a convenient water source was a necessity for Asklepios'[s] shrines."[48] Similarly in Athens, the nymphs were associated with the site of the Round Spring House, and their "healing emphasis" along with the "abundant water ... necessary for the god's healing operations" made the south slope of the Acropolis a "logical place" to establish the new male healing god.[49] "Asklepios'[s] cult was introduced to the site in 420–19, when Telemachos donated the first Asclepieion building. Two small caves, an upper and lower, were incorporated into the shrine at some point. The lower cave contains a spring and was built into an early third-century Doric stoa as the Round Spring House. In this area were discovered the earliest known Attic nymph relief, dedicated to Archandros, and other nymph reliefs, including one dedicated by a priest of Asklepios."[50] So here in Athens, as at many other ancient sites, healing practices—nourishing life itself—were originally governed by female divinity.

Bronze Age Connections

Turning to the Bronze Age, I can now consider specific healing deities who may have been transferred in various forms through Mycenaean culture and contact to Archaic and then Classical mainland Greece.[51] Perhaps most fascinating of all is the possibility that healing incubation of a very similar ritual was practiced in Bronze Age Minoan civilization. Recent scholarship proposes that the numerous gold seal rings that depict figures reclining against or "hugging" a rounded rock, with epiphanies of divine female figures appearing in the atmosphere, are in fact incubating.[52] These figures are within the holy sanctuary, where the "baetyl," the sacred stone, named for the Semitic house-of-god, can still be seen even today, as within the open-air central courtyard at Malia. It is now considered that these figures are not worshipping the stone (considered by some cultures a meteorite), but rather experiencing epiphanic dreams. While Nanno Marinatos believes that these Minoan figures are ecstatics experiencing the presence of divine entities that appear in the form of birds, insects, and shooting stars, I would additionally propose that the incubation may in fact be for the more specific purpose of epiphanic healing. Those "incubating" are often in conjunction with other figures who are shaking trees; while this had been thought of as a way to invoke the presence of the divinity, or to hear her or him (as with the oracular rustling of the oak tree at Dodona), I propose that the incubating figure may be shown by the goddess particular plants for the purpose of healing particular ailments. Additionally, there are mysterious symbols in the sky that may also be specific cures revealed, that then promote either immediate or subsequent relief: an eye, and an ear, as well as other strange non-organic forms that have the qualities of medical or other instruments or emblems float above the reclining figures and may relate to an organ cured or the means towards this. According to Janice Crowley in her study of Minoan rings and seals, "two possibilities are that the eye and ear could represent the all-seeing and all-hearing goddess in a symbolic epiphany ... or that they could be votives for good sight and good hearing."[53] She also believes that the floating objects that had been considered as possible "shooting stars" or "comets" and yet appear more plant-like than celestial have now been clearly identified (with a new signet discovery), as ears of grain.[54] Grain often symbolizes the renewal of life, as at Eleusis in later practice, revealed at the climax of the mystery rites in the Telesterion. I suggest that the Minoan gold rings were worn to depict the entire timeline of healing and regeneration, including prayers for a cure and votive thank-offerings.

It is also remarkable that votive objects have been discovered in the form of body parts—healed—at Minoan peak sanctuaries and were also evidenced at the numerous Greek asklepieia centuries later. At these later healing sanctuaries—such as Epidauros, Corinth, Athens, and Pergamon— many examples have been found, and particularly prevalent—in large numbers—are terracotta hands, feet, ears, eyes, genitals, and wombs.[55] Key here is that at various peak sanctuaries in Crete millennia earlier—where Bronze Age Minoan ritual activity is confirmed by evidence of sacred feasting, ceremonies, and votive offerings—body parts (primarily made of clay) have also been discovered, and except in one instance "do not represent entire living organisms but merely parts" with arms and legs prevailing.[56] As found at Maza, Petsofas, Philioremos, Traostalos, Vrysinas, and Youkhtas, "they are characteristic of those peak sanctuaries that survive into the Neopalatial period."[57] According to Marinatos, these votive limbs "do not refer to human sacrifice and dismemberment, but rather express a desire for healing."[58] Walter Burkert wonders, "could these be votive gifts for a healing [male] god?" but counter-suggests that the peak sanc- tuaries evidence fire rituals where "the earthen figures were thrown onto the glowing embers," similar to later Greek fire festivals that were typi- cally "in honour of a goddess."[59] And we have evidence of specific and named goddess figures worshipped at peak sanctuaries! For example, the mother goddess Demeter is attested—implying, I would emphasize, that during the Bronze Age (and most likely prior to this time) healing was the province of a maternal, life-nourishing female divinity.[60] It was only later, as patriarchy increased, that matriarchal nurturing was eclipsed by a male-dominated pantheon—and yet never entirely erased—and so is still there to be rediscovered and illuminated. In Titane, not far from Corinth on the Greek mainland (and close to a temple of Athena whose wooden statue bespeaks a very early origin), Pausanias describes that Alexanor, son of

Machaon and grandson of the mortal Asklepios, built a Bronze Age sanctuary to Asklepios. The geographer himself saw there, nearly two thousand years later in the 2nd century CE, a statue of Hygieia that "one cannot see easily because it is so surrounded with the locks of women, who cut them off and offer them to the goddess, and with strips of Babylonian raiment."[61] The implication is that women, especially, flocked to Hygieia for help, and I would like to imagine the same relationship to the even more ancient female healing deities, including Athena as well—known at Knossos and beyond in Mycenaean Linear B as A-ta-na and whose worship was adopted from the Minoans on Crete and spread to the mainland during the Bronze Age. This all suggests that Athena Hygieia was potent and persistent!

Skoteino Cave and Beyond

Now I turn to Skoteino Cave in central Crete, where further ancient associations of female divinity, cave sites, water, and healing can be teased out from obscurity. This massive enclosure has four levels and is 160 meters deep; water drips from stalactites and is concentrated in two or three troughs below; the earliest worship here is thought to be of a Minoan goddess, possibly later called Britomartis. While current names for the various rooms include "Great Temple," "Altar" (where libations may have been poured into a crack in the floor), "Hall of Worship," and "Hall of Prayer," it is notable that townspeople call a deep (and difficult to access) narrow room the "chapel" or "church."[62] Mircea Eliade noted that "at the end of the 2nd level are two cult idols, set up above, and in front of, a stone altar.... In front of these two statues, the fragments of vessels ... chronologically ... follow one another without a break from the beginning of the 2nd millennium BCE to the end of the Roman period. The sanctity of the cave has persisted [to this] day. Very nearby is a small white chapel dedicated to the Parasceve (Good Friday). On [each] July 26, there is an assemblage at the entrance to the cave. It consists of the entire population of the valley of the Aposelemi and of the Chersonese region; there is dancing in two areas under the vault and heavy drinking, and love songs are sung as ritually as mass was heard in the nearby chapel."[63,64] I want to note that three bronze statues of the male adorant variety were found here dating from the Late Minoan period—probably votive offerings to a female goddess as similarly depicted in gold seal rings. And, the later use of the site includes the remains of a small Byzantine "temple" dedicated to the female Christian Agia Paraskevi (which was destroyed by the Turkish), with an 1840 CE church to this saint rebuilt above the cave. It is fascinating that Agia Paraskevi was considered a healing saint following the story of her various tortures by the Roman Emperor Antonius Pius, which included immersing the devout woman in boiling oil and tar, which (unaffected) she then hurled as a test of its heat at the Emperor, blinding him—further explaining that only the Christian God could cure him, at which he regained his sight and ended Christian persecution under his rule. When Marcus Aurelius came to power and Christians were blamed for a pestilence, Agia Paraskevi was again captured and this time "she was thrown into a pit with a large snake. The Saint made the sign of the cross and the snake did not harm her.... Realizing that a great and mighty power guarded Paraskevi, she was again set free to teach others about Christianity."[65] After a final persecution and beheading, she became known as a "healer of the blind, because of the miracle she performed in restoring the sight of Antonius Pius."[66] I find it amazing to locate at Skoteino a healing female saint who has a sacred relationship with snakes at a cave known for its worship of the "goddess" as far back as the Minoan period (and perhaps earlier), and bringing into consideration that this more ancient divinity was a female healing deity associated specifically with snakes!

Snakes have been considered as apotropaic (rather than specifically "healing") at Mycenae and have been associated with women both here and in Athens (as noted earlier), guarding inhabitants of the home or palace—again, protecting life itself.[67] In the subterranean "House of the Idols" in the cult center of Mycenae, numerous clay coiled snakes were found, in a religious complex replete with goddess images.[68] From recent discoveries of approximately 240 Linear B tablets at Thebes, "it is possible to suggest that the term e-pe-to-i refers to a group of snakes, represented by terracotta figures in a sanctuary called *63-te-ra(-de), which are given libations of wine as sacred guardians of the palace."[69] As for Crete, it is interesting to speculate, but impossible to determine the exact use and symbolism of the serpent, and of the Postpalatial Mycenaean-era clay "snake tubes" found at Gournia, and similarly for the famous "snake goddess" figurines found at Knossos.[70]

Also on mainland Greece, snakes associated with regeneration (and women) are found in relationship to the goddesses Demeter and Kore at

Eleusis; while they are depicted winding protectively around the sacred kiste with its hidden mysteries, they also appear around the arms of Demeter as she displays the ears of grain and poppies in the now iconic Roman-era relief. Eleusis may be related etymologically as well to the goddess Eileithyia,[71] who is most well attested in Crete, is specifically associated with childbirth, and who was venerated in a "holy" cave at Amnisos located near Knossos—dating back to the Bronze Age and earlier—and as described in Homer's Odyssey (19.185–6).[72] In Classical mainland Greece, sanctuaries for Eileithyia are found in many locations, including Athens, Megara, Korinthos, Argos, Mycenae, Sparta, and Olympia. In Elis, Greece, the goddess is specifically associated with a serpent! According to Pausanias, a dream prompts the saving of a peoples through the agency of a child-turned-snake-turned-god, and the birth of this being is venerated—and it is a woman who nurtures and tends the snake-god with water and honey cakes.[73] To me, it is apparent again that renewal, regeneration, fertility, birth, death, and healing are variations on the same theme and thus connotations of the snake—safeguarding and preserving life—are intimately connected to maternity itself.

Messenia

Lastly, I describe the Mycenaean tholos tomb in Messenia, which may have been equated with that of Asklepios's Bronze Age physician son Machaon, which Pausanias records at Gerenia on mainland Greece. According to R. Hope Simpson, this tomb held two lead statuettes of the Cretan type, a male figure wearing "the Minoan peaked cap and loin-cloth," and a female figure "also dressed in Minoan costume [with] tight bodice and wide skirt.... If she originally held snakes in her hands, as Stais conjectured, it is possible that the two figures formed a group of the type of 'Goddess with male worshipper.' It is quite likely that the two statuettes were actual Cretan imports."[74] While Minoan gold signet rings, a warrior seal, and other like items have been discovered recently at the tomb of the Mycenaean "Griffin Warrior" in Pylos,[75] it is fascinating to find this particular female figurine at the proposed tomb of Asklepios's renowned Bronze Age physician son. I believe that it points to a possible earlier female presence at this site as well, in which snakes figured. I propose here, again, a transferal of deities—or at least influence—from Crete to the Greek mainland, where a heroic healer became syncretized locally (or in any case was intentionally buried),[76] and where further clues are revealed for the inclusion of snakes and women to the later cult of the hero-god Asklepios, amplifying the desired healing power. Near the tomb site, according to Pausanias, "is a mountain, Calathium; on it is a sanctuary of Claea with a cave close beside it; it has a narrow entrance, but contains objects which are worth seeing."[77] Claea is an Oreiad, a nymph of mountains and grottoes; caves have been found near Zarnata in Messenia which contain Neolithic pottery, and may include the very cave named by Pausanias—yet another telling aspect to the complex and layered history of this locale.[78] Given this evidence, perhaps the family of Asklepios and his son Machaon was associated with an unknown female healing deity very early on, whether Athena Hygieia as proposed at Titane, or yet another! This would—again—re-tell the origin of healing on the mainland, as on Crete, as a divine and primarily matriarchic function that could be invoked through human women and men.

Conclusion

Complete health includes balance of the active and passive principles, which means that an exclusively male god of healing is intrinsically out of balance and, by extension, unhealthy. Ignoring the historical tradition of healing goddesses exacerbates such an imbalance. Hence, there are manifold logical, emotional, and spiritual reasons why the "wife" and "daughters" of Asklepios, and especially Hygieia, were included in the god's myth once he became deified—not the least of which is to honor and perpetuate a more ancient tradition of the healing goddess or goddesses dating back at least to the Bronze Age Aegean. Certainly including women, water, and snakes in the cult of Asklepios added greatly to the god's appeal because they conjoined with a potent history that was still felt by all as it echoed through the centuries—and where a greater balance between female and male divinity—and between nature and humanity— was acknowledged as essential for healing and regeneration. Hygieia, or "Health," remained a healing partner to the god Asklepios for a millennium, providing blessed relief for those in terrible distress, and inspiring hymns to invoke her ever-beneficial presence. The Orphics sang the praise of this nurturing, serpent-wielding goddess, and I hope that we too can enlist her bounteous aid even now ... perhaps especially now!

Charming queen of all,
lovely and blooming,
blessed Hygeia, mother of all
bringer of bliss, hear me.
Through you vanish
the illnesses that afflict man.
Through you every house
blossoms to the fullness of joy.
The arts thrive when the world
desires you, O Queen,
loathed by Hades,
the destroyer of souls.
Apart from you all is
without profit for men:
wealth, the sweet giver of abundance
for those who feast, fails,
and man never reaches
the many pains of old age.
Goddess, come, ever-helpful
to the initiates,
keep away the evil distress
of unbearable diseases.

—Orphic Hymn, ca. 3rd century CE[79]

References

Athanassakis, Apostolos N. *The Orphic Hymns*. Translated by Benjamin M. Wolkow. Baltimore: Johns Hopkins University Press, 2013.

Blayney, Keith. *The Caduceus vs the Staff of Asclepius*. October 2005. Accessed October 30, 2017. www.drblayney.com/Asclepius.html.

Bulkeley, Kelly. *Dreaming in the World's Religions*. New York: New York University Press, 2008.

Burkert, Walter. *Greek Religion*. Translated by John Raffan. Cambridge, MA: Harvard University Press, 1985.

Connelly, Joan Breton. *The Parthenon Enigma*. New York: Vintage Books, 2014.

Crowley, Janice L. "In the Air Here or From the World Beyond? Enigmatic

Symbols of the Late Bronze Age Aegean." In *Metaphysis: Ritual, Myth and Symbolism in the Aegean Bronze Age*, edited by Eva Alram-Stern et al., 89–95. Leuven-Liege: Peeters, 2016.

Edelstein, Emma, and Ludwig Edelstein. *Asclepius: A Collection and Interpretation of the Testimonies*, Vols. I and II. Baltimore: Johns Hopkins Press, 1945.

Eliade, Mircea. *A History of Religious Ideas: From the Stone Age to the Eleusinian Mysteries*. Translated by W. Trask. Chicago: University of Chicago Press, 1978.

Garcia, Carlos Varias. "'Snakes' in the Mycenaean Texts? On the Interpretation of the Linear B Term E-PE-TO-I." In *KE-RA-ME-JA: Studies Presented to Cynthia W. Shelmerdine*, edited by Dimitri Nakassis et al., 179–88. Philadelphia: INSTAP Academic Press, 2014.

Gimbutas, Marija. *The Language of the Goddess.* New York: Harper & Row, 1989.

Homer. *The Iliad.* Translated by Robert Fitzgerald. New York: Doubleday, 1974.

Homer. *The Odyssey.* Translated by Robert Fitzgerald. Garden City, NY: Doubleday, 1961.

Hurwit, Jeffrey M. *The Athenian Acropolis.* Cambridge: Cambridge University Press, 1999.

Johnston, Sarah Iles. *Ancient Greek Divination.* Oxford: Wiley-Blackwell, 2008.

Jones, Donald W. *Peak Sanctuaries and Sacred Caves in Minoan Crete: A Comparison of Artifacts.* Jonsered: Aströms, 1999.

Kyriakidis, Evangelos. *Ritual in the Bronze Age Aegean: The Minoan Peak Sanctuaries.* London: Duckworth, 2005.

Lang, Mabel L. *Cure and Cult in Ancient Corinth: A Guide to the Askelepieion.* Princeton, NJ: American School of Classical Studies at Athens, 1977.

Larson, Jennifer. *Greek Heroine Cults.* Madison: University of Wisconsin Press, 1995.

Larson, Jennifer. *Greek Nymphs.* Oxford: Oxford University Press, 2001.

Luraghi, Nino. *The Ancient Messenians.* Cambridge: Cambridge University Press, 2008.

MacGillivray, J. Alexander. "The Minoan Double Ax Goddess and Her Astral Realm." In *Athanasia: The Earthly, the Celestial and the Underworld in the Mediterranean from the Late Bronze and the Early Iron Age*, edited by Nicholas Chr. Stampolidis et al., 115–28. Rhodes: International Archaeological Conference Proceedings, 2009.

Marinatos, Nanno. *Minoan Kingship and the Solar Goddess.* Urbana: University of Illinois Press, 2010.

Marinatos, Nanno. *Minoan Religion: Ritual, Image and Symbol*. Columbia: University of South Carolina Press, 1993.

Martin, Thomas R. "An Overview of Classical Greek History from Mycenae to Alexander." Accessed December 21, 2017. www.perseus.tufts.edu/hopper/textt%3A1999.04.0009%3Achapter%3D10%3Asection%3D1%3Asubsection%3D6

Mitropoulou, Elpis. *Deities and Heroes in the Form of Snakes*. Athens: Pyli Editions, 1977.

Municipality of Cheronissos—Crete. "Land of Experiences," Skoteino Cave, n.d. Accessed December 1, 2017. www.landofexperiences.gr/travels/skoteino/

Nilsson, Martin P. *The Minoan–Mycenaean Religion and Its Survival in Greek Religion*, 2nd Revised Edition. Lund: C.W.K. Gleerup, 1968.

Patton, Kimberley C. "Ancient Asklepieia: Institutional Incubation and the Hope of Healing." In *Imagination and Medicine: The Future of Healing in an Age of Neuroscience*, edited by Robert Bosnak and Stephen Aizenstat, 3–34. New Orleans: Spring Journal, 2009.

Pausanias. *Description of Greece*. Translated by W.H. Jones and H.A. Ormerod. Cambridge, MA: Harvard University Press, 1926.

Richardson, Rachel. Team discovers a rare Minoan sealstone in the treasure-laden tomb of a Bronze Age Greek warrior. November 6, 2017. Accessed December 21, 2017. www.phys.org/news/2017-11-team-rare-minoan-sealstone-treasure-laden.html

Schouten, J. *The Rod and Serpent of Asklepios: Symbol of Medicine*. Amsterdam: Elsevier Publishing Company, 1967.

Simpson, R. Hope. "Identifying a Mycenaean State." *The Annual of the British School at Athens*, vol. 52 (1957): 231–59.

"St. Paraskevi the Roman," True Orthodox Diocese of Western Europe, accessed March 13, 2022, www.trueorthodox.eu/st-paraskevi-the-roman-2.

Strabo. *Geography*, n.d. Accessed December 12, 2017. www.perseus.tufts.edu/hopper/text?doc=Perseus:text:1999.01.0198:book=8:chapter=4

Theoi Greek Mythology. *Eileithyia Cult*, n.d. Accessed December 20, 2017. www.theoi.com/Cult/EileithyiaCult.html

Theoi Greek Mythology. *Gorgones & Medousa*, n.d. Accessed December 1, 2017. www.theoi.com/Pontios/Gorgones.html

Tyree, L., et al. *Inferences for Use of Skoteino Cave During the Bronze Age and Later Based on a Speleological and Environmental Study at Skoteino Cave, Crete*. Academia.edu, 2005–2006, www.academia.edu/29962456/

Inferences_for_Use_of_Skoteino_Cave_during_the_Bronze_Age_and_Later_
Based_on_a_Speleological_and_Environmental_Study_at_Skoteino_Cave_
Crete_1

Zeke, Andras. "Goddess Eileithyia and her Snakes." *Minoan Language Blog.*
September 29, 2010. www.minoablog.blogspot.com/2010/09/goddess-eileithy-
ia-and-her-snakes.html (accessed December 1, 2017)

Endnotes

1 Emma Edelstein and Ludwig Edelstein, *Asclepius: A Collection and
Interpretation of the Testimonies*, vol. 2 (Baltimore: Johns Hopkins Press,
1945), 53.

2 Ibid., 2: 62.

3 Kelly Bulkeley, *Dreaming in the World's Religions* (New York: New York
University Press, 2008), 158.

4 Edelstein and Edelstein, *Asclepius*, 2: 65.

5 Asklepios reigned for more than a millennium as the blameless and gentle
physician who could cure the most chronic and hopeless of diseases, wounds,
and afflictions. The cult's personalized care for the suffering of mortals *regardless* of age, gender, and economic or political status created a following that
perpetuated well into the Christian era. While Asklepios's most famous early
sanctuary in Epidauros came to prominence in the 5th century BCE, as late as
the 5th century CE, the famed Athenian philosopher Proclus was living in the
house "next door to the Asclepieion" and to which he went "to pray to the god
for the sick girl. For the city still enjoyed the god's presence at that time and
still held the temple of the Savior unravaged." See Edelstein and Edelstein,
Asclepius, 1: 323–24.

6 See Jennifer Larson, *Greek Heroine Cults* (Madison: University of Wisconsin
Press, 1995), 63. Larson also notes here that a sacrifice was made to both
Asklepios and Hygieia in Athens on the day of the Dissoteria.

7 Larson adds that "at the annual festival at Epidauros, a male–female symmetry
was achieved by offering the male deities of the family a bull, while the female
deities received a cow." See ibid., 63.

8 Machaon was considered "the representative of surgery, that is, of the treatment of wounds," and Podalirius was "in charge of the cure of internal diseases"
(see Edelstein and Edelstein, *Asclepius*, 2: 12). While scholars dispute whether
these two sons were additions to the legend of Asklepios, there is certainly
evidence that they existed, and Bronze Age Greece did have medical specialists.
Pausanias references both a tomb of Machaon and a holy sanctuary in Gerenia
(see Pausanias, *Description of Greece*, trans. W.H. Jones and H.A. Ormerod,
2: 3.26.6–10 [Cambridge, MA: Harvard University Press, 1926]), as well as a

sanctuary of Machaon's sons at Pharae (4.3.1–4). Interestingly, as relates to the tomb for Machaon in Gerenia, "archaeological and epigraphic evidence points to a Mycenaean tholos as the complex Pausanias refers to." See Nino Luraghi, *The Ancient Messenians* (Cambridge: Cambridge University Press, 2008), 272. In Gerenia, according to Strabo, there is also "a temple of Triccaean Asklepios, a reproduction of the one in the Thessalian Tricca," and he notes a "heroum" of Podalirius located in Daunia, Italy, "on a hill known as Drium. By the hero-shrine of Podalirius there flowed a stream believed to cure animals of any diseases" (see Strabo, *Geography*, 8.4.21 and 6.3.9).

9 While "we often find that heroes do not stand alone but exist in a familial context," no mention is made of Asklepios's daughters (or Epione) in any of the early accounts. Certainly if they were skilled, mortal healers as their brothers or husbands were, their names and prowess would presumably have been handed down in legend. It is further important to note that, in evidence from Archaic and Classical cultures, "heroines rarely take on the role of general healers, presumably because the customs of Greek society prevented real women from practicing medicine except as midwives. Thus it is very unusual to find a heroine presiding over a temple in which healing incubation is practiced." See Larson, *Greek Heroine Cults*, 5–13.

10 Edelstein and Edelstein, *Asclepius*, 2: 87.

11 Ibid., 86–88.

12 Ibid., 88.

13 Ibid., 87.

14 Ibid., 90.

15 Ibid., 88.

16 Ibid., 88–89.

17 Ibid., 89.

18 Ibid., 89, and quoting vol. 1, Testimony 282 [Aelius Aristides' Oratio XXXVIII, 22], 138.

19 Emma and Ludwig Edelstein offer a cogent explanation for why Hygieia (Health) became associated with the god, an association that persisted, unchanging, for the remainder of the cult's existence. "Asklepios, certainly from the fourth century B.C., was venerated not only as the healer of diseases but also as the giver and preserver of health, as the hymns written in his honor clearly show. The worship paid to him by the inhabitants of whole cities at regular intervals, by those who enjoyed perfect health, was directed toward the god who keeps men healthy rather than toward him who restores them to health. The twofold activity which was thus attributed to the god reflects the twofold activity of the human physician who was supposed to take care not only of the sick, but of the healthy as well; health no less than disease, in the opinion of these generations,

required medical supervision. The god of medicine, the deified physician, therefore, was obliged likewise to take care of both health and sickness. Since originally he had been only a healer of diseases, a savior from deadly illness, Hygieia was made his daughter, and he retained her as his associate. Only in this way could the concept of the preserver of health become part of his own god-head." "Health and freedom from disease" had become paramount in the Greece that welcomed Asklepios and his daughters. Whereas "in Homeric centuries the warrior, the hero, found his sole aim in glory; he was intent only on battle, on victory" and "health to him was no value in itself.... [I]n post-Homeric centuries, however, physical well-being became more important and began to assume a place among the goods for which men were striving.... It was health even more than beauty or riches that constituted the summum bonum of later generations; to be healthy seemed the indispensable pre-requisite of all joy and happiness." See Edelstein and Edelstein, *Asclepius*, 2: 90–123.

20 Ibid., vol. 11: 8–9.

21 Larson, *Greek Heroine Cults*, 9.

22 Edelstein and Edelstein, *Asclepius*, 2: 51.

23 Elpis Mitropoulou, *Deities and Heroes in the Form of Snakes* (Athens: Pyli Editions, 1977), 15.

24 Joan Breton Connelly, *The Parthenon Enigma* (New York: Vintage Books, 2014), 46.

25 Marija Gimbutas, *The Language of the Goddess* (New York: Harper & Row, 1989) 121.

26 J. Schouten, *The Rod and Serpent of Asklepios* (Amsterdam: Elsevier Publishing Company, 1967), 35, 39.

27 Keith Blayney, "The Caduceus vs the Staff of Asklepios," October 2005. Accessed 12/1/17. www.drblayney.com/Asclepius.html

28 Kimberley Patton, "Ancient Asklepieia: Institutional Incubation and the Hope of Healing" in Stephen Aizenstat and Robert Bosnak, Editors, Imagination & Medicine: The Future of Healing in an Age of Neuroscience (New Orleans: Spring Journal, 2009), 13.

29 Edelstein and Edelstein, *Asclepius*, 1: 219, quoting Aristophanes, Plutus.

30 Ibid., 1: Testimony 301 [Macrobius, *Saturnalia* I, 20, 1-4], 149.

31 Mitropoulou, *Deities and Heroes in the Form of Snakes*, 184.

32 Connelly, *The Parthenon Enigma*, 46–47.

33 Ibid., 135.

34 Ibid.

35 Ibid., 46.

36 Nilsson further notes, "On a well-known relief vase from Kertsch, representing the contest of Athena and Poseidon and believed to be a copy of the central part of the western pediment of the Parthenon, a snake coils round the olive tree in the centre. The snake is also sometimes associated with Athena in vase paintings. A late red-figured lid of a pyxis in the National Museum of Copenhagen shows her chariot drawn by two huge snakes. A late red-figured lekythos at Athens shows Paris and Athena and at her side a snake as large as the goddess herself, and a black-figured lekythos depicts Cassandra flying from Ajax and taking refuge by the statue of Athena, from in front of which a snake issues forth against the sacrilegious hero. A black-figured hydria in Berlin represents a sacrifice to Athena; the goddess is seated with a phial in her right hand and her helmet in her left; at her feet the forepart of her snake appears." See Martin P. Nilsson, *The Minoan-Mycenaean Religion and Its Survival in Greek Religion*, 2nd rev. ed. (Lund: C.W.K. Gleerup, 1968) 496–97.

37 Connelly, *The Parthenon Enigma*, 132.

38 Jeffrey M. Hurwit, *The Athenian Acropolis* (Cambridge: Cambridge University Press, 1999), 199.

39 Ibid.

40 Ibid.

41 Jennifer Larson, *Greek Nymphs* (Oxford: Oxford University Press, 2001), 4.

42 Ibid., 20.

43 As at Pergamon, other asklepieia are intentionally located at the sites of springs (e.g., at Corinth, Epidauros, and Athens). See ibid., 5.

44 Sarah Iles Johnston, *Ancient Greek Divination* (Oxford: Wiley-Blackwell, 2008), 65–66.

45 Larson, *Greek Nymphs*, 9.

46 Ibid., 16–27.

47 Ibid.. Note that "at Eleusis, the caves that make up the Ploutoneion were part of Demeter's sanctuary, and Iphigeneia's tomb site in a cave was part of the sanctuary of Artemis Brauronia." See ibid., 227.

48 Ibid., 188.

49 Ibid., 129–30.

50 Ibid., 130. Larson also notes that some scholars consider instead the South Slope Spring House as the site of the early Athenian asklepieion and that this had also been the site of a shrine of the nymphs and (later) Pan, although she remarks that the evidence is not convincing.

51 See Gimbutas, *The Language of the Goddess*, 134, for a description of Hera as a "likely descendent of the prehistoric Snake Goddess."

52 Nanno Marinatos, *Minoan Kingship and the Solar Goddess* (Urbana: University of Illinois Press, 2010), 88–91.

53 Janice L. Crowley, "In the air here or from the world beyond? Enigmatic symbols of the Late Bronze Age Aegean," in *Metaphysis: Ritual, Myth and Symbolism in the Aegean Bronze Age*, ed. Eva Alram-Stern et al. (Leuven-Liege: Peeters, 2016), 92.

54 Ibid., 93.

55 At Corinth were found "ten legs with thighs, nine feet to the knee, nine entire arms, three hands to the elbow, one upper arm, five feet with their original finished top, some twenty feet probably belonging to larger limbs, and some twenty hands" along with "remains of at least 125 hands," "remains of some sixty-five female breasts, offered singly or in pairs, and thirty-five male genitalia," and a number of ears "singly or in pairs," eyes, torsos, and heads. See Mabel L. Lang, *Cure and Cult in Ancient Corinth: A Guide to the Asklepieion* (Princeton, NJ: American School of Classical Studies at Athens, 1977), 15.

56 Evangelos Kyriakidis, *Ritual in the Bronze Age Aegean: The Minoan Peak Sanctuaries* (London: Duckworth, 2005), 163.

57 Ibid., 163–64.

58 Nanno Marinatos, *Minoan Religion: Ritual, Image and Symbol* (Columbia: University of South Carolina Press, 1993), 117.

59 Walter Burkert, *Greek Religion*, trans. John Raffan (Cambridge, MA: Harvard University Press, 1985), 27.

60 At the peak sanctuary "Agios Georgios sto Vouno" above the Minoan settlement of Kastri on the island of Kythera (from which point one can see Crete), a black steatite vase bears a Linear A inscription that is likely to be translated to "DA-MA-TE"—similar to the proposed Linear A "I-DA-MA-TE" found on a gold votive double ax from the Arkalochori cave on Crete, dated to approximately 1550–1500 BCE. See J. Alexander MacGillivray, "The Minoan Double Ax Goddess and Her Astral Realm," in *Athanasia: The Earthly, the Celestial and the Underworld in the Mediterranean from the Late Bronze and the Early Iron Age*, edited by Nicholas Chr. Stampolidis et al. (Rhodes: International Archaeological Conference, 2009), 120. These inscriptions are considered, potentially, to read "Demeter" and "O Demeter" and point to a mother goddess specifically named and venerated, at a peak sanctuary. On the one hand, there are intimations that Bronze Age healing deities may have been both male and female; the ancient male "Paean" or physician of the gods who became replaced by Apollo and then Asklepios is known from Mycenaean-era Linear B inscriptions at Knossos, Crete and most likely dates back even earlier, to Minoan civilization, to that unknown pantheon of gods from a "prehistory" without as yet a translated language to refer to. Yet, given the peak sanctuary finds, it may be that evidence for early healing goddess figures

assisting mortals is even more prevalent.

61 Pausanias, *Description of Greece*, trans. W.H. Jones and H.A. Ormerod (Cambridge, MA: Harvard University Press, 1926), 2.11.5–6.

62 Municipality of Cheronissos—Crete, "Land of Experiences," Skoteino Cave, n.d., www.landofexperiences.gr/travels/skoteino/

63 Mircea Eliade, *A History of Religious Ideas: From the Stone Age to the Eleusinian Mysteries*, trans. W. Trask (Chicago: University of Chicago Press, 1978), 138.

64 Also notable: "Water from the catch basins was at one time used in modern festivities at the cave. When the volume of water diminished in recent times, the water collected from the stalactites was incorporated into the dough for holy bread during the annual blessing of domestic animals." See L. Tyree, et al., *Inferences for Use of Skoteino Cave during the Bronze Age and Later Based on a Speleological and Environmental Study at Skoteino Cave, Crete* (2005–2006), 52–57, accessed December 1, 2017, www.academia.edu

65 "St. Paraskevi the Roman," True Orthodox Diocese of Western Europe, accessed March 13, 2022, www.trueorthodox.eu/st-paraskevi-the-roman-2.

66 Ibid.

67 Carlos Varias Garcia, "'Snakes' in the Mycenaean Texts? On the Interpretation of the Linear B Term E-PE-TO-I" in KE-RA-ME-JA: Studies Presented to Cynthia W. Shelmerdine, ed. Dimitri Nakassis, et al. (Philadelphia: INSTAP, 2014), 185–87.

68 Burkert, *Greek Religion*, 32.

69 Garcia, "'Snakes' in the Mycenaean Texts?", 186.

70 Burkert believes that the epiphany gesture with two upraised hands is the mark of a goddess rather than mortal/priestess figure "who stands at the centre and towards whom all eyes are directed," and that the "two faience figurines from a magazine at Knossos are therefore almost certainly goddesses, the Snake-Goddesses, especially as the snakes of the one and the panther on the head-dress of the other point to superhuman status." He further notes, "in later Greek times, the snake symbolizes the world of the dead, of heroes, and of the subterranean gods; similar snake tubes also appear in the cult of the dead. Nothing in the Minoan finds, however, points to the grave or the dead; here, as Evans and Nilsson saw, the snake appears as guardian of the house. The house snake is a familiar figure in European folk-lore, and real, harmless snakes may still be seen being fed in houses in Balkan villages. Tiny bowls, as if for milk, which were found next to snake tubes in a room in the palace at Knossos could similarly have been used to feed real snakes; but in the Minoan cult here, too, the symbolic representation may be sufficient." See Burkert, *Greek Religion*, 23–30.

71 Nilsson, *The Minoan-Mycenaean Religion*, 520–23.

72 According to Burkert, pottery is found at the Amnisos cave dating from Neolithic to Roman times, with abundant use beginning during the Late Minoan III period. Additionally, "strange rock formations are found: not far from the entrance is an oval elevation like a belly with a nave.... At the very center of the cave is a stalagmite resembling a female figure ... [with] an altar-like stone block pushed in front of it; the stalagmite seems to have been touched, smoothed, and polished by countless human hands. Pools of mineral water from which water was obviously drawn are found at the very back of the cave. Here, people must have come to seek help in contact with the mysterious powers. A tablet from Knossos records: 'Amnisos, for Eleuthia, one amphora of honey.' This name, although here testified for the Bronze Age, is to be understood in precisely this form as pure Greek.... Eleuthia is an individually named goddess with a specific function [i.e., childbirth].... The marked differences between the finds from the [caves of] Kamares and Psychro, or Amnisos and Skotino indicate that even in Minoan times there were a number of different gods, each with a specific function, rather than one universal cave deity. And in spite of discontinuities and new beginnings, the example of Eleuthia-Eileithyia argues for at least a partial continuity from Minoan to Greek." See Burkert, *Greek Religion*, 25–26. Further note that "the earliest record of the cult of Eileithyia is the Linear A tablet KH5. The goddess is named there as A-RA-U-DA (*Alauta), and worshipped at WI-NA-DU (*Winatu = Inatos) directly corresponding to the goddess E-RE-U-TI-JA (*Eleuta) mentioned on the Linear B tablets from Knossos. From the Mycenean name, the classic Greek terms Eileithyia, Eleithya, Eiléthyia, Eleuthya (Ionic), Eleusia (Laconian doric), Eleiuthya (Cretan doric), and Eileitheia (Northwestern Greek) were born—from one of them comes Latin Ilithia. The origin of the name seems to be Indo-European," a speculation found on the website www.minoablog.blogspot.com/2010/09/goddess-eileithyia-and-her-snakes.html.

73 Pausanias relates that, "At the foot of Mount Kronios [at Olympia, Elis], on the north, between the treasuries and the mountain, is a sanctuary of Eileithyia, and in it Sosipolis (Saviour of the State), a native Elean deity, is worshipped. Now they surname Eileithyia Olympian, and choose a priestess for the goddess every year. The old woman who tends Sosipolis herself too by an Elean custom lives in chastity, bringing water for the god's bath and setting before him barley cakes kneaded with honey. In the front part of the temple, for it is built in two parts, is an altar of Eileithyia and an entrance for the public; in the inner part Sosipolis is worshipped, and no one may enter it except the woman who tends the god, and she must wrap her head and face in a white veil. Maidens and matrons wait in the sanctuary of Eileithyia chanting a hymn; they burn all manner of incense to the god, but it is not the custom to pour libations of wine. An oath is taken by Sosipolis on the most important occasions. The story is that when the Arkadians had invaded the land of Elis, and the Eleans were set in array against them, a woman came to the Elean generals, holding a baby to her breast, who said that she was the mother of the child but that she gave him,

because of dreams, to fight for the Eleans. The Elean officers believed that the woman was to be trusted, and placed the child before the army naked. When the Arkadians came on, the child turned at once into a Drakon. Thrown into disorder at the sight, the Arkadians turned and fled, and were attacked by the Eleans, who won a very famous victory, and so call the god Sosipolis. On the spot where after the battle the snake seemed to them to go into the ground they made the sanctuary. With him the Eleans resolved to worship Eileithyia also, because this goddess to help them brought her son forth unto men." See Pausanias, *Description of Greece*, 6.20.2.

74 Jewelry—a "bronze ear scoop" and "an agate seal with a design of two Cretan wild goats"—were also found. See R. Hope Simpson, "Identifying a Mycenaean State," *The Annual of the British School at Athens* 52 (1957): 238.

75 Rachel Richardson, "Team Discovers a Rare Minoan Sealstone in the Treasure-laden Tomb of a Bronze Age Greek Warrior," Phys.org, accessed December 21, 2017, www.phys.org/news/2017-11-team-rare-minoan-sealstone-treasure-laden.html.

76 According to Thomas R. Martin, "Particularly important both to the community and to individuals were what we call hero-cults, rituals performed at the tomb of a man or woman, usually from the distant past, whose remains were thought to retain special power. This power was local, whether for revealing the future through oracles, for healing injuries and disease, or for providing assistance in war." See "An Overview of Classical Greek History from Mycenae to Alexander," www.perseus.tufts.edu/hopper/text?doc=Perseus%3Atext%3A1999.04.0009%3Achapter%3D10%3Asection%3D1%3Asubsection%3D6, accessed December 21, 2017.

77 Pausanias, *Description of Greece*, 3.26.11.

78 R. Hope Simpson, "Identifying a Mycenaean State," *The Annual of the British School at Athens* 52 (1957): 239.

79 Apostolos N. Athanassakis, *The Orphic Hymns*, trans. Benjamin M. Wolkow (Baltimore: Johns Hopkins University Press, 2013), 54–55.

A MIDRASHIC LOOK AT QUEEN MICHAL: THE TRAGIC LOVER-HERO OF THE DAVIDIC NARRATIVE

HANNAH IRISH

The Bible includes stories of strong women, such as the Hebrew matri-archs (Sarah, Rebecca, Leah, and Rachel); and Deborah; Naomi; Ruth; and Esther. However, in much traditional exegesis and biblical scholarship, there are many other women whose stories are typically valued only in their relation to important men (Rahab and Miriam), overlooked almost altogether (Tamar and Hannah), or viewed almost entirely negatively (Eve and Bathsheba), to name a few. Michal most often belongs to the latter group. The youngest daughter of King Saul, who becomes David's first wife prior to his kingship, Michal is a biblical character who, traditionally, many commentators love to hate—or pity. As a member of the mad king's family, and as a character often contrasted with David, a quick look at some of the literature about Michal shows that she is most often vilified due to her angry confrontation with David when he brings the Ark of the Covenant back to Jerusalem (perhaps the biblical episode for which she is best known). In a literary analysis tied distressingly loosely to the biblical text, Buckner B. Trawick claims that Michal's story is "one of the most pathetic domestic stories"[1] in the Davidic narrative, and that "David punishes her by refusing thenceforth to cohabit with her."[2] Edward Edinger interprets the story as a typical mythological pattern: by marrying her, David rescues Michal from her father. In turn, Michal helps David escape from Saul. However, Edinger interprets Michal's accusations as envious of David's devotion to God, and, like Trawick, he sees her childlessness as punishment.[3]

Others, however, see Michal as a victim, a powerless woman who is merely a pawn in the men's game of king-making. Alice Ogden Bellis calls Michal a helpmate who is also a victim,[4] and distinguishes her as "the dissatisfied daughter/wife of divided loyalties."[5] Irene Nowell calls Michal's story a tragedy: Forced to return to David, whom she loved and whose life she saved, but who uses her only as a claim to the throne, she is taken from Palti, "the only man who truly loved her." She concludes that Michal is "a sacrifice to the claims of Israel's monarchy."[6]

However, rather than accept Michal as villain or victim, there is a more subversive view that venerates her. Benjamin Morse argues that "the proliferation of commentary that 'confines', 'erases', and 'murders' Michal does not seem to do justice to the compelling persona that surfaces."[7] It is in this vein that the passages concerning her in 1 and 2 Samuel are explored, with emphasis on her rescue of David from Saul's plot and her final confrontation with David after the Ark of the Covenant is returned to Jerusalem. Far from a villain, and having far more agency than other biblical victims—though she is a tragic figure in many respects—I use the midrash tradition to argue that Michal is a strong character in her own right, despite being overshadowed and manipulated by the men in her story.

Briefly, midrash is a Jewish tradition of scriptural exegesis in which the teacher interprets or elaborates upon a text from the Hebrew Bible in order to provide religious teaching that is often beyond the literal or plain meaning of the employed text. In this tradition, we look at passages from the book of Samuel (paraphrased from *The New Oxford Annotated Bible with Apocrypha: New Revised Standard Version*) to tell Michal's story from the perspective that she is the hero of her own story, and not a villain or victim in David's.

Michal Is Married to David (1 Samuel 18:17–27)

Saul's daughter, Michal, loves David. When Saul finds out, he thinks he can use her against David. Saul tells David that he can marry Michal in exchange for one hundred Philistine foreskins. David takes him up on it, as he likes the idea of being the king's son-in-law. When David succeeds, in what Saul had hoped he would die endeavoring, Saul marries him to Michal.

Michal's introduction includes two things: she is Saul's daughter and she loves David. Much has been made of Michal's love for David, though

Fig. 8. David Escapes through a Window.
From https://commons.wikimedia.org/wiki/File:073.David_Escapes_through_a_Window.jpg.

the scene sounds like little more than political marriage negotiations. Morse notes, however, that she is the only woman in the Hebrew scriptures said to love a man,[8] while Robert Alter notes that nothing is said about David's feelings for her.[9] This question of David's feelings toward Michal is important to keep in mind, as well as noting the continual emphasis on Michal as Saul's daughter, which Hayyim Angel suggests implies that her familial ties and royal lineage are paramount to David.[10]

Michal Rescues David from Saul (1 Samuel 19:11–17)

Not long after their marriage, Saul decides to kill David, and Michal finds out. She tells David, "If you do not run tonight, tomorrow you will be killed." She helps David escape out the window and he flees. Then she makes a decoy by laying an idol in their bed. When Saul's messengers come to take David, she tells them he's sick. When Saul sends them back to bring David anyway, they discover the decoy. Saul asks Michal, "Why did you lie and help my enemy escape?" Michal replies, "David said to me, 'Let me go; why should I kill you?'"

Michal's love for her husband is evident in her loyalty to him rather than to her father. She heroically risks a great deal, likely her own life, to save David. Again, there is no mention of David's feelings toward Michal for saving him.[11] However, in the process of choosing David over her father, as Bellis points out, Michal loses David: he escapes, but there is no plan for his return.[12]

Michal Is Married to Palti (1 Samuel 25:42–44)

About seven years after Michal helps David escape, while still hiding from Saul, David takes two new wives. Also, Saul has married Michal to Palti, son of Laish, who was from Gallim.

This event in Michal's story is a simple narrative statement comprised of one sentence. The text nowhere indicates that Michal has any voice in this matter; as in her original marriage to David, she is a pawn in the men's political power struggle.

Michal Is Returned to David (2 Samuel 3:12–16)

After another seven years, in which Saul and his son Jonathan have died in battle, David has rallied the tribes of Judah; defeated Saul's son, Ishbaal, and Ishbaal's general, Abner; acquired four additional new wives; and had sons by all six of his wives. Rather than continue fighting, Abner offers a truce, to which David agrees, but only on the condition that Abner brings Saul's daughter Michal back to him. Then David tells Saul's son Ishbaal, "Give me my wife Michal, for whom I paid the bride price of one hundred Philistine foreskins." Ishbaal sends Abner to take her from her husband Palti, the son of Laish. But her husband follows her, weeping as he walks behind, until Abner tells him, "Go back home!" So he goes home.

John Kessler notes an implied narrative criticism of David: prior to his demand for Michal's return, David's six other wives and all his sons are listed, emphasizing that David will deprive Palti of his only wife.[13] We also know that David is removing Michal from a real relationship, with a person whose name and family are known.[14] Further, Angel notes that David first calls Michal "Saul's daughter," emphasizing her political significance in unifying the northern and southern kingdoms,[15] rather than any personal value. Then, when he does call her "my wife," he immediately states the bride price he paid, emphasizing his legal ownership of her. Ellen White rightly remarks that these are not the actions of a heart-broken husband who wants his beloved wife back, but rather those of a man check-mating his enemy.[16] This contrasts sharply with the image of the husband Michal is being taken from.

Though little is known about Palti, his following Michal in tears, suggests love and devotion.[17] However, as moving as Palti's response is, nothing is said about Michal's feelings regarding leaving Palti or returning to David. Her reaction to yet another maneuver by the men in power is conspicuous in its absence. It seems Michal, in herself, is meaningless[18]; she is just the final sign that David has defeated Saul.

Michal Confronts David (2 Samuel 6:20–22)

Following another seven years—in which David is anointed king over all of Israel, moves the royal quarters to Jerusalem, and conquers the Philistines—David determines to move the Ark of the Covenant back to Jerusalem. As he returns with the Ark, David, girded with a linen ephod, dances before the Lord. When David gets home, Michal, the daughter of Saul, says to him, "How the king of Israel honored himself today, uncovering himself today before the eyes of his servants' maids, as any vulgar fellow might shamelessly uncover himself!" David responds, "It was before the Lord, who chose me in place of your father and all his household, to appoint me as prince over Israel, that I have danced. I will make myself more contemptible than this, and be abased in my own eyes; but by the maids I shall be held in honor."

Until this moment, the text indicates no interaction between David and Michal since Michal helped David escape.[19] We can only speculate as to how she has felt the last twenty-one years. Though there is debate over what, exactly, David's being girded with a linen ephod connotes—whether he was garbed as a priest[20] or was wearing only a loincloth-like garment[21]—Michal's statement indicates that David reveals his body in a way she deems unfitting for the king to do in front of his people on the street. It is worth noting that she addresses David in the third person, using his public title rather than a personal one,[22] and that Michal, again, is referred to in this instance as Saul's daughter, rather than David's wife,[23] highlighting her political position rather than a personal one.

If David is wearing a priestly garment, Morse suggests that Michal is offended by it in accordance with the prophetic distrust of kings, and that she resents David for buying into the celebrity cult of kingship.[24] If David is wearing only a loincloth while dancing ecstatically in the streets, as is the common understanding, then his entire body is publicly exposed. In either case, it seems that Michal's assessment is fair: David has behaved without propriety, humility, or modesty before God and his people.

Michal referencing the maids brings attention to two things: David's arrogance and Michal's position as his wife. If David is wearing a priestly garment, David Clines calls out David's pride in assuming the "king-priest" role, something to which his right to do is contested.[25] If he's wearing a loincloth, Alter states that the idea of the maids enjoying David's near-nakedness suggests justified sexual jealousy, as well as political resentment, in Michal's anger.[26] After all, David acquired six wives in Michal's absence (thus rendering her sexually disposable) and the text nowhere indicates his current relationship with her is anything but political. White calls this the final insult in what seems a humiliating marriage: since Michal holds the highest status possible for an Israelite woman—wife of the king—by exposing himself in public, taking what is rightfully hers and giving it to any who would look, David effectively strips Michal of her marital status.[27] Thus, Michal's indignation over David's behavior proves warranted.

At this point, if Michal's accusations are misguided, David has the opportunity to explain himself. A common interpretation of David's actions is that he is humbly and jubilantly serving God, with no regard for his royal status. However, David's defensive and haughty reply to Michal is inconsistent with this; if he truly believes his actions are innocent, that his humility and purity of heart need no defense, his response to his wife would also be humble and pure. Rather, as White notes, David lashes out aggressively, further demeaning Michal; not only does David show no compassion for his wife, he taunts her further by saying the maids honor him, and never does he show any love for her, the woman who put her own life at risk to save his.[28]

Michal Had No Children (2 Samuel 6:23)

And Michal the daughter of Saul had no child
to the day of her death.

Immediately following their quarrel, Michal's story ends. The common reaction is to deduce cause and effect: because of Michal's actions, she is barren. (It is worth noting, though, that the biblical text does not use the word "barren.") However, this is not so simple. First, there are two issues of translation. While the *NRSV* begins the verse, "And Michal," other versions, such as the *King James Version*, begin the verse with "So" or "Therefore." Alter translates the verse, "And Michal daughter of Saul had no child till her dying day,"[29] and notes that "[m]odern translators generally destroy the fineness of the effect of rendering the initial 'and' as 'so,'"[30] and *Young's Literal Translation* says, "As to Michal daughter of Saul, she had no child till the day of her death." While "so" commonly implies cause and effect, "and" does not. Nor does "As to Michal," which is fitting wording considering that the verse wraps up her story in the books of Samuel, and does so in a manner that is common in narrating the histories of the kings of Israel.

Additionally, in an essay regarding the mention of Michal's five sons in 2 Samuel 21:8, J.J. Glück comments on the original Hebrew in which "the literal translation of the phrase ... in English suggests 'never' ... [whereas] in Hebrew it means 'never after.'"[31] As none are mentioned in the text, it is likely that Michal never bears children to David, either before or after their quarrel. However, if the five sons of 2 Samuel 21:8 are Michal's by

Palti, as Glück argues they are, then at one point in her life Michal does fulfill the role of mother. And if she was torn away from her children by David's demand for her return, that adds an additional layer to her feelings toward him at the end of their story. Alternatively, as Glück also points out, the five may be sons of Merab, Michal's sister, adopted by Michal after Merab's death. Therefore, whether they are Michal's biological children or not, the assumption that she never mothered is strongly contradicted by 2 Samuel 21:8.

Further, if Michal is in fact childless, as Morse points out, barrenness in the Bible is never explicitly a divine punishment.[32] Thus, it is unprecedented to assume that Michal's childlessness is God's doing. If it is not God's will, many assume it is David's, as he retaliates by refusing to sleep with her.[33] There are, however, two other possibilities. One of them is that Michal, not David, puts an end to the sexual relationship,[34] which, in light of Michal's actions up to this point, is quite plausible. Clines suggests it's unlikely that a woman who despises a man the way Michal appears to despise David would choose to bear him children.[35] And even if it is David's choice, is Michal not better off having no sons contending for David's throne?[36] And, even if it is true that to be childless is the greatest dishonor a woman could face, can it really be worse than what Michal has already suffered, being deserted by her first husband, then ripped away, by him, from her second husband, to be kept as nothing but a political prize?[37]

Finally, it is possible that Michal having no children is simply biological—while David fathers children later in life (as men do), Michal may be past childbearing age—she was a young woman when she was married and over twenty years passed since then. White suggests that the ambiguity may be the narrator's indication that no fault should be assigned.[38]

Conclusion

With so much left unsaid in the biblical text (we know almost nothing of the twenty years between Michal and David's initial separation and their final confrontation, nor do we know how Michal feels during those years), it is possible to fill in the gaps in a variety of ways and writers in both the Jewish and Christian traditions have done so. Thus, I argue that Michal is a multidimensional character who cannot be summed up or tied down by labels such as "villain" or "victim," nor only by "tragic figure" nor by "heroine." Rather, she is a "tragic lover-hero."

Of the six episodes explored above, in three of them Michal is acted upon by her father, King Saul, and or her husband, King David; in two of them she acts first and decisively; and the final is simply a concluding comment. With her father the mad king, we can imagine that she survives a tense home life after David's escape, and that she worries about her father, her brothers, and her husband during the civil war between Saul and David. If she knows of David's other marriages, we can imagine that she feels hurt, disappointed, betrayed, or angry, or probably some combination. In this case, perhaps she welcomes her new marriage to Palti. If she does not know of David's marriages, then she may be devastated by being married off to Palti.

In either case, seven years is long enough for her to develop some affection toward her new husband, even if she never feels the level of devotion and love toward him that his weeping at her departure indicates he feels toward her. However, after seven years of apparent peace with Palti, we can imagine that she feels a sense of loss at leaving him. Further, if she has biological children with him, we can imagine that she is devastated at being torn away from them. We can also imagine that she is wary, at best, of David's reason for demanding her return. However, she may be excited to return to the man she once loved. Or perhaps she is angry at his initial abandonment of her and now demand for her return over a decade later. Or, even more likely, she feels some combination of these emotions. Thus, from these episodes, we see a complex and multidimensional woman who has known many extremes in life, both good and bad, and can genuinely be described as a "tragic lover."

Considering, now, the two episodes in which Michal is the primary agent, a strong figure emerges. In rescuing David, Michal shows herself to be a woman who will act on her convictions, despite the risk. She first acts on her love and loyalty to her new husband by warning him, quickly and concisely, of the danger and helping him escape out the window. She acts courageously in defying her father, the king, and she bravely risks her own life to save the man she loves. It is reasonable to assume that, had she not acted, David would have been murdered by Saul in the morning. To buy David more time to get as far away as possible before Saul sends anyone to find him, Michal quickly concocts a clever ruse to stall her father's murderous intentions. Finally, when Saul confronts her over rescuing David, she once again acts with quick wit, telling her father what will hopefully protect her from his wrath (that David threatened her life) but that gives no explanation as to why Michal hides the truth from Saul after David escapes through the window. This lack of a "real" answer defies Saul's authority as her father and her king, and it does not betray her love of or loyalty to David. Thus, Michal actively takes on the role of "hero."

When Michal confronts David after the return of the ark, she once again courageously acts on her convictions, despite the potential fallout. Over twenty years have elapsed since she saved her young husband from her mad father. In that time she has endured a great deal; she has been abandoned by her first husband, whom she loved, after risking her life for his; given to a second husband, who seems to have loved her a great deal; mothered five children, whether biological or adopted; and then forced to return to her first husband who has given no indication that he has ever had any personal feelings for her whatsoever, including any gratitude or appreciation for her heroic act two decades ago, and who married six other women, and had children by all of them, in the approximately fourteen years that Michal and David were separated. As the text provides no reason to assume that Michal's feelings for David have remained unchanged since she was a young woman, it is logical and reasonable to assume that, while she may still respect and esteem him as her husband and king, the love and devotion of her youth has faded, if not completely died. It is also reasonable to assume that she is hurt and angry about the way he has treated her. Thus, her choice to confront David, whatever the outcome, is a choice to act with dignity and integrity, and in righteous anger.

When David further demeans her by his angry and haughty response, rather than the narrator "giving her no reply," as many commentators suggest, Michal chooses not to reply. With dignity, integrity, and strength, she walks away from a pointless fight. She lets it go, and lets him go, removing him from her life, as much as possible, including refusing to share his bed. She is a woman of strength, not impious or jealous or ashamed, and certainly not to be pitied for bearing no children to David. Thus, I agree with Alter and Clines. Though David's kingship may be divinely ordained, Alter states that "theological rights do not necessarily justify domestic wrongs, and the anointed monarch of Israel may still be a harsh and unfeeling husband to the woman who has loved him and saved his life."[39] And, rather than seeing Michal as a never vindicated victim, Clines asks, "is not her dignity and her sarcasm sufficient vindication, in the eyes of readers at least? And is David a character who is 'flawed but favored', or is he not rather a truly nasty piece of work who has too many lucky breaks?"[40] Thus, she is truly a "tragic lover-hero." As this episode wraps up Michal's story, we see a woman who once loved a man and heroically saved his life, who now, as before also, must be her own hero, asserting herself while at the same time accepting, with great dignity, the end of her own tragic love story.

References

Alter, Robert. "Characterization and the Art of Reticence." In *Telling Queen Michal's Story: An Experiment in Comparative Interpretation*, edited by David J. A. Clines and Tamara C. Eskenazi, 64–73. Sheffield, England: Sheffield Academic Press, 1991.

Alter, Robert. *The David Story: A Translation with Commentary of 1 and 2 Samuel.* New York: W.W. Norton and Company, 2000.

Angel, Hayyim. "When Love and Politics Mix: David and His Relationships with Saul, Jonathan, and Michal." *Jewish Bible Quarterly* 40, no. 1 (2012): 41–51. https://search-ebscohost-com.pgi.idm.oclc.org/login. aspx?direct=true&db=a2h&AN=70079336&site=ehost-live&scope=site.

Bellis, Alice Ogden. *Helpmates, Harlots, and Heroes: Women's Stories in the Hebrew Bible.* Louisville, KY: Westminster/John Knox Press, 1994.

Clines, David J. A. "The Story of Michal, Wife of David, in Its Sequential Unfolding." In *Telling Queen Michal's Story: An Experiment in Comparative Interpretation*, edited by David J. A. Clines and Tamara C. Eskenazi, 129–40. Sheffield, England: Sheffield Academic Press, 1991.

Edinger, Edward F. *The Bible and the Psyche: Individuation Symbolism in the Old Testament.* Toronto, Canada: Inner City Books, 1986.

Eskenazi, Tamara C. "Michal in Hebrew Sources." In *Telling Queen Michal's Story: An Experiment in Comparative Interpretation*, edited by David J.A. Clines and Tamara C. Eskenazi, 157–74. Sheffield, England: Sheffield Academic Press, 1991.

Glück, J. J. "Merab or Michal." *Zeitschrift Für Die Alttestamentliche Wissenschaft* 77, no. 1 (1965): 72–81. EBSCOhost: pgi.idm.oclc. org/login?url=https://search-ebscohost-com.pgi.idm.oclc.org/login. aspx?direct=true&db=rfh&AN=ATLA0000708971&site=ehost-live&scope=site

Kessler, John. "Sexuality and Politics: The Motif of the Displaced Husband in the Books of Samuel." *Catholic Biblical Quarterly* 62, no. 3 (2000): 409. https://search-ebscohost-com.pgi.idm.oclc.org/login. aspx?direct=true&db=aph&AN=3745897&site=ehost-live&scope=site

Morse, Benjamin. "The Defence of Michal: Pre-Raphaelite Persuasion in 2 Samuel 6." *Biblical Interpretation* 21, no. 1 (2013): 19–32. doi:10.1163/15685152-1049A0002

The New Oxford Annotated Bible: New Revised Standard Version with the Apocrypha, 5th ed. Edited by Michael D. Coogan, Marc Z. Brettler, Carol A. Newsom, and Pheme Perkins. New York: Oxford University Press, 2018.

Nowell, Irene. *Women in the Old Testament.* Collegeville, MN: The Liturgical Press, 1997.

Trawick, Buckner B. *The Bible as Literature: Old Testament History and Biography.* New York, NY: Barnes and Noble, 1963.

White, Ellen. "Michal the Misinterpreted." *Journal for the Study of the Old Testament* 31, no. 4 (2007): 451–64. doi:10.1177/0309089207080051

Endnotes

1 Buckner B. Trawick, *The Bible as Literature: Old Testament History and Biography* (New York: Barnes and Noble, 1963), 101.

2 Ibid., 102.

3 Edward F. Edinger, *The Bible and the Psyche: Individuation Symbolism in the Old Testament* (Toronto: Inner City Books, 1986), 86.

4 Alice Ogden Bellis, *Helpmates, Harlots, and Heroes: Women's Stories in the Hebrew Bible* (Louisville, KY: Westminster/John Knox Press, 1994), 140.

5 Ogden Bellis quoted in Ogden Bellis, *Helpmates, Harlots, and Heroes*, 151.

6 Irene Nowell, *Women in the Old Testament* (Collegeville, MN: The Liturgical Press, 1997), 107.

7 Benjamin Morse, "The Defence of Michal: Pre-Raphaelite Persuasion in 2 Samuel 6," *Biblical Interpretation* 21, no. 1 (2013): 21.

8 Ibid.

9 Robert Alter, *The David Story: A Translation with Commentary of 1 and 2 Samuel* (New York: W.W. Norton and Company, 2000.), 115.

10 Hayyim Angel, "When Love and Politics Mix: David and His Relationships with Saul, Jonathan, and Michal," *Jewish Bible Quarterly* 40, no. 1 (2012): 48.

11 Ibid.; Alter, *The David Story*, 120.

12 Ogden Bellis, *Helpmates, Harlots, and Heroes*, 145.

13 John Kessler, "Sexuality and Politics: The Motif of the Displaced Husband in the Books of Samuel," *Catholic Biblical Quarterly* 62, no. 3 (2000): 45–16.

14 Ibid., 417.

15 Angel, "When Love and Politics Mix," 49.

16 Ellen White, "Michal the Misinterpreted," *Journal for the Study of the Old Testament* 31, no. 4 (2007): 458.

17 Alter, *The David Story*, 211.

18 White, "Michal the Misinterpreted," 458.

19 Alter, *The David Story*, 228.

20 Morse, "The Defence of Michal," 26.

21 Alter, *The David Story*, 227; David J. A. Clines, "The Story of Michal, Wife of David, in Its Sequential Unfolding," in *Telling Queen Michal's Story: An Experiment in Comparative Interpretation*, edited by David J. A. Clines and Tamara C. Eskenazi, 129–40 (Sheffield, England: Sheffield Academic Press, 1991), 138.

22 Morse, "The Defence of Michal," 23; Alter, *The David Story*, 229.

23 Angel, "When Love and Politics Mix," 49.

24 Morse, "The Defence of Michal," 27.

25 Clines, "The Story of Michal," 139.

26 Alter, *The David Story*, 229.

27 White, "Michal the Misinterpreted," 460.

28 Ibid., 460–61.

29 Alter, *The David Story*, 230.

30 Robert Alter, "Characterization and the Art of Reticence," in *Telling Queen Michal's Story: An Experiment in Comparative Interpretation*, ed. David J. A. Clines and Tamara C. Eskenazi (Sheffield, England: Sheffield Academic Press, 1991), 73.

31 J. J. Glück, "Merab or Michal," *Zeitschrift Für Die Alttestamentliche Wissenschaft* 77, no. 1 (1965): 73.

32 Morse, "The Defence of Michal," 31.

33 Ibid.

34 Ibid., 32.

35 Clines, "The Story of Michal," 139.

36 Ibid.

37 Ibid.

38 White, "Michal the Misinterpreted," 462.

39 Alter, "Characterization," 72.

40 Clines, "The Story of Michal," 140.

SHÂMARAN (SHAHMARAN):
THE LOST GODDESS OF KURDISTAN[1]

DILŞA DENIZ

Fig. 9. Contemporary example of Shaymaran.
From http://ku.wikipedia.org/wiki/W%C3%AAne:Salname_2004.jpg

The first time I saw her, she was painted on the left and right borders of a small mirror. I was a child then, fascinated by this image of a half-woman, half-snake—and saddened, too, intuitively sensing what she was trying to tell me. Years later I heard her story, and realized that as a child I had grasped that she had been betrayed and murdered. Then, with my involvement in the women's struggle, I also realized she was telling the history of women, as well as a history of the Kurds. She is *Shahmaran*; her name "*sha*" (shah) and "*mar*" (*snake*) means "Sha[h] of the snakes" in Kurdish. There are variant spellings; I use the Shâmaran version here.[2]

The Kurds and the History of a Goddess[3]

There are an estimated forty million Kurds in Greater Kurdistan, and about fifty million in the world. They are the largest stateless group in the world, despite their strong ethnic identity for over two thousand years. According to Izady, as the Indigenous inhabitants of the land, "there are no 'beginnings' for Kurdish history and people. Kurds and their history are the end products of thousands of years of continuous internal evolution and the assimilation of new peoples and ideas introduced sporadically into their land."[4] Thus, genetically, Kurds are considered to be the descendants of all those who ever came to settle in Kurdistan, such as the Guti, Kurti, Mede, Mard, Carduchi, Gordyene, Adianbene, Zila, and Khaldi,[5] and also Indo-European tribes who migrated to the Zagros Mountains some four thousand years ago.[6,7]

Archaeological findings in the region show early agricultural development and domestication of farm animals such as sheep, goats, hogs, and dogs. The earliest evidence of a unified and distinct culture (and possibly, ethnicity) of people inhabiting the Kurdish mountains dates back to the Halaf culture of 8,000 to 7,400 years ago. There are also traces of recordkeeping, fired pottery making and glazing, weaving, metallurgy, and urbanization dating between 8,000 and 12,000 years ago in Kurdistan.[8]

Robson indicates that the first mention of the Kurds in historical records is from Sumerian cuneiform writings about "the land of the Karda" in 3000 BCE. From the earliest times the Kurds followed their tribal leaders with very limited interference from outsiders. The lack of interference was mostly due to the inaccessibility of the area in which they lived, and also their reputation as fierce warriors. Even so, in their early history they were, at times, dominated by the Sumerians, Akkadians, Babylonians, Assyrians, Parthians, Persians, Romans, and Armenians.[9]

Cyrus's conquest of Medes, an early Kurdish state, brought it under Persian dominion. Mingling of these two cultures is referred to as the Medo-Persian process. George Smith states that "in order to conceal the subjection of their country to Media, the Persian annalists identified those Median sovereigns who had ruled over their land as their own kings."[10] This outcome seems similar to use of *"sha[h]"* as a title in the first records by Cyrus after his conquest of the Median kingdom. According to legend, Cyrus was the grandson of Medes king Astyages, who also raised him.[11] In that instance, it is not wrong to say that Cyrus was more Medes, suggesting that "sha[h]" was probably an appropriated Median (sacred) ruling title. Moreover, the word "sha[h]" is Median[12]; however, it is currently used to refer to Persian/Iranian monarchs as the Medes no longer exist.

Due to the Medo-Persian process, cultural mythologies were similarly appropriated. For instance, the Kurdish legend of Kawa and Dehhaq turns into the Persian historical legend of Kawah and Zouhak. Persian poet Ferdowsi's *Shahname*[13] is similar to Kurdish *Shahnamehs*. It is interesting to note the Kurdish prefix "Sha[h]" in both *Shahnameh* and *Shâmaran* and its implications.

Shâmaran—an important, semi-sacred being—had, and continues to have, a dynamic and intense relationship with the Kurdish people. The demotion from sacred to semi-sacred was most probably due to thousands of years of monotheist Islamic pressure as well as patriarchal dominance before and during monotheism. Despite that pressure, her myth—orally transmitted from generation to generation—and image, a traditional feature of Kurdish homes and everyday life—have been preserved. The Kurds have enduring myths such as the blacksmith Kawa, but Shâmaran is one of few images and the only surviving female being from antiquity who continues to have an important role in daily life into the present.

Despite her diminishing stature through time, Kurds still tell her story from generation to generation, making sure she has a place in their homes. For instance, I was born in Dersim, a Kurdish city in eastern Turkey where Shâmaran's story and image thrived in the memories of its occupants. Her snake–woman image was painted on a mirror, hanging on guest room walls, as the only female who (symbolically) had access to such a reserved public sphere for men. Her physical features matched beauty standards of Kurdish society: big black eyes, long nose, very elegant lips, and lush black hair, with full-blown roses framing her head. Her long, strong tail was almost hovered over her, as if protecting her head and nicely ornamented neck.

I grew up gazing at her picture. I remember our elders telling us throughout childhood about Shâmaran, the "sha[h]" of the snakes. We continued to hear the story in different places from different people as we entered adulthood and beyond. Despite slight differences in stories, the unchanged part was how she was betrayed by a man (mankind)—that is, she was enslaved to a sick brutal king, and her medical knowledge was transferred to the man she loved, who then caused her death.

She is known to everyone, as her image appears on walls, mirrors, embroideries, copper trays and housewares, and so much more. The demand for her images for centuries has created one of the Kurds' oldest occupations, including—male and female artisans who specialize in painting, engraving, and weaving her image on countless surfaces and textiles.

To understand her cultural (and economic) importance in Kurdish daily life, we need to ask why people would still need her image in their daily lives. The answer most probably is that her aesthetic, beauty, embodies "well-being," that is, protection from illness, harsh ecological conditions, dangerous outsiders, family enemies, wild animals, and so on. It also includes fertility, abundance, protection of domestic animals, and the flourishing of agriculture. Only a being with strong mystical power can be depended on to oversee such a wide range of circumstances. Many indicators show that Shâmaran is that kind of sacred being even after thousands of years of colonization by Abrahamic religions, mainly Islam. Her powers remained deeply embedded in the collective unconscious collective. Recently she has become a symbol of Kurdish women's struggle for equality as well as of Kurds in general; her name and image are common among women's NGOs.

Shâmaran's dynamic presence in daily Kurdish life is especially remarkable given Islamic prohibitions against and punishment for (including the death penalty) displays of artistic work depicting human images. According to Islam only God can create a human (image). Nonetheless, Kurds have not stopped painting, engraving, printing, and embroidering her image or displaying it on walls. Even after many centuries of the dominant Abrahamic version of Genesis—woman and snake depicted as evil—and of Islam have failed to alter the Kurds' positive regard for Shâmaran. This might be why the Kurds are not seen as "proper Muslims" by other Muslims and why their Arabic and Turkish Muslim neighbors denounce them as "the children of evil or children of sin." "Evil" in this context most probably refers to antiquity when Kurds worshipped a goddess and women were greatly honored in Kurdish society.

The situation of women in Kurdish society today still retains important traces of traditional women's power in both the sacred realm and
in daily life. In spite of the Kurdish patriarchy, the secondary position of women and thus, their limited educational opportunities and (of
course) domestic violence, Kurdish women have always enjoyed a certain amount of independence, respect, and power compared to women in
neighboring Arabic and Turkish regions. For instance, Kurdish women
have always been unassailable in public spaces. As I recall from childhood (and also presently), women freely traveled through villages and
towns without a male companion. I should also mention that all such
travel in the past was done on foot, taking several hours through high
mountains, deep valleys, remote villages, and so on. It was unthinkable
to disturb or harass any woman.[14]

Such relative freedoms can be apprehended as the Kurds' strong connection with their past belief system(s) in which women have sacred roles
and are granted a certain amount of privilege and esteem. As Bruinessen
states, many Kurdish authors accept the same "as proof of the respected
position enjoyed by women in their society, or even as the remnants of an
old tradition of gender equality."[15] Naomi Gale underlines Kurdish Jewish
women's freedom, stating that "even [though] the Kurds are a patriarchal
society, ... the Kurdish Jewish woman enjoys much more freedom than her
Jewish sisters" in other nations.[16]

Another point that should be mentioned here is that Kurds are known
for blood feuds among themselves. Despite such a tradition, if any woman
comes upon such a scene and removes her veil—mostly the white *lecheg*—
and drops it on the ground, all men engaged in the fight must stop.[17] This
can be understood as an example of the woman's sacred role in society
from the deep past, and most probably, a symbolic representation of the
goddess's command that society still obeys. Consequently, I believe that
the image of Shâmaran—as a deity, as a goddess of the land of Kurdistan,
as a lost goddess—embodies these traditions. Accordingly, in the midst of
tribal or familial conflicts, women are rarely harassed or targeted.

Kurdish women's involvement in the struggle against ISIS is another
example of this tradition. Although the Kurds have no nation-state supporting them, they continue to fight against the most recent criminal power
created in the name of religion that is also widely involved in committing
crimes against women. While other Islamic countries maintain silence,

Kurds—the most secular society in the Middle East—has fought with female combatants against ISIS. Kurdish armed organizations, such as KOMALA, PKK, YPG, and PEJAK, have female guerrillas and unit commanders as well. All Kurdish organizations in Turkey, and now in Rojava (the Syrian area of Kurdistan), are co-chaired, with one chair designated for a woman.[18] There is also a quota system for seats reserved for women in the pro-Kurdish parties in the parliament.[19] All Kurdish mayors have female co-chairs despite the Turkish state's declaration that this practice is illegal and subject to retribution.

Methodology Matters

Mythological tales act as non-material archaeological artifacts and, thus, can serve as historical evidence, according to Marija Gimbutas. Tracing the role of women in the sacred realm through diverse historical processes, cultures, and civilizations can be revealing. Because Kurdish lands have been occupied by four states and three nations, there have been purposeful attempts by the occupiers to block or erase historical evidence relevant to the Kurds and their past. Compared to other nations, quite recently Kurds have received academic opportunities; thus Kurdish researchers[20] have just started writing about their culture, history, language, land, mythology, and so on. Yet, Kurdish researchers continue to encounter countless obstacles due to population displacement and the ongoing colonialization of Kurdistan. For example, Kurdish cultural artifacts have often been registered in the name and the languages of the occupying states. More importantly, in some of these countries, the Kurdish language is either prohibited, or has become inaccessible after years of its elimination from educational systems. Due to ideologically-driven translations, as well as lack of centralization and codification in Kurdish language produced by segregation by the colonizers and assimilation processes, the words in the Kurdish language have many versions in different locales, as is the case for the name of Shahmaran/ Shâmaran.

Because colonizer states and respective researchers often argue that the cultural artifacts belong to them, Kurdish researchers require even more support and special attention than their peers. As such, Kurdish studies are simultaneously decolonization studies, by which researchers have to anticipate additional hardships and obstructions. For instance, Kurdish studies scholars' articles in the peer-review process may be blocked by academic gatekeepers who support the state. Kurdish scholars' work may be rejected based on biased references produced by colonizers' nationalist academics.

In brief, this chapter is grounded in de-colonizing ethnic and religious perspectives. Therefore, Shahmaran/Shâmaran is used as a non-material archaeological remnant in this study, and has become the subject of the content and discourse on both myth and image. Accordingly, I use *Shâmaran* in its original spelling and pronunciation among Kurdish Alevis, my target population here.[21]

The Shâmaran Myth

She lives in the underworld with her people, the snakes. One day a young man stumbles upon a cave—in some versions, he falls into a hole, and in others, four friends found a cave full of honey. In all versions, the protagonist(s) dig in the earth. At the end of digging, one remains in the well and enters her world. Or, when he regains his bearings after the fall, he realizes he is surrounded by snakes and is taken to Shâmaran. Shâmaran welcomes him and informs him that nobody was supposed to know about her world; thus he could never return, as harm would come to her and her people; she adds that he would be safe living with them.

As the years pass, he becomes homesick. Meanwhile, Shâmaran falls in love with him. He asks to be set free as he does not belong there, but Shâmaran denies his request. As he becomes very upset and unhappy, Shâmaran worries that he will die. Eventually, she decides to let him go, but under certain conditions. She forbids him from ever bathing in public, because the body of any human who has seen Shâmaran in person becomes covered with distinctive marks every time he or she come into contact with water. He agrees to heed this warning and thanks her many times before returning to the world. He keeps a low profile and decides to live at a distance from the city to avoid being seen.

At the time, the country was ruled by a very cruel king who had a fatal disease; he was examined by nearly all physicians in the realm, but no one of these was able to cure him. The king is informed that the only remedy for his illness was the blood (in some versions, flesh) of Shâmaran. Therefore, a proclamation is issued stating that anyone who has seen Shâmaran must inform the authorities. Some time later, the young man is seen bathing in the river and people saw the marks on his body, and the authorities were notified. So he is captured and asked about Shâmaran's location. He refuses to answer and is subjected to torture, but remains silent. (In some versions, he confesses, while in others, he is offered a post as vizier, and he accepts.) The king's agents were afraid that he would die; they could not risk his death as he was the only person who knew the whereabouts of the goddess. Hence, they released him but had him followed. For a time he does nothing, waiting until he believes the king's people are no longer watching. At that time, he decides to travel to Shâmaran's abode to warn her. He is followed yet again, and Shâmaran is captured and brought to the king's palace. The young man, consumed by sorrow, blames himself for her capture and certain death.

When Shâmaran is taken to the palace to give her blood to the king, she asks for a favor. She says that since the young man has caused her death, she would like to take revenge. She tells the king that the blood (flesh in other versions) from the left side of her body is poison, while that from the right side has medicinal properties (in some versions the sides are reversed, other versions replace sides with tail and head). She tells the king, "You need the medicine in order to recover from your illness. Drink it. But I would like the blood from the poison side to be given to the man who disclosed my location." The king accepts with pleasure. Shâmaran is slaughtered moments afterward (in some versions the man was forced to kill her), and blood from her left side is given to the young man while blood from the right is given to the king. After a short time, the king starts choking, turns purple, and dies, but the young man survives. Thus, it is understood that Shâmaran intentionally killed the tyrant king and saved her lover; moreover, transferred her wisdom to him through her blood. The young man becomes a medicine man and leaves the palace for the countryside to enhance his medical knowledge. In the end, he becomes an immortal healer called Loqmanê Hekim.[22]

Shâmaran: The Body of Sacred Unity

As seen in the image of Shâmaran, the whole is built from a series of contrasts or dualities: human/animal, woman/man, femininity/masculinity, woman/snake, hot/cold, death/rebirth. Despite the apparent physical contrast of two seemingly incompatible creatures, perfect balance is achieved as they are forged into a single entity at the opposite ends of each body. The Shâmaran image and myth represent the perfect map showing how dualistic balance is achieved. Alongside the female part, the masculine is represented by the features of the snake: strong long neck, plain style of adornment, the ruler's crown atop the head, and the snake's stance as a protector.

The American anthropologist of comparative religion, E.O. James, points out the dualism of death and life, equivalent to regeneration through death, as one of the main qualities of goddess worship. The female is a nature-based symbol for the concept of the fundamental unity of organic life as expressed through death and rebirth, the sowing and harvesting of crops in the soil, and so forth. A half-male/half-female divinity, or masculine and feminine merging into one, expresses the same principle.[23] Thus, the balance of contrasts as the principal context for goddess worship is clearly depicted in the myth and image of Shâmaran and its horizontal (societal) formation, which is contrary to the key feature of monotheist dualism. In the latter, everything is classified as bad or good, and accordingly used to construct a vertical hierarchy—man becomes good and thus master, women and the snake become devilish and bad, and therefore must be kept under control. As a result, men were granted full dominance over women, and religion became a male-dominated sphere. Vertical hierarchy removed goddesses from the sacred realm and all women from the public sphere. Consequently, as Gimbutas states, independent, parthenogenetic (creating life without male participation) goddesses gradually turned into the brides, wives, and daughters of the (Indo-European) gods.[24]

Goddess worship represents both gendering and androgyny, as clearly seen in the Shâmaran image. For instance, the serpent/male melds with the upper half of the woman/human torso to transform the figure into an androgynous unity. Worshipping this bisexual/androgynous quality is emphasized by Westenholz, an Assyriologist and expert on ancient Near Eastern gender studies. She indicates that the vizier deity of Ninshubur was an androgynous character. He was male when ministering to male gods and female when ministering to female gods. She argues that "originally they had no gender, but were differentiated in this way only at the point of taking on human form."[25] This androgyne form is a very logical representation of the entire population comprised of men and women.

The process of gods and goddesses taking on human form is believed to have occurred sometime in the third millennium BCE.[26] Later this androgynous duality was turned into a paired or dual divinity, and later still, gods' consorts, lovers, and so on. In Indian mythology, this was expressed through the myth of Ardhanārīśvara. Ardhanārīśvara is translated along the lines of "the Lord who is half woman," or "the half woman Lord"[27]—a male–female composite of the Hindu god Shiva and his consort, Parvati. The myth appears in the Brihadaranyaka Upanishad and is explained as "the same size and kind as a man and woman closely embracing. He caused himself to break into two pieces, and from him a husband and wife were born."[28] Examples of the divine pair are Shiva and Parvati and Vishnu–Lakshmi (Indian); Isis and Osiris (Egyptian); Paris and Helen, Persephone and Hades (Greek); and Anšar and Kišar (Mesopotamia). While they can be partners or spouses, they can also be mother and son, and according to Marija Gimbutas, in matrilineal societies, sister and brother.[29] Shâmaran presents as an androgynal form that predates the pair divinity process.

The most important aspect of the Shâmaran myth is ownership of healing knowledge, a typical occupation of goddesses. In the Shâmaran image, the female part symbolizes owning knowledge/wisdom, the serpent part symbolizes action based on knowledge, the medicine. Despite the fact that the serpent's main power is its venom, the snake has been the symbol for medicine since ancient times. Gimbutas states that "in the cycle of life, the feminine force—the goddess—not only manifested in birth, fertility and life sustenance, she also embodied death, decay, and regeneration. As death wielder, she loomed as a terrifying raptor, a poisonous snake."[30] Shâmaran, via her serpent part, owns the venom, thus the killing or destructive power. Besides, as E.O. James states, "[t]he wonderful ability of the serpent to slough its skin and so renew its youth has earned for it throughout the world the character of the master of the mystery of rebirth."[31] So again, in the dualist character of goddess worship, woman's body is the source of birth, her venom the source of killing/death. So this is the cycle of life as death and rebirth, and thus immortality. All these dualistic symbolisms are clustered in the same body, as it contains both venom and antidote, death and life, immortality, eternity, and, fertility, and as such represents the basic circle/spiral of life.[32]

Shâmaran as a goddess of fertility and healing alludes to the cycles of physical existence and fertility that then encompass physical/societal existence and regeneration. Elements that appear to be complete opposites actually highlight the contribution of union/unity to a cooperative or cohesive existence. In this unified body there is no representation of masculine or feminine superiority. Furthermore, as understood from the position of the snake's head, the goddess/woman in the image is the "principal head." Despite the way in which the whole image is positioned, the principal head does not create a vertical hierarchy. Instead it depicts horizontal power and shared responsibility. As understood from the image and also the myth, the formula for ruling is both physical power and knowledge/wisdom. Neither can be qualified as good or bad, and in isolation, neither can survive.

This union has another layer of symbolic representation for the potent reinforcement of social unity. At least 5,000 years old, the androgynous image of Shâmaran[33] unites both sexes in one body, and is a kind of a map of balance and continuity in both physical and social life. Shâmaran uses her wisdom, strength, goodness, and consciousness to place eternal knowledge into responsible hands. She suggests a way of safeguarding knowledge by handing it over to a third party who will allow humankind to benefit from it or, at the very least, will not use it to their detriment. In contrast, according to the monotheistic Abrahamic Genesis, woman, snake, and, in fact, man as well, are expressly forbidden from being the carriers or producers of knowledge. While Adam is represented as one who has no interest in knowledge and Eve and the serpent as evil for desiring knowledge, Shâmaran has high praise for knowledge and wisdom and transfers the knowledge of healing to a man. Knowledge here is not something dangerous, but the most valuable resource.

It can also be said that Shâmaran's image and myth create a powerful objection to the violent seizure of valuable knowledge. Handing over knowledge to an "ordinary man" who is forbidden to pursue knowledge shows that the Shâmaran myth is in direct opposition to the monotheist discourse that followed. Goddess ownership of knowledge is a codification of a common resource from which all can benefit, and thus is handed down as a whole—a challenge to the most powerful discourse of the Abrahamic myth of creation.

The symbolic narrative of her killing suggests that the period of goddess worship was forced to give way during a time of social upheaval. It expresses the imposition of a new and dominant discourse/ideology on an existing social mechanism and the subsequent disruption of its balance. The Shâmaran myth represents the advent of a new patriarchal, monotheist social formation that came about through the violent destruction of a pre-existing social order, belief system, and ideology.

Shâmaran destroys (the cruel king) with the snake part of her body, the female part (healing knowledge) is immortalized in the body of the man she loves. Of course, this is not a voluntary gift because it is her only choice and it is made in desperation as the only way to protect knowledge. This is a narrative of rebirth of her essence into a new vessel, a form of resistance. The myth also contains the metaphor that knowledge was hijacked from women to then become possessed by men, which continues today in science, medicine, and academia. Perhaps this is the narration of generational oppression and thus the resistance of women/goddesses in history. Thus it is quite logical to say that Shâmaran—the goddess—is still fighting, and possibly through us, in a period, or even a place, where she was thought to have been defeated.

In conclusion, Shâmaran, through her myth and image, has been transmitted from generation to generation in Kurdish communities. She is the one who has survived more than 5,000 years with a very successfully integrated/aggregated symbolic figure[34] and a dense imagery map in which a series of contrasts are represented, collated, balanced, and woven into multiple layers of goddess philosophy and knowledge.[35] With all these qualities of goddess worship, Shâmaran is an academically unregistered and/or lost goddess[36] of Kurdistan. Her goddess-worship–based text contains a series of meanings that answer social needs from multiple angles. The balance is the intermediate stage where contrasts and opposites intersect.

In summary, the continued existence of Shâmaran in Kurdistan can be interpreted not only as resistance against the new(er) masculine/monotheistic form of religion, but definitely, if only partially, an insistence on the Kurdish ancient-time form of religion. Hanging Shâmaran's image on the "guest room" walls can be interpreted as a form and/or statement of resistance by her worshippers. It is an indication that after thousands of years, there are still followers; and that even a kind of secret resistance to monotheistic religion is still alive in this land. That is how and why Shâmaran, a goddess, has been preserved among her people, the Kurds.

References

Britannica. "Ardhanarishvara," last modified April 9, 2015. https://www.britannica.com/topic/Ardhanarishvara

Britannica. "Shah," last modified September 15, 2019. https://www.britannica.com/topic/shah

Bruinessen, Martin van. "From Adela Khanun to Leyla Zana: Women as Political Leaders in Kurdish History." In *Women of a Non-State Nation: The Kurds*, edited by Shahrzad Mojab, 95–112. Costa Mesa, CA: Mazda Publishers, Inc., 2001.

Cook, Helena. *The Safe Haven in Northern Iraq*. London: Kurdish Human Rights Project, 1995.

Deniz, Dilşa. "Kurdish Alevi Belief System, Rêya Heqî, Raa Haqi: Structure, Networking, Ritual and Function, in Kurdish Alevis." In *Kurdish Alevis and the Case of Dersim: Historical and Contemporary Insights*, edited by A. Kerim Gültekin-Erdal Gezik, 45–73. Lexington Books, 2019.

Deniz, Dilşa. "The *Shaymaran:* Philosophy, Resistance and Defeat of the Lost Goddess of Kurdistan." *The Pomegranate* 22, no. 2 (2020).

Erel, Umut, and Necla Acik. "Enacting Intersectional Multilayered Citizenship: Kurdish Women's Politics." *Gender, Place & Culture* (June 2019): 1–23. DOI: 10.1080/0966369X.2019.1596883.

Frye, R.N. "Cyrus the Great." Encyclopedia Britannica, April 10, 2020. https://www.britannica.com/biography/Cyrus-the-Great

Gale, Naomi. "Kurdish Women." In *The Shalvi/Hyman Encyclopedia of Jewish Women*, February 27, 2009. Accessed March 9, 2021. https://jwa.org/encyclopedia/article/kurdish-women

Gimbutas, Marija. *The Living Goddesses*. Berkeley: University of California, 1999.

Gunter, Michael M. "Gender Issue in Kurdistan." *Georgetown Journal of International Relations*, December 30, 2019. Accessed March 8, 2021. https://gjia.georgetown.edu/2019/12/30/gender-issues-in-kurdistan/

Izady, Mahrdad. "Are the Kurds Descended from the Medes?" *Kurdistanica*, 1994. Accessed June 15, 2020. http://kurdistanica.com/are-kurds-descended-from-the-medes/

Izady, Mehrdad. "Origin of the Kurds." *Kurdistanica*, 1992. Accessed June 15, 2020. http://kurdistanica.com/origin-of-the-kurds/

James, E.O., *The Cult of the Mother Goddess: An Archaeological and Documentary Study*. New York: Frederic A. Praeger, 1959.

Lagace, Phil. "Ardhanārīśvara in Tiruchengode, Tamil Nadu: A Case Study." Master's thesis. University of Saskatchewan, 2016.

Murdock, Maureen. "The Goddess and Marija Gimbutas." 2016. Accessed June 25, 2020. http://jungatlanta.com/articles/spring16-marija-gimbutas.pdf

Oracc Museum. "Ancient Mesopotamian Gods and Goddesses." Last modified February 11, 2013. http://oracc.museum.upenn.edu/amgg/technicalterms/index.html#abzu

Robson, Barbara. "Iraqi Kurds: Their History and Culture." Washington, DC: Center for Applied Linguistics, 1996. Accessed June 13, 2020. http://www.culturalorientation.net/learning/backgrounders

Saeedpour, Vera. *Meet the Kurds*. London: Cobblestone Publishing, 1999.

Smith, George. *Gentile Nations: Or, the History and Religion of the Egyptians, Assyrians, Babylonians, Medes, Persians, Greeks, and Romans*. New York: Carlton & Phillips, 1854.

Skjærvø, Prods Oktor. *An Introduction to Old Persian*. Cambridge, MA: Harvard University, 2003.

Westenholz, Joan Goodnick. "Goddesses of the Ancient Near East 3000–1000 BC." In *Ancient Goddesses, the Myths and the Evidence*, edited by Lucy Goodison and Christine Morris, 63–82. Madison, WI: University of Wisconsin Press, 1998.

Yildiz, Kerim, and Mark Muller. "Introduction." In *The European Union and Turkish Accession: Human Rights and the Kurds*, edited by Kerim Yildiz and Mark Muller, xi–xvii. London: Pluto Press, 2008.

Endnotes

1 I would like to thank my colleague and friend Svetlana Peshkova for reading this manuscript and providing me with insightful feedback. Many thanks to the Institute of International Education-Scholar Rescue Fund (IIE-SRF) for their support. I would also like to thank the editors of this volume for providing me with valuable feedback that greatly improved the quality of the chapter. Finally, I very much appreciate ASWM for its valuable work that I am honored to be part of.

2 Despite the widespread use of "Shahmaran," I prefer to use "Shâmaran" here, as this version is used among Kurdish Alevis.

3 This chapter derives from a forthcoming book titled, *Shâmaran: The Goddess of the Kurds*.

4 Mahrdad Izady, "Are the Kurds Descended from the Medes?" *Kurdistanica* (1994), http://kurdistanica.com/are-kurds-descended-from-the-medes/

5 Helena Cook, *The Safe Haven in Northern Iraq* (London: Kurdish Human Rights Project, 1995), 6.

6 Vera Saeedpour, *Meet the Kurds* (London: Cobblestone Publishing, 1999).

7 Kerim Yildiz and Mark Muller, *The European Union and Turkish Accession: Human Rights and the Kurds*, edited by Kerim Yildiz and Mark Muller, xi–xvii (London: Pluto Press, 2008), 4.

8 Izady, "Are the Kurds Descended from the Medes?"

9 Barbara Robson, "Iraqi Kurds: Their History and Culture" (Washington, DC: Center for Applied Linguistics, 1996), 7–8, accessed June 13, 2020. http://www. culturalorientation.net/learning/backgrounders

10 George Smith, *Gentile Nations: Or, the History and Religion of the Egyptians, Assyrians, Babylonians, Medes, Persians, Greeks, and Romans* (New York: Carlton & Phillips, 1854), 254.

11 Richard N. Frye, "Cyrus the Great, King of Persia," *Britannicca* https://www. britannica.com/biography/Cyrus-the-Great, last modified 2020.

12 Prods Oktor Skjærvø, *An Introduction to Old Persian* (Cambridge, MA: Harvard University, 2003), 149.

13 See John Andrew Boyle, "Ferdowsī, also spelled Firdawsī, Firdusi, or Firdousi, pseudonym of Abū al-Qasem Manṣūr (born *c.* 935, near Ṭūs, Iran— died c. 1020–26, Ṭūs), Perisan poet, author of the *Shāh-nāmeh* ('Book of Kings')," *Britannica*, https://www.britannica.com/biography/Ferdowsi, accessed February 14, 2021.

14 This situation continues to a certain extent due to the Turkish military presence and the village guard system by the state that aimed at destroying Kurdish cultural domination in the region, as well as the pressure of urbanization, which somewhat diminishes traditional cultural codes.

15 Martin van Bruinessen, "From Adela Khanun to Leyla Zana: Women as Political Leaders in Kurdish History," in *Women of a Non-State Nation: The Kurds*, ed. Shahrzad Mojab (Costa Mesa, CA: Mazda Publishers, 2001), 95.

16 Naomi Gale, "Kurdish Women," in *The Shalvi/Hyman Encyclopedia of Jewish Women*, February 27, 2009, accessed March 9, 2021, https://jwa.org/ encyclopedia/article/kurdish-women>

17 See "Kültürümüzde Kavgayı Durduran Laçik (Leçek) Gerçeği," *Yeni Muşun Sesi*, May 20, 2017, , http://www.yenimusunsesi.com/haber/kulturumuzde-kav-gayi-durduran-lacik-lecek-gercegi-5039.html, accessed March 8, 2021; Bejan Matur, "Başörtünü Yere Bırak," *Haber* 7, September 26, 2004, https://www.haber7.com/ yasam/haber/15045-matur-basortusunu-yere-birak, accessed March 9, 2021.

18 Umut Erel and Necla Acik, "Enacting Intersectional Multilayered Citizenship: Kurdish Women's Politics," *Gender, Place and Culture: A Journal of Feminist Geography*, 27, no. 2 (2019): 15–16. DOI: 10.1080/0966369X.2019.1596883; Michael M. Gunter, "Gender Issue in

Kurdistan," *Georgetown Journal of International Relations* (December 2019), https://gjia.georgetown.edu/2019/12/30/gender-issues-in-kurdistan/, accessed March 8, 2021.

19 Umut Erel and Necla Acik, "Enacting Intersectional Multilayered Citizenship: Kurdish Women's Politics," *Gender, Place & Culture* (June 2019): 11–12, DOI: 10.1080/0966369X.2019.1596883

20 Such as Celile Celil, Hamit Bozarslan, Amir Hasanpour, Nazand Begikani, and so on.

21 Alevism is a religion that is often presented as a sect of Islam. In reality, Alevis do not consider themselves Muslims, nor does the state and Muslims in general. Alevis might not argue against this; misleading identification for security reasons. Muslims and the state, while not accepting Alevism as a Muslim sect, wish to reduce the visibility of Alevi communities, and most importantly, to force them into assimilation via Islamic practices. The number of Alevis in Turkey, although there are no credible numbers, has been estimated at 15 to 20 million. A large proportion of Alevis in Turkey are Kurdish. Alevis do not follow the five pillars of Islam, and unlike Muslims, they believe in reincarnation. One must be born Alevi (i.e., conversion is not possible), and killing (including unnecessary killing of animals) is prohibited. Alevis do not practice gender segregation, nor veiling (except by older generations in communities where it is traditional). For further information, see Dilşa Deniz, "Kurdish Alevi Belief System, Rêya Heqî, Raa Haqi: Structure, Networking, Ritual and Function, in Kurdish Alevis," in *Kurdish Alevis and the Case of Dersim: Historical and Contemporary Insights*, ed. A. Kerim Gültekin-Erdal Gezik, 45–73. Lexington Books, 2019.

22 Dilşa Deniz, "The *Shaymaran:* Philosophy, Resistance and Defeat of the Lost Goddess of Kurdistan," *The Pomegranate* 22, no. 2 (2020): 224.

23 E.O. James, *The Cult of the Mother Goddess: An Archaeological and Documentary Study* (New York: Frederic A. Praeger, 1959), 244–245.

24 Marija Gimbutas, *The Living Goddesses* (Berkeley: University of California, 1999), 164.

25 Joan Goodnick Westenholz, "Goddesses of the Ancient Near East 3000–1000 BC," in *Ancient Goddesses, The Myths and the Evidences*, eds. Lucy Goodison and Christine Morris, 63–82 (Madison: University of Wisconsin Press, 1998), 68.

26 Oracc Museum, "Ancient Mesopotamian Gods and Goddesses," 2013, accessed June 25, 2020, http://oracc.museum.upenn.edu/amgg/technicalterms/index.html#abzu

27 Phil Lagace, "Ardhanārīśvara in Tiruchengode, Tamil Nadu: A Case Study" (master's thesis, University of Saskatchewan, 2016), 35.

28 Britannica, "Ardhanarishvara," April 9, 2015, https://www.britannica.com/topic/Ardhanarishvara, accessed June 28, 2020.

29 Maureen Murdock, "The Goddess and Marija Gimbutas," 2016, 10, accessed June 25, 2020, http://jungatlanta.com/articles/spring16-marija-gimbutas.pdf.

30 Gimbutas, *The Living Goddesses*, 19.

31 James, *The Cult of Mother Goddess*, 179.

32 Deniz, "The *Shâmaran*," 239.

33 Shâmaran likely first appeared in third millennium BCE (Orracc Museum, 2013) in the pre-human form, which means she is at least 5,000 years old. In that regard, when Turks invaded the region starting at 1071 CE, she had arrived at least 4,000 years previously in the region. Note that the etymology of the term "Shâmaran" shows no relation to the Turkish language. The word "*Sha[h]* (ruler)," as explained, is derived from Iranian languages that Turks borrowed from Persian, and *"mar"* is "snake" in Kurdish and Persian. In Turkish the word for "snake" is *"yılan."*

34 This expression was conceptualized by the author to describe the existence of multiple symbolic discourse/layers/images within a single symbol.

35 Deniz, "Th," 245.

36 Ibid., 245.

SECTION 3

MYTH AND GRIEF:
REWRITING OUR STORIES,
HEALING OUR WOUNDS

THE CREATION OF KUNSIKEYA TAMAKOCE

LUSHANYA ANDREA ECHEVERRIA

My Mother's Womb

The year was 1975, and that was the year I met my first Creator—my mother Beverly Littlethunder. I met her essence first in the womb of her belly, a cramped, yet warm and moist nook where I would live, grow, and develop for nine months. As soon as the tiny folds on the sides of my head could hear, I began to hear my first Creation stories. Soon after I learned I had been created by this woman, and that her womb's purpose was for nourishing, sustaining, and giving me life. We grew together; her belly swelled as my limbs swelled, her blood was my blood, her breath was my breath, and her heartbeat became my verve.

Once I made the journey to the light and left the womb of my mother, I was immediately taken to another womb, the Inipi Ceremony, or sacred house of prayer, that my Lakota people considered to be the "womb of Mother Earth." Sitting in this womb did not feel as snug, soft, or comfortable as my mother's womb, yet in time I felt safe, warm, and spiritually connected to another Creator, the Great Spirit. Thus began a childhood of dissonance because I soon realized that after my birth, my mother's stories of Creator disappeared, and I only heard the voices of the fathers and grandfathers as the voice of our sacred creation.

Each time I entered the *Inipi* womb, my spirit reverberated with my mother's womb. While I listened to the *Inipi*'s elders' stories about how Mother Earth came to be, warning the youth against harmful actions, and how to interpret the sacred teachings of the Great Spirit, I listened for my mother's womb stories. Yet, no matter how I twisted or turned, I could only hear the voice of a father, never my mother. In the *Inipi*, I would learn that the sacred stones placed in the center were called "grandfathers." I would learn that the great star in the sky that provided life to Mother Earth is called "father Sun." The great thunder beings treading across the sky would be the "grandfather tatanka." Those omnipresent winged ones who flew as high as the clouds would be called "grandfather wambli." The undulating swords from the sacred fire would be called "grandfather pheta." This confusion presented itself repeatedly in the traditional Lakota society in which I grew up.

The Lakota stories I grew up with, also called "modern-day" creation stories, were stories told by the elders, from their elders. Often, the elders told stories of being raised on reservations or attending boarding schools. The intent of the stories was to weave the lifestyle of pre-colonization with that of post-colonial days. In pre-colonial times, there were particular skills needed to live in balance with Native American traditions and practices. Post-colonial times are called "modern" because they occurred after colonialism. Our elders were committed to sharing teachings with the youth, and their intent was to help the emerging generations fare well in today's society.

We young ones would all gather around the elders, listening intently. Through these teachings, we learned the practical skills of our ancestors. We learned, sometimes told solely in the Lakota language, lessons and values we would need for daily living, and the adaptations we would make for modern-day living. Every conversation, every teaching, every learning experience was infused with male-dominated language, and strata upon strata emerged as evidence that women's only role was to birth children.

For a young Lakota child, the language of these modern-day stories was the connective tissue between the traditional past and Euroamerican present. These stories would be the foundation of our learning, and mimicked throughout our childhood by adults, family members, and children within the community. These were "colonized stories" that embedded patriarchal experiences as the primary meaning into the intellectual, moral, and spiritual development of our tribe's youth. These stories were a sacred hide designed to protect us from the colonists' mental diseases. Yet, in each story, a sacred undercurrent was cloaked: the spirit of the traditional matriarchal Indigenous past. The language of these stories did not calibrate with what I had learned in my mother's womb, nor with her voice as a spiritual leader. I have spent my entire life wondering, *Where did we bury the creation stories of all of our mothers and how do we call them back?*

My Mother's Story

During my childhood, Beverly was a mother to five children, married to a Lakota man, and an active member of the American Indian Movement. When she wasn't taking nursing classes, organizing civil rights protests, spending time with Indigenous elders, providing spiritual guidance for community members, or preparing ceremonial spaces for community, Beverly could be found at home sewing ceremonial regalia for her children, teaching her children how to bead on a loom, or tending to the squash, tomatoes, and flowers in her garden. From this vantage point, Beverly was the embodiment of what Buffalo Calf Pipe woman recognizes as a woman who catalyzes the evolution of family growth and healing in order to contribute to the safety of the tribal community, or a "woman who makes the family move."[1] Beverly blessed her life with the memories of the traditional ways and lived to pass those ways on to her children, to be used throughout their lifetimes and the seven generations to come. This was the traditional Lakota woman's way of life.

Yet, just like there are two sides to the Indian head nickel, there were two sides to Beverly, and the eclipse of Beverly's life was her equally devout political activism in the women's liberation movement, accompanied by her intimate, tender feelings for women. In the traditional era, if Beverly had shared with her elders details of the dual role she was living, they may have believed her to be a dreamer of the "double woman's appearance," or a person who embodied both the feminine and male spirits, and she would have been revered within her community as an elder, teacher, and storyteller. However, in the modern-day era, when Beverly disclosed her feelings to her spiritual community, she was referenced as a lesbian whose behavior was considered a sexual perversion and taboo in nature.

Beverly's story then became one of isolation, perseverance, and love. In her memoir, *One Bead at a Time*,[2] my mother's story vividly illustrates her Native American activism, pain and hardship endured from being rejected by her spiritual community, and same-sex domestic violence. Beverly shares the intimate details of her life, as well as highlighting the many struggles that she and many other queer Native American people faced in a modern colonized society.

Being a true storyteller, Beverly's stories provided a glimpse of Lakota beliefs and practices, empowerment for women in ceremonial roles and leadership, and resiliency. Most importantly, Beverly's stories shed light on the toxic gender dynamics that are prevalent within Native American communities. Beverly's story is beautiful, deep, and empowering.

My Story

I am a two-spirit Lakota woman, who was removed from my traditional Lakota community during early adolescence because my mother admitted to our spiritual community that she loved women. When I was nine years old, I watched my mother come out as a "lesbian" to our community. I watched the faces of the medicine men and women—the same community members who willingly took everything my mother had to offer for almost a decade—turn from respect to disgust. I peeked from under the tipi liner to watch my mother as she spoke with her "sisters" and "brothers," the same people I called "auntie" and "uncle," only to see tears streaming down her face as she walked away from their scowling faces and shaking heads. She walked quickly toward our camp, as if that was the only safe space in the world; and then only to hear the sounds of her muffled sobs and wails coming from our family tipi, when she thought everyone was away. And, eventually came the sound of the suitcases zipped, the truck being loaded, and the start of the engine as we drove away, or really were turned away, from every ceremony where we had once been welcomed with tobacco, sage, and a feast.

In my despair, I didn't want to believe the rejection was true. I saw my mother in service to our patriarchal community every day of my childhood life. I replayed the many years of watching my mother lead women through sacred ceremonies, providing a safe haven for Indigenous women who were being chased by inebriated husbands and partners, and cooking deer meat stew and fry bread for hundreds of people. Yet, I saw so many members of her community turn their backs when she took off her cloak of silence and declared her love for women.

The summers of my early adolescence were the loneliest of my life to that point; I had spent every summer until then preparing for and being in ceremony with my relatives. As soon as school closed for the year, I would hear the sounds of my mother's sewing machine whirring away at all hours of the night making ceremonial clothes for me and my siblings. The house would be an ever-turning spiral of women and children, the women learning how to bead, sew, and cook from my mother. Women and children would be in the garden. I took it upon myself to keep the kids out of the adults' way by showing off my favorite neighborhood trees, hiding places, and swimming holes. Every child in my spiritual community knew without a doubt that summers were about new outfits for the Sundance ceremony, learning new pow-wow dance moves, picking zucchini, eating stew, and making homemade fry bread and strawberry ice cream. That summer, there were no new relatives to come to our camp, or to caravan our way back home. We went home alone.

Yet, throughout this heartbreaking journey, with those two small folds on the sides of my head that had grown into a "sonar dish," I began to hear faint reverberations of my mother's Creation stories once again. I watched my mother build a new community. Every weekend there was a group of women at our home who at first participated in pipe ceremonies. I listened to my mother teach about how each person would share how they were doing, and then she would pass the sacred *chanupa* to each of them and ask them to say a prayer. After a few months of that, I heard my mom and her new partner talk about the need for a space to have a sweat lodge. Soon, we were building a sweat lodge once again and it was full of women and beautiful stories.

As our family evolved further away from the patriarchal, very Westernized, beliefs of my Lakota people, stories of strong ethnically diverse women began to emerge. Throughout my adolescence and young adulthood, I learned there were women, not necessarily Lakota women, who freely shared stories of women with very special strengths, talents, skills, and ways of serving their communities through ceremonial and other types of leadership. I was regularly exposed to hearing stories of women who believed in women's power, while the ingrained patriarchal stories ebbed and flowed in and out of my consciousness as I became an adult.

Although my mother persevered and introduced me to a new way of being in ceremony, where women were honored for their strengths as ceremonial leaders, I always carried the painful memories of my spiritual aunties, uncles, cousins, and elders turning their backs on me in ceremony when my mother came out. I, too, had come out as a two-spirit woman, and my experience as a child created a chronic inner turmoil whose message expressed, "You will never be welcomed to be yourself in any Indigenous ceremony." This inner voice caused fear and anxiety, and I found myself hiding behind my mother's story and matriarchal teachings. As I grew older, I realized I had been hiding my own identity and matriarchal upbringing when attending heterosexual traditional ceremonies.

For decades, I freely shared the teachings I have been given by my mother, which place emphasis on the strength of women embodying traditional ceremonial roles. In women's communities, sharing stories about Great Spirit as non-binary is welcomed. In mixed-gender, heterosexual communities, I became aware that I was developing severe anxiety when asked to share my traditional Lakota teachings.

Recently, I attended a ceremony and was asked to share the traditional Lakota flood story. Thus began a journey of exploring the trauma of being taught matriarchal values in a patriarchal society. I researched Lakota creation stories. I read them and practiced retelling them, seeking to find the one that resonated with my values and beliefs. And, I was heartbroken to realize that none of these stories felt natural coming from the tradition in which I had been raised. And so, I prayed.

This is the story that came to me on the night of my prayer. This is the story I had heard in the womb of my mother. This is the story I wish my elders and teachers had shared with me in the *inipi*. This is the story that passed from my mother's blood to mine. And this is the story that I hope gets passed to the next seven generations to come. *Hiya Mitakuyasin.*

How the Earth Came from Grandmother Turtle's Back

A long, long time ago, the beings on Mother Earth were so divided that they retreated to opposite sides of the planet. The weight of their sorrow, grief, rage, and hate from both sides, grew so much the earth began to form a natural dividing fracture right in the middle. Over time, no amount of prayers, no known ceremony would repair the split and soon the earth's edges began to sink into the ocean waters. As the despair grew, the tears of the people fell into the ocean and the great regret pulled the earth apart and no earth was left to be seen. All of the tears fell to the ocean floor and filled the ocean and covered the earth.

All animals adapted to the water except for the winged ones. The eagle wingeds heard the prayers of all of their relatives and soared to the greatest heights to connect with the Great Mysteries. Yet, their wings soon grew tired from not having any place to rest. The wingeds pleaded with the Great

Fig. 10. Grandmother Turtle. Painting by Raine Dawn Valentine, 2022.

Mysteries of the universe—the Sun, moon, and stars. They pleaded to have a bit of earth placed above the water, so they could have a place to rest and continue to carry and lift the prayers of their relatives to the ancestors. The Great Mysteries agreed to bring together all of the elements to sustain a piece of land if the wingeds could produce a piece of earth from the bottom of the sea.

With the blessing of the Great Mysteries, the wingeds returned to the waters and relayed the request for one of their relatives to dive deep to the bottom of the ocean to retrieve a bit of earth. Otter eagerly volunteered. "I know how to navigate the waters and I will swim to the depths of our mother ocean and bring some earth." All of the relatives agreed that Otter was the best choice for the job. Otter dove deep, deep, deep into the depths of the ocean, yet soon returned to the surface gasping for air. "I am sorry. No matter how hard I try, I cannot get to the ocean floor." All relatives agreed Otter had done their best.

Next, Beaver eagerly volunteered. And all of the relatives grew excited and agreed, as Beaver had experience navigating earth and water and would be an ideal servant. Off went Beaver, diving deep, deep, and deep, and deeper into the depths of the ocean waters, yet soon returned to the surface gasping for air. "No matter how hard I try, I cannot go to the ocean's floor." All relatives agreed Beaver had done their best.

Soon came Eel: "My ancestors navigate both land and water, and I can stretch my body, and I can easily get to the ocean floor." Once again, all of the relatives grew excited and agreed. Off went Eel, gliding deep, deep, deep, deeper, and deeper into the depths of the ocean waters, yet soon returned to the surface gasping for air. "No matter how hard I try, I cannot go to the ocean floor." All relatives agreed Eel had done their best.

And then Turtle bobbed to the water's surface. "My ancestors navigate both land and water, and I have many sea relatives who can help me get to the ocean floor." All of the relatives were skeptical, yet they agreed. Off went Turtle, not going directly to the ocean depths, taking her time to swim and play with her relatives. She took the time to share the hard times that were happening above the surface of the ocean. And with each depth of the ocean, she met new relatives and shared with them her endeavor of gathering a piece of earth from the sea.

Soon, Turtle was not alone, as many of her newfound relatives had agreed to support her as she journeyed to the bottom of the sea. And when she reached the bottom, each of her relatives helped fill her back with earth. They helped lift her to the surface of the waters when she struggled. They gave her a place to rest when she needed to rest. And, at last, with the help of all of her relatives, she bobbed to the surface of the ocean with the earth upon her back.

The Great Mysteries planted sacred medicines and created new human life on Turtle's back. The sacred medicines healed the humans and they began once again to live in harmony with one another. With a place to rest, the wingeds carried the humans' innermost prayers and hopes for a new world to the Great Mysteries. And soon, life on the Turtle's back grew and grew.

Turtle had the wisdom to share the vision with her relatives, accept their support, and the patience to allow the Great Mysteries to build a new world with prayers of the people being lifted to the universe. And that is why to this day we say Earth was built on Grandmother Turtle's back, and that is how Turtle Island came to be.

References

Hassrick, Royal B. *The Sioux*. Norman: University of Oklahoma Press, 1964.

Little Thunder, Beverly, as told to Sharron Proulx-Turner. *One Bead at a Time: A Memoir*. Toronto: Inanna, 2016.

Endnotes

1 Royal B. Hassrick, *The Sioux* (Norman: University of Oklahoma Press, 1964), 125.

2 Beverly Little Thunder, as told to Sharron Proulx-Turner, *One Bead at a Time: A Memoir* (Toronto: Inanna, 2016).

LOVING MEDUSA, REDEEMING ATHENA: RESTORYING FEMALE BLOOD, SOVEREIGNTY, AND AGENCY

JAFFA V. FRANK

Mythic Restoration of Female Blood

The way we understand and narrate experience is shaped by and shapes our sense of self and reality. While material facts have objective concreteness, it is the reflective, creative, and integrative articulation of events through the imagining mind that transforms facts into coherent, meaningful stories—life stories, mythic stories. Through stories we co-create our well-being and dis-ease. The capacity to engage the experiencing body, creative imagination, and narrating mind in a healing collaboration in response to life's inevitable difficulties is a form of grace—a mystery that transforms the experience of hardship without denying the truth of suffering.

I call this approach to life's challenges "embodied mythopoesis," and ground it in the understanding that reality, including story and the body, is enlivened by archetypal energies. Essentially, biological experiences have archetypal meaning and coherence. In other words, these experiences are both an embodiment of myth and a mythic embodiment. By embodiment of myth I mean that we have the capacity to recognize our lived experience within the great stories. By mythic embodiment I mean that the archetypal meaning of our experiences can be apprehended through a process of embodied mythopoesis wherein we locate archetypal (mythic) energy in the body and relate to it imaginally. Embodied mythopoesis engages with physiological processes and symptoms archetypally through lived experience, imagination, and mythic story. The process seeks the symbolic, soulful meaning that underlies the living, evolving story by turning toward embodied experience and symptom asking questions such as "who's visiting?"; "what's the body experiencing?"; and "what myth might be playing out?" By relating to embodied experience as archetypal visitation, pathology can be rendered sacred and approached compassionately to reveal meaning.

While female blood is not pathology, it and its processes—menstruation, pregnancy, and menopause—have often been pathologized, demonized, controlled, and steeped in disempowering taboos. Yet, these processes link us intimately with life as it truly is, with birth, death, and regeneration inextricably interrelated and reciprocal. Through our female blood, we can contemplate what it means to be human in an embodied relationship with the divine.

For me and over 176 million other women, the story of our female blood is dominated by endometriosis.[1] Endometriosis is an inflammatory disease in which tissue like that lining the uterus occurs elsewhere in the body where it reacts to monthly hormone fluctuations by swelling and bleeding.[2] Often misunderstood and minimized, this disorder is a leading cause of pelvic pain,[3] infertility,[4] and female hospitalizations.[5] During the forty-five years that I've suffered from this chronic, incurable disease, it has inflicted pain, loss, and even death. It began with increasingly intense menstrual pain as a teenager. The disease progressed, despite treatment, and caused my uterine artery to rupture and hemorrhage, resulting in the stillbirths of the twins I was carrying and my own near-death experience. Invasive endometriosis strangulated my ureters, threatening my kidney function, and penetrated my colon causing perilous blockages. Diseased tissue infiltrated my bladder and uterus and encased my reproductive organs in a calcified condition called "frozen pelvis." I've undergone multiple abdominal surgeries and lived with chronic and acute pain and complications. In addition to the physical suffering, I, like so many girls and women with endometriosis, have faced a perplexing medical and psycho-social landscape dominated by uncertainty, misconceptions, contradiction, and shockingly dismissive misogynistic attitudes and taboos.[6]

What I have discovered through research is that endometriosis simply amplifies the larger experience of misogyny and taboo that surrounds the female body and its blood processes. The extremity of my experience compels me along the path of meaning. But, while endometriosis colors my menstrual lens, the healing mythopoesis I see emerging transcends both the disease and my personal story to reveal the mythic wisdom of female blood.

Through embodied mythopoesis, I engage the afflicted body and mythic material in a multidisciplinary approach that integrates soma, psyche, and relationship. This process facilitates meaning-making and incubates a new narrative that transcends victimhood and nourishes psycho-spiritual resilience and healing. From this perspective, while my story (and yours) is overtly personal, a mythic grounding can situate it as potentially healing for the community as well; as poet and mythologist Dennis P. Slattery argues, "There is a healing of a cultural wound through myth that aids us in repatterning our existence."[7] This stance is also supported by trauma specialist Peter A. Levine who emphasizes that "it is universally true that the renegotiation of trauma is an inherently mythic-poetic-heroic journey."[8] Healing is individual and collective, human and archetypal.

The story I am sharing grows out of the mythopoetic soil of the chthonic great goddesses and weaves threads of female blood with the mythic strands of Medusa and Athena into a single expression of the creative imagination. Healing emerges by seeing through the concrete in life and myth to the archetypal—reconciling and integrating events into meaningful experiences that engage the deeper significance underlying the manifest.[9] This requires that we simultaneously accept distinct, opposing realities as equal in value and archetypally true even when these realities seem rationally antithetical. The process also asks that we embrace the body's centrality as a locus of concrete memory and creative mythopoesis.

I have already shared a brief summary of my female blood story, a concise narrative of concrete facts. Now, I reflect mythopoetically on one part of the narrative with curiosity, asking "who" and "what" questions, imagining if this event were a dream what the psyche might be telling me. I consider symptoms, associations, intuitions, emotions, and sensations all as valuable information. Objective facts interrelate with subjective, embodied experience and soulful mystery. In this way, understanding deepens from the facts of "my story" into a new context of "mystory"—a narrative that engenders psycho-spiritual meaning. While the mythic kaleidoscope through which I gaze is Medusa–Athenan, I do not assert a monistic interpretation of Medusa, Athena, menstruation, or endometriosis. Myth and archetype are living, organic, and evolving; they are concrete, but never literal.

Embodied Mythopoesis:
Girlhood in Patriarchy and Mythic Revelation

Myth does not provide Medusa with a childhood; she first appears as a *parthenos* (a menstruating virgin). Athena's childhood is obscured by her Olympian birth as the fully-grown *parthenos* springing from her father Zeus's head. Luckily, we have glimpses of Athena's girlhood in other mythic accounts. Scholars—Jane Ellen Harrison, C. Kerényi, Robert Graves, Marija Gimbutas, Miriam Robbins Dexter, Barbara Smith, and Sandra Edelman—alongside ancient poets and scholars—Homer, Apollodorus, and Hesiod—paint a more complete picture of Athena, her birth, adventures, and allegiances. We learn she loses her mother, Metis, who, though wise and primordial, is consumed by the power drives of ascending patriarchy when Zeus swallows her. Athena suffers the effects of this unintended maternal abandonment in her suppression of her connection to her maternal, earth origins, which she projects onto other females, perhaps engendering her need to integrate them into her. For example, there is a story about Pallas, Athena's childhood foster-sister from Africa whom the goddess accidentally slays and whose identity Athena takes for herself as evidenced in the widely used moniker, Pallas Athena. Later, Athena incorporates Medusa and wears the Gorgon's face as an *aegis* (protective shield) upon her chest.

Stories also demonstrate that Athena is acquainted with the threat of violation inherent in her *parthenos* state and the general threat of violence, particularly sexual violence, engendered in patriarchal views of masculinity and male prerogative. She deals with these threats in various ways. Pre-Greek Athena, from a less phallocentric tradition, dispatches a perpetrating father figure with righteous agency and wears his flayed pelt as her protective *aegis*.[10] Later, in Greek myth, she adopts the protective persona of father's daughter, and handmaiden and shieldmaiden of Olympus. Despite her adaptation, Athena sometimes smolders with resentment against her father.[11] Further, according to Aeschylus in his play *The Eumenides*, she preserves the chthonic feminine as sacred—even its most demonized forms—covertly within the patriarchy, "hidden" in her temple center as

Fig. 11. Raging Medusa. Fiberglass, Cristina Biaggi, 1988.

the Eumenides and upon her breast as the Gorgoneion (Gorgon-faced *aegis*). Much of Athena's identity is obscured by her Apollonian image and she easily literalizes into a vision of the promise and prestige available to women who repress feminine values; in my experience, to its favorite daughters, patriarchy bestows power and inclusion. Classical scholar Christine Downing echoes the pain inherent in a woman's confrontation with the version of Athena privileged by patriarchy: "[I]t means looking at the hitherto least explored aspects of my life: the negative side of my love for my father, my ever-repeated tendency to divert energy from my own creative work into relationships, the still present temptation to understand my assertiveness and intellectual acumen as masculine attributes."[12] To fall into identification with this Athena is to risk petrifying perfectionism, but it can seem like a small price to pay for the rewards.

If I reflect upon my youth as revealed in Athena's mirror, I comprehend how I actively—if unconsciously—cultivated my position as a father's daughter in my family and in my stance in the world. Unfortunately, my Athena was exclusively the father's daughter, and I took her denial of the feminine literally, at face value. Athena's myth shows that the father's daughter role can serve as a survival mechanism; it did so for me. My affiliation with Athena runs deep. My childhood was also marked by early maternal attachment disruption, interpersonal trauma and violence, and the constant tension of feeling paternal estrangement and identification. I also benefited from a link to chthonic nature and an Athena-like temperament—strong, strategic, dexterous, protean, and self-reliant. Within this childhood myth, I see seeds of a pragmatic and unconsciously antagonistic relationship with my female body, its specifically female processes, and endometriosis. Psychologically, I was in thrall to a patriarchal version of Athena. Archetypally, Athena was visiting and her presence provided me pragmatic adaptability, strategic vigilance, and the power to succeed in "a man's world."

Because of the unconscious nature of my communion—or more precisely, my ego-identification with a one-sided version of the goddess—I ascended to striving and perfectionism so that in attending her altar I both worshiped and defended against the dominant masculine principle, taking on its "potentially overwhelming ... power by assimilating it in [my] own being," as Downing warns.[13] This assimilation replicated the patriarchal hierarchy within me so that my adaptive ego related to my female body by exploiting its pleasures while disciplining and judging it, and suppressing its needs and symptoms as secondary inconveniences.

My father's daughter persona was belied by my female blood; Medusa in my veins and flowing from my body. Perhaps the only way I could look at the rage of my denigrated Gorgon heritage and my own wounding was reflected through my endometriosis—knowing Medusa through her awful (rather than awe-full) manifestations of pain and death. Rather than an empowering, "protective *aegis*," my endometriotic Gorgoneion was a "defensive mask, made necessary by dread of annihilation"[14] as the ever-threatened fate of the vulnerable *parthenos* for whom patriarchy has demonized feminine creativity and female agency, and delimited her worth in sexual terms. If I had looked fully upon the face of my embodied misogyny, I would have turned to stone—as encounters with chthonic rage will do. Perhaps my endometriotic Gorgoneion served as ironically apotropaic, deflecting the full force of shame engendered in my gender. As a patriarchal female, the terrible Gorgoneion came to rest in the part of my body so frequently judged to be the face of terror, evil, shame, and sin; the embodied center of the dynamic tension of the feminine and her sex as "sacra, sacred and accursed"[15]—the female reproductive organs and their blood processes.

Myth says seeing Medusa's face turns you to stone. But then, looking at any deity has a similarly overwhelming, annihilating effect according to myths throughout the world. Why is this demonized in Medusa's case? Her dual nature as goddess and mortal woman seems relevant in pondering the question. Historically, woman's prerogative to participate so overtly in life's creation and destruction through her biological capacity to bear children and menstruate (bleed without dying and seemingly, spontaneously heal) made her powerfully taboo[16] such that the image of her reproductive organs and genitals often became seen as monstrous.[17] Despite being misunderstood and marginalized in ancient Greece, females and their menstrual processes were regarded as threateningly powerful,[18] in many ways more horror than mystery—the stony face of the terrible Gorgoneion as the evil eye.[19]

Misogynistic attitudes persist in modernity, finding their way into psyches. Woman's most Indigenous biological processes have been medicalized and characterized as the bane of the female and proof of her original sin and defiled nature. For me, it is as if as I unconsciously adapted myself to dominant patriarchal values, even my body took on that perspective and when confronted with the reality of its divine, chthonic feminine nature through menses, it turned to stone, petrified like the polarized patriarchal attitude of scorn or appetite that confronts Medusa in the myths.

In this way, I perceive my endometriosis as a metaphoric mask of embodied misogyny. I see Medusa as an image of the archetypal energy pattern expressing the deeply regenerative, chthonic sacred carried in menstrual blood, and literalized and scorned as femaleness. At an early age, I apprehended the victim–victimizer dynamic at play in the world and perceived the patriarchal position as forcefully dominant and of superior power. In a dangerous, competitive world of scarcity and rigid standards, force and power can seem to be of superior value to feeling and connection. By aligning with this attitude, I wore an internalized *aegis* of feminine outrage. In compensation, my soul began its lifelong mythopoesis toward redeeming the wholeness of the feminine, and my dis-eased body became a concrete context. Through the mythic mirror, endometriosis, still a physical disease with all that that implies and requires, deepens into a particular and meaningful visitation. I apprehend it as a complicated life companion and teacher; an amplification of denigrated female blood.

When I began exploring the myths of Athena and Medusa, I contemplated the possibility that Athena represented woman's adapted ego—forming itself according to the patriarchal philosophical, religious, psychological, and social ideal of heroic ego-hood. In this story, Medusa represented the estranged female body as carrier of shadow and shame. Athena was all rational reasonableness and Medusa irrational rage. I resented and admired Athena for her assimilation. I championed and loathed Medusa's rage.

While this story expressed the split that I had observed in myself and other women, the interpretation failed to foster healing; perhaps because it was an image of the split, emblematic of the tension, but not of what might emerge from the tension. Being focused on the split, I was caught in the dynamic of identifying with one pole or the other; possessed by the complexes constellated around wounds. Neurobiologically, this behavior strengthens the neural pathways associated with trauma and short circuits healing by reinforcing the neurochemistry of activation. From a depth psychological view, living the split defends against feeling the tension engendered by the schism—a tension that, if felt, can stimulate the healing transcendent function of the psyche.[20]

Then the psychological question, which let me feel the tension and simultaneously facilitate resolution of the tension, came to me: What is the meaning of Athena's orchestration of Medusa's beheading? I had thought of it as the splitting off of female sexuality and the co-opting of female power for use by the adapted feminine hero-ego in service to patriarchy. But, could it possibly be a reuniting of archetypal feminine wholeness?

In fact, Athena and the Gorgoneion Medusa are not split, they are a body, spirit, and soul—whole and complete. This completeness is achieved by way of the beheading. Further, there is reciprocity within the relationship between Athena and Medusa, which is the energy of functional wholeness. Athena *Gorgopis* is two-faced and whole, uniting—through chthonic and Olympic imagery—the divine androgyny manifest throughout creation and in the act of creating. Athena does not simply contain and wield the terrible Gorgoneion. The Gorgon is part of Athena's identity, relating her to her own regenerative, gynocentric, chthonic beginnings.[21]

According to Ovid,[22] Apollodorus,[23] and others, Athena—father's daughter who disavows her maternal lineage and proclaims that she is "always for the male"[24]—is instrumental in both creating and beheading the Gorgon, and redeeming *man*kind from the petrifying menace. However, Athena's beheading of the Gorgon (with or without Perseus's assistance) does not render Medusa benign, for Athena's Gorgoneion is potently apotropaic. The great goddesses once signified a unified multiplicity and the Gorgon Medusa is one face of the often vilified, sometimes rageful, multivalent visage of unmitigated feminine potency also mirrored in female blood. Medusa's paradoxical masks range from beautiful victim to apotropaic protector to emblem of the evil eye, menstrual taboos, and embodied misogyny.[25] In her lineage and at her core, the Gorgon carries the blood of life, death, and renewal; the mysterious sacred *tremendum*.[26] The Gorgon expresses a chthonic, mysterious, nonrational reality, but not necessarily an evil.[27] However—when denigrated and scorned—the Gorgon manifests as "gratuitously destructive of whatever [comes] into view,"[28] including the organs of the human body.

Here, it is vital to understand that I do not claim the psychological experience of misogyny literally causes menstrual disorders like endometriosis. This is the sort of literal, linear attitude that has created real suffering for women repeatedly told that their pain is "all in your head." What is efficacious is the mythopoetic experience of disorder as a meaningful visitation of the deity that engenders resolution of victimhood into agency. The resolution is not a physical cure or cessation of the biological process, but rather a pattern of response available as demonstrated by Athena in her restoring of Medusa's honor and reverence at the level of the heart as the apotropaic Gorgoneion—not Gorgon as evil eye. Through the beheading, Athena integrates the rejected, demonized shadow of the so-called feminine principle of relatedness—what we might call the quality of objective eros—raising it into consciousness and displaying it in its proper place in the natural order.

Archetypally, Athena *Gorgopis* reunites subjective and objective eros, and signifies an embodied, sovereign feminine consciousness. Through her right relationship with the unmitigated feminine potency of the Gorgon, Athena establishes her own untouchable sovereignty—she is ever virginal, belonging only to herself; "she is 'one-in-herself.'"[29] No matter what happens to her, her soul, the essence of who she is, is inviolable, her integrity intact. Through this mythic lens, dis-ease offers reconciliation and integration into greater wholeness within the body and psyche. My endometriotic experience incites my transformation so that I can begin to wear my Medusan *aegis* properly, with the awe-full Gorgoneion radiating from my heart. This transformation is toward a particular kind of consciousness, a form of objective, unconditional loving that facilitates reverential acceptance of the whole of creation, and which is beyond ego preference, attraction or aversion, appetite or scorn.

My time at Medusa's altar has disillusioned me of the belief that I should, or could, redeem her from her fundamental nature by transforming her. It is she who is the redeemer, she who is the transformer. Unburdened by patriarchal perspectives, the myths reveal that it is Medusa who redeems Athena, restoring the goddess from the split engendered in her adaptation to the phallocentric demands of one-sided patriarchy; an adaptation likely demanded to some extent of every daughter of the patriarchy. The Gorgon's visitation offers the wisdom to accept the forces she represents—including life, death, and regeneration—and to cultivate reverential love for the sacredness of life as it is, within and outside of us. Through deep engagement, stories of female empowerment, agency, and sovereignty emerge and grow from the fertile relationship between mythic material, the experiencing body, creative imagination, and narrating mind. The profoundly sacred nature of every-woman's Medusan body, including the numinous *tremendum*, is reclaimed with a critical piece of instruction so easily missed and yet communicated by Athena with her Gorgoneion *aegis* upon her breast: The wisdom of the Gorgon must be held at the level of the heart, in the field of transpersonal love and the seat of spiritual rebirth—virgin birth.

References

Aeschylus. *The Eumenides*. In *Aeschylus I*. Translated by Richmond Lattimore. Edited by David Grene and Richmond Lattimore, 133–71. Chicago: University of Chicago Press, 1953.

Apollodorus. *The Library of Greek Mythology*. Translated by Robin Hard. Oxford: Oxford University Press, 1997.

Ballweg, Mary Lou. "Research Reveals Disease Is Starting Younger: Delayed Diagnosis." *Endometriosis: The Complete Reference for Taking Charge of Your Health*, 343–60. Chicago: Contemporary, 2003.

Blundell, Sue. *Women in Classical Athens*. London: Bristol Classical Press, 2001.

Cook, Andrew S. *Stop Endometriosis and Pelvic Pain*. Femsana Press, 2012.

Dexter, Miriam Robbins. *Whence the Goddess: A Source Book*. New York: Pergamon Press, 1990.

Downing, Christine. *The Goddess: Mythological Images of the Feminine*. New York: Author's Choice Press, 1981.

Edelman, Sandra. *Turning the Gorgon: A Meditation on Shame*. Woodstock, CT: Spring Publications, Inc., 1998.

Endometriosis Foundation of America. "Disease Information and Support: FAQs," 2017. www.endofound.org/faq.

Frank, Jaffa V. *Eyes of the Gorgon: Endometriosis, Mythic Embodiment, and Freedom*. Sacramento, CA: Mandorla Books, 2019.

Freud, Sigmund. "Medusa's Head." Translated by James Stache. PEP Archive, EBSCO, 1922.

Gimbutas, Marija. *The Goddesses and Gods of Old Europe: Myths and Cult Images*. Berkeley: University of California Press, 1982.

Graves, Robert. *The Greek Myths: The Complete and Definitive Edition*. New York: Penguin, 2011.

Harding, Esther M. *Woman's Mysteries: Ancient & Modern*. Boston, MA: Shambhala, 1971.

Harrison, Jane Ellen. *Prolegomena to the Study of Greek Religion*. Princeton, NJ: Princeton University Press, 1991.

Hesiod. *Theogony. Works and Days; Theogony; The Shield of Herakles*. Translated by Richmond Lattimore. Ann Arbor: University of Michigan Press, 1991.

Hillman, James. *Re-Visioning Psychology*. New York: Harper & Row, 1975.

Homer. "Homeric Hymn 28." *Theo Texts Library*. Translated by H. B. Evelyn-White. Compiled by A. J. Astma. 2000–2017. www.theoi.com.

Jung, C. G. Psychological Types. In the *The Collected Works of C. G. Jung*. Translated by R. F. C. Hull. Princeton, NJ: Princeton University Press, 1971.

Kerényi, C. *The Gods of the Greeks*. London: Thames and Hudson, 1982.

Levine, Peter A. *Waking the Tiger: Healing Trauma*. Berkeley, CA: North Atlantic Books, 1997.

Lubell, Winifred Milius. *The Metamorphosis of Baubo: Myths of Woman's Sexual Energy*. Nashville, TN: Vanderbilt University Press, 1994.

Ovid. *Metamorphoses*. Translated by David Raeburn. London: Penguin, 2004.

Slattery, Dennis P. *The Wounded Body: Remembering the Markings of Flesh*. Albany: State University of New York Press, 2000.

Smith, Barbara. "Greece." *The Feminist Companion to Mythology*. Edited by Carolyne Larrington, 65–101. London: Pandora, 1992.

Thomson, George, quoted in Delaney, Janice, Mary Jane Lupton, and Emily Toth. *The Curse: A Cultural History of Menstruation*. Urbana: University of Illinois Press, 1988.

World Endometriosis Society. "Facts about Endometriosis." May 27, 2017. www.endometriosis.org/resources/articles/facts-about-endometriosis/.

Endnotes

1 "Facts about Endometriosis," World Endometriosis Society, May 27, 2017, www.endometriosis.org/resources/articles/facts-about-endometriosis/.

2 Andrew S. Cook, *Stop Endometriosis and Pelvic Pain* (Los Gatos, CA: Femsana Press, 2012), 7.

3. Ibid., 59.

4 "Disease Information and Support: FAQs," Endometriosis Foundation of America, 2017, www.endometriosis.org/faq.

5 Cook, *Stop Endometriosis*, 45.

6 Mary Lou Ballweg, "Research Reveals Disease Is Starting Younger: Delayed Diagnosis," *Endometriosis: The Complete Reference for Taking Control of Your Health* (Chicago: Contemporary, 2001), 357–58.

7 Dennis P. Slattery, *The Wounded Body: Remembering the Markings of Flesh* (Albany: State University of New York Press, 2000), 134.

8 Peter Levine, *Waking the Tiger: Healing Trauma* (Berkeley, CA: North Atlantic Books, 1997), 119.

9 James Hillman, *Re-Visioning Psychology* (New York: Harper & Row, 1975), x.

10 C. Kerényi, *The Gods of the Greeks* (London: Thames and Hudson, 1982), 121.

11 Homer, *The Iliad*, trans. Robert Fagles (New York: Penguin, 1990), 4:26–27.

12 Christine Downing, *The Goddess: Mythological Images of the Feminine* (New York: Author's Choice Press, 1981), 104.

13 Ibid., 113.

14 Sandra Edelman, *Turning the Gorgon: A Meditation on Shame* (Woodstock, CT: Spring Publications, Inc., 1998), 111.

15 George Thomson quoted in Janice Delaney, Mary Jane Lupton, and Emily Toth, *The Curse: A Cultural History of Menstruation* (Urbana: University of Illinois Press, 1988), 8.

16 Sue Blundell, *Women in Classical Athens* (London: Bristol Classical Press, 2001), 16, 19.

17 Sigmund Freud, "Medusa's Head," trans. James Stachey (PEP Archive, EBSCO, 1922).

18 Barbara Smith, *The Feminist Companion to Mythology*, edited by Carolyne Carol Larrington (London: Pandora, 1992), 87, 92.

19 Winifred Milius Lubell, *The Metamorphosis of Baubo: Myths of Woman's Sexual Energy* (Nashville, TN: Vanderbilt University Press, 1994), 111.

20 C. G. Jung, "Psychological Types," in *The Collected Works of C. G. Jung*, trans. R. F. C. Hull (Princeton, NJ: Princeton University Press, 1971), par. 824.

21 Jaffa Frank, *Eyes of the Gorgon. Endometriosis, Mythic Embodiment, and Freedom* (Sacramento, CA: Mandorla Books, 2019), 165.

22 Ovid, *Metamorphoses*, trans. David Raeburn (London: Penguin, 2004), 4: 770–785.

23 Apollodorus, *The Library of Greek Mythology*, trans. Robin Hard (Oxford: Oxford University Press, 1997), II.4.2.

24 Aeschylus, *The Eumenides*, in *Aeschylus I*, trans. Richmond Lattimore, edited by David Grene and Richmond Lattimore (Chicago: University of Chicago Press, 1953), lines 736–738.

25 Frank, *Eyes of the Gorgon*, ii.

26 Ibid., 82.

27 Ibid., 166.

28 Edelman, *Turning the Gorgon*, 106.

29 Esther M. Harding, *Woman's Mysteries: Ancient and Modern* (Boston: Shambhala, 1971), 103.

GRIEF AND THE MOTHER/S ODYSSEY: PERSONAL RECKONING AND COLLECTIVE RESPONSIBILITY

ANGELINA AVEDANO, PhD

Introduction

In 2015, I gathered a group of women to discuss the archetype of the grieving mother. After several conversations with three mother-scholars, all pursuing graduate degrees at Pacifica Graduate Institute, something began to coalesce. Each of us had experienced profound grief related to motherhood; and our interest in mythologies gave us a common language. We also shared another understanding: our pursuit of mythological studies had become a "call" to a unique kind of empathy and embodiment related to our work. We presented our panel "Rage, Ravages, and Rapture: Applying Goddess Wisdom to the Grieving Mother" at the 2016 conference for the *Association for the Study of Women in Mythology (ASWM)*.[1] At the time, I was immersed in academia, finishing my third graduate program. Therefore, my tendency was to intellectualize *everything*, to turn the most profound emotional experience into a theoretical inquiry. So, while the *ASWM* conference was a welcome professional opportunity, it was also another exercise in compartmentalizing and intellectualizing my personal grief passage. What I did not know was that this event was a herald for a more vigorous personal descent into a Mother/s Odyssey that would lead to a book, a workshop, and this article.

What is the "Mother/s Odyssey," and what is the significance of the forward slash? First of all, the Mother/s Odyssey is a grief passage. However, one does not need to be a mother to encounter a grief passage, just as one does not need to be the son of God to endure (or comprehend) a metaphorical "crucifixion." The "mother" in Mother/s Odyssey indicates profound grief characterized by unbearable loss. The loss of a child is considered the epitome of grief. As such, the grieving mother archetype is something to which most can relate. Inevitably, every individual will experience a powerful loss; although, not all are mothers, all have been born from mothers. So, while the experience of the mother/child relationship is subjective, on a collective level, the brutality of the broken mother/child bond becomes a symbol for profound loss—the loss of someone or something of supreme value, or the loss of some aspect of oneself. Representations of the grieving mother archetype therefore illuminate the Mother/s Odyssey and have the potential to offer solace in the face of devastating loss.

"Mother" also indicates the primal or fundamental nature of grief, and the origin (and nourishment) of personal growth. The grief passage—the *mother* of all journeys—is an initiation, to be sure. Encountering a most traumatizing heartbreak, one dies to oneself, and must let go of their dreams for their beloved. The "beloved" symbolizes an attachment to a loved one, or one's health, identity, or *anything* that carries profound importance. Although some may argue that nothing compares to the loss of a child, grief is deeply personal. It cannot be measured or compared. Profound loss is a trauma; and a mythological approach to grief can catalyze this trauma into transformation. My work here is a project in what I call "shamanic scholarship,"[2] which is an investigative process by which one is transformed, and therefore begins to facilitate change in the world through research, study, application, and most importantly, embodiment and compassionate engagement. To my mind, this is the primal power and life-altering force of mother energy; it is what creates the momentum toward transformation on the Mother/s Odyssey.

The forward slash in Mother/s Odyssey is a nod to the work of feminist theologian, Elisabeth Schüssler Fiorenza, who utilized it to challenge the ways in which gendered language has traditionally been used, explaining in her own words: "In order to lift into consciousness the linguistic violence of so-called generic, androcentric [that is male-centered] language which eliminates wo/men from the cultural and religious records, I use the term "wo/men" and not "men" in an inclusive, generic way."[3] Schüssler Fiorenza recognizes the importance of language as it relates to identity and subjective experience. She expands her reasoning for using the forward slash: "Wo/

men includes men, she includes he, and female includes male. Feminist studies of language have elaborated that Western, kyriocentric [that is slave master, lord, father, male centered], language systems understand language as both generic and as gender specific."[4] This feminist perspective calls into question the exclusionary dilemma women have faced, always wondering if they are included when generic terms like "men" (or even "human") are used. Schüssler Fiorenza encourages her readers to "think twice," asking if we are included in the conversation and challenging us to be more inclusive with our language.[5]

For this reason, I use "Mother/s" Odyssey. I am uncomfortable with the singular "Mother" Odyssey, even though it resonates deeply with my personal experience and seems appropriate considering many of the archetypal representations I focus on are rooted in motherhood. However, since profound grief is not exclusive to women or mothers, I sought to acknowledge this reality. Schüssler Fiorenza's forward slash allows me to create an expanded awareness of grief encounters, to include those who may not see themselves as women or mothers, but none-the-less know what it is to endure profound loss.

Without a doubt, 2020 was a time of profound collective grief. A) Many continue to grieve literal loss of life on an unprecedented scale in the face of a global pandemic. B) Still more are grieving what we have come to depend on: our worldviews and our experience of ourselves in the world as we have known it. C) There is also unresolved grief over deep social wounds that have festered far too long. Collective racial/ethnic[6] trauma demands to be recognized, refusing to be silenced, placated, or ignored any longer. D) And finally, profound grief resulting from the planetary devastation humanity has wrought on Earth, while last on this list, is undeniably at the root of many other grief encounters. How appropriate then to recognize as coextensive the travails of our fundamental "Mother" (Earth) alongside our personal Mother/s Odyssey. If we are to respond to collective grief with collective healing, the work begins by acknowledging our pain, telling our stories, and listening to the stories of others, including personal, fictional, and mythological tales of grief. What emerges from these stories are transformative patterns and processes marked by phases of enduring, emerging, embracing, and ensouling.. The forthcoming examples (including my own) reveal facets of the Mother/s Odyssey, and demonstrate how a mythological lens might be applied to the grief passage.

A Personal Reckoning

It was two years after the *ASWM* conference in Massachusetts, when I had an opportunity to travel to the island of Oahu for five weeks to attend a summer program at The University of Hawai'i-Mānoa. If I were awarded a grant from the National Endowment for the Humanities, it would enable me to travel to see my son for the first time in six years. Steven had been living on and off the street for almost a decade.[7] Sometimes he would surface for a time, but mostly, he lived a vagabond life. My son had been diagnosed with schizoaffective disorder years before. In 2012, he spontaneously boarded a one-way flight to Honolulu; I had not seen him since.

In fact, there were and still are long periods of time when I am unsure whether Steven is alive or dead. As a result, I endure ongoing cycles of grief; my son might call from a jail, hospital, or shelter and I will be relieved to know he is safe, for a time. Relief is always brief however, because the system is not set up to help him end this cycle. He is caught in what seems like a web of arbitrary bureaucratic nonsense; and since he is now over thirty years old, I can no longer intervene. Routinely, he has been institutionalized for a few days, months, even years only to be discharged without a plan to help him reacclimate. He will then reabsorb himself back into the homeless subculture until picked up on some infraction: breaking and entering, loitering, theft, or (believe it or not) jaywalking. In 2018, Steven had been remanded to a state facility on the island only a few miles from the University of Hawai'i. If everything went as planned, I would visit him three or four times a week while I attended the program.

However, seeing my son in a completely dysregulated state was devastating. What was for most travelers an island paradise was my living hell, and my five-week stay was a defining moment in my personal Mother/s Odyssey. As such, Hawai'i became the alchemical vessel for my personal metamorphosis. In an attempt to cope with grief, I began to write; and what had been a somewhat detached, academic approach in 2016, became full-fledged embodiment during my stay on the island, leading to my book, *Living Grief: A Mother/s Odyssey of Surrender, Renewal, and Mad Joy.*[8] The result was a deep appreciation for the grief passage and its transformative potential, as well as a recognition that each individual's personal journey may in fact mirror an unfolding global Mother/s Odyssey.

Now, after the publication of *Living Grief* and the development of a workshop entitled "Transforming Loss," I am thoroughly convinced that we are collectively—in communities, nations, and as a planet—in the painful descent of the Mother/s Odyssey. Many have lost faith in systems that were put in place to guide, protect, and serve us. Even more have grieved the loss of loved ones, as well as their way of life and livelihoods as a result of COVID 19. However, these personal and collective upheavals are symptoms of a greater and more catastrophic loss due to climate change and its imminent global impact.

Conversations like those at Harvard T.H. Chan School of Public Health, are sounding the alarm for a collective recognition of the connection between climate change and the pandemic. Director of the Chan Center for Climate Health and the Global Environment (C-CHANGE), Dr. Aaron Bernstein, emphatically points out: "The separation of health and environmental policy is a dangerous delusion."[9] He explains that climate change has a direct impact on the spread of infectious diseases, and the forced migration of animal species specifically creates conditions for exposure to and mutation of viruses like COVID 19 (Bernstein).[10] Furthermore, the director points out that human activities like deforestation, excessive use of resources, and agricultural practices contribute to the global threat, as the world's current extinction rate is expected to surpass the age of the dinosaurs 65 million years ago when half of all life on earth became extinct.[11] At this point, the losses with which we must contend are incalculable. Mother Earth is in sorrow and travail; the Mother/s Odyssey is occurring whether or not we wish to acknowledge it. Unless we recognize and actively engage in our personal grief passages, we may be unable to serve as midwives to the regeneration of our planet.

Some may assume that the Mother/s Odyssey is simply a reappropriation of Joseph Campbell's hero's journey,[12] but this is not so. For purposes of this abbreviated analysis, I focus on three main characteristics that distinguish the Mother/s Odyssey from the hero's journey. First, the Mother/s Odyssey is specifically a grief passage—and grief becomes a catalyst for transformation. Secondly, the hero on the hero's journey often undertakes his passage by choice. For example, Odysseus embarks on his voyage to fight in the Trojan War; and Christ accepts his "cup" to willingly endure crucifixion. The Mother/s Odyssey, on the other hand, is undertaken not by choice, but by necessity, which leads to its third defining characteristic. This grief passage is initiated by the loss of someone or something considered extremely precious; and there is a component of complete powerlessness to prevent our own torment or the suffering of someone we love.[13] For example, Odysseus' absence sets in motion his mother's self-destruction and descent into Hades; and Mary, the mother of Christ endures her own annihilation at the foot of her son's torture device.

One *can* ultimately choose to learn from one's experience with grief or not. The point is that a Mother/s Odyssey is not initiated by the one who grieves; it is a result of grieving for someone or something to which we are closely bonded, and it demands surrender to that which is not in our control. Therefore, it can feel as if we have no choice but to endure this agonizing passage. The Mother/s Odyssey requires complete disintegration before reconstitution can begin. This process is easily observed in countless myths and stories, four of which elaborate the movement between enduring, emerging, embracing, and ultimate ensouling or integration characteristic of the Mother/s Odyssey.

Enduring - Inanna

How does one begin to understand grief as a catalyst for transformation while enduring excruciating pain? Stories and myths can be a portal to this kind of reframing. During my collaboration with the three mother-scholars with whom I began this conversation seven years ago, two myths became vital to fleshing out the archetype of the grieving mother: the Sumerian myth of Inanna, and the Greek myth of Demeter and Persephone. While our individual grief encounters were vastly diverse, both stories were touch-stones for our common emotional experience.

Inanna, Queen of Heaven, began her descent into the Underworld upon the death of her sister's husband.[14] Here, the archetypal signature of the Mother/s Odyssey is evident—the grief passage is initiated by a loved one. Inanna sought to pay her respects and comfort her sister, Ereshikigal, Queen of the Dead. However, her sibling was less than welcoming. She demanded that Inanna be systematically stripped of everything signifying her status as queen. Brought before Ereshkigal fully exposed, Inanna was condemned to death.[15] There she remained, her naked corpse suspended on a hook in the bowels of the deep.

However, the Queen of Heaven was clever, instructing her handmaid to appeal to the gods if she did not return within three days. In response, the god Enki dispatched two divine emissaries to come to Inanna's aid, carrying with them the food and water of life. These two otherworldly beings were given three specific instructions: empathize with Ereshkigal's grief, validate her intense emotions, and once those tasks were complete, resuscitate Inanna with divine nourishment. As a result, Inanna was able to return to the land of the living.[16]

What is to be ascertained from such a brutal tale? First, Inanna's journey was initiated by grief (the death of her brother-in-law and her sister's profound loss). The horror of her divestiture and execution becomes an apt metaphor for such a traumatic experience. For me, Hawai'i became the "hook" on which I hung. I was stripped of all coping mechanisms I had built over the years when I had learned to manage my son's schizophrenia at a distance. However, seeing him in such a dissociative state, in what I perceived to be a frightening and oppressive environment left me raw and exposed. Everything I had come to depend on had to die: my dreams for Steven's life, my longing for our relationship as it once was, and the hope that maybe things would get better. However, like Inanna, over the course of my Mother/s Odyssey, I too was visited by "divine emissaries" who came to offer compassion, presence, and nourishment. Sometimes, they seemed to be unlikely ambassadors, but they nevertheless showed up.[17]

Today, as we endure a collective Mother/s Odyssey on an epic scale, we bear the responsibility to listen, empathize, and carry the food and water of life into our communities both large and small. For those who are besieged by grief, they may experience overwhelming rage like Ereshkigal, or feel vulnerable and brutalized like Inanna. If one has experienced these emotions, they recognize the violence and terror grief can evoke. In fact, the intensity of profound grief often presents as rage and retribution, just as it did for Ereshkigal. The Sumerian myth of Inanna illustrates extreme emotions must be attended to if we are to come through the process. We do this by allowing rage over injustice, as well as the agony of grief to be expressed, not to mention, a total disorientation that results from the loss of one's identity and worldview. Those who have traveled this path are able to descend into the depths where grief is endured and expressed. Once there, they may coax others back to life by witnessing without judgement. By their compassionate presence, they inspire those who grieve to find a way to reemerge from the realm of the dead.

Emerging - Demeter

The Greek myth of Demeter and Persephone is another primary text for the archetype of the grieving mother. Even the great Goddess of the Harvest (Demeter) does not have the power to avoid the Mother/s Odyssey. The abduction of her daughter impels her grief passage, emphasizing that her journey is not by choice—she is forced. Moreover, her passage is indicative of the "tandem descent," that occurs when one initiation instigates another.[18] Persephone's rite of passage triggers her mother's harrowing transformation.

When Demeter discovered that her brother Zeus was complicit in her daughter's abduction, she was beside herself.[19] Searching everywhere for Persephone, the Mother Goddess became so enraged that she threatened to destroy the Earth by refusing to allow anything to grow. At this point in the story, Clarissa Pinkola Estés' version offers a refreshing perspective by introducing Baubo (or Iambe), the crone goddess.[20] Baubo's presence was a turning point for Demeter. In an irreverent pose, the crone lifted her skirt and made wise cracks with her vulva. The dark humor of the crone was able to penetrate Demeter's despair; and laughter broke the spell of a mother's profound grief. Estés emphasizes the healing power of the irreverent and rebellious feminine seen in the ironic, crude, and unsavory aspects of life force represented by the crone.[21] The crone has seen it all; she embraces life and death and thumbs her nose at both. Baubo represents mature feminine energy: fearless, decisive, sardonic, and wise.

Grief can choke the life out of everything. Anyone who has experienced profound loss understands Demeter's desire to shut down, and are unfazed by her impulse to wreak havoc on everything around her. The psychic, emotional, and spiritual malaise that prolonged sorrow elicits reduces everything to ash; it is nothing less than complete annihilation. Personally, I felt it as detachment in my day-to-day routine whenever Steven was off the grid. "Not knowing" created a level of anxiety that was impossible to sustain. Part of me had to disengage in order to survive. I felt it again as numbness after my visits with my son in June of 2018.

Countless individuals described a similar numbness due to the lingering uncertainty over COVID-19. High levels of fear, frustration, and grief took a remarkable psychological toll. Several reported becoming detached and listless as the months passed. For many, normal social routines were upended, and they found themselves existing in a surreal kind of stasis (like Demeter), watching and waiting for signs of life. Perhaps Baubo offers some guidance here as well. Could it be that the wisdom of the crone is a key to working through collective grief? How might mature feminine wisdom be applied to losses related to the virus?

On the other hand, Demeter's reluctance to nurture and sustain life was certainly warranted. I resonated with that internal pressure that sometimes lashed out, seeking to destroy anything or anyone who perpetrated some injustice against my son. Even more insidious was the self-hatred, guilt, and shame that could bring me to my knees. Such emotions turned inward easily became overwhelming and self-destructive. The opposite of life-affirming, these powerful forces were a death knell.

Shifting the focus to the global community, suppressed rage and despair have led to eruptions of violence, as individuals "act out," wreaking havoc wherever they can. If this kind of emotion is natural in response to an individual loss (like Demeter's loss of Persephone), how much more for a collective body? According to Demeter's story, rage and grief can go hand in hand. As such, it is essential to acknowledge (or descend into the depths of) grief that provokes such intense levels of anger and violence. Rather than labeling extreme emotion as a nuisance, an over-reaction, or a calculated political maneuver, a mythological approach makes space for all expressions, not just those that are socially acceptable. Remember, it was the empathy, validation, and nurturing provided by Enki's messengers that broke the spell of Ereshkigal's wrath; the same could be said of the crone. How might we collectively attend to racial wounding and desperation expressed today? Control, coercion, and criticism have no place in the mythology of grief, and therefore prove to be ineffective measures for healing the collective body. The stories show that for the Mother/s Odyssey to progress one must fearlessly enter the realm of grief, engage in active compassion, and provide nourishment in order to enliven the desperate souls who languish there.

Embracing - Anticlea

Whereas Inanna and Demeter proceeded through the Mother/s Odyssey with all its savagery and pain, Anticlea's story is a tragic tale of one who either tries to control grief, or is unable to fully engage in or complete the grief passage. Homer's *Odyssey* recounts the ten-year ordeal of Anticlea's son, Odysseus, who endeavored to return to Ithaca after already being away for a decade-long siege on Troy.[22] Thrust into an emotional tempest over her son's absence, Anticlea died from heartbreak; in other accounts it is said that she took her own life.[23] Anticlea then languished in the Underworld. Although she was briefly reunited with her son when he arrived to seek the advice of the prophet Tiresias, because she was in the land of the dead, Odysseus at first did not recognize her. Once he did, he tried to embrace his mother. Sadly, since Anticlea was now one of the souls trapped in Hades, Odysseus could not touch her, and she could not feel (or experience) the love she had been so desperately missing. Odysseus had to leave Anticlea behind in order to find his way home. So, there she remained, unable to embrace her son, forfeiting the opportunity to celebrate his homecoming. Whether Odysseus' mother ended her own life or died from a broken heart, her demise is symbolic of the complete annihilation that accompanies profound grief.

Anticlea's Mother/s Odyssey stalls. Her inability to accept her son's absence causes her death. Instead of embracing the grief passage (in other words, *feeling* it) and therefore integrating it, her passage ended in self-sacrifice. Her sacrifice was pointless, however, since Odysseus already made the sacrifices required by the gods (for ultimately, they were his to make). Anticlea's misplaced martyrdom yields nothing but eternal alienation from her son, the very thing she tried to avoid in the first place. Not only that, but she also became isolated from all those she loved, sentenced to eternity in her own personal hell.

As it relates to the Mother/s Odyssey and specifically managing profound grief that exists outside the bounds of one's control, acceptance promises life. Resistance to inevitable and undeniable loss, on the other hand, promises alienation and death. This is the simplest, yet most difficult lesson to be learned as one makes their way through a grief passage. For me, resisting the reality of my son's schizophrenia—a condition that mirrored Anticlea's ability to see, but not reach her son—was a path straight to hell. I experienced it every time I struggled against circumstances that I had no power to change. It has taken almost two decades to embrace my grief, to accept the loss of my relationship with my son as it once was, and to stop fighting the tide. Mental illness is as arbitrary and unforgiving as the gods; and Anticlea's message to those of us who grieve is clear: resistance is a dead end.

As the global pandemic evolves, the challenge is to recognize where acceptance is warranted and where resistance is needed. Obviously, our entire way of life is changing: the ways we work, socialize, and coexist. This too is a profound loss. Resisting the realities of a global pandemic is a hellish path. At the height of the lockdown, all one had to do was to watch the news or go out in public to observe the various ways individuals were handling their loss of control. Many were either paralyzed by fear or emboldened by denial. Anticlea's story is a reminder. When it comes to controlling or resisting profound grief, the question is: Will we choose to accept what is, or force the hand of the gods? Climate change and the coronavirus would seem to indicate that the gods are playing the winning hand. Have we become so invested in our denial that we are ignorant to our demise?

Furthermore, it is nihilistic to ignore collective grief due to racism, separatism, and discrimination (ongoing plagues on humanity), or the action required to address this blight. Action begins with a personal reckoning, a willingness to face the ugly truth about ignorance, denial, and complicit participation in systems of oppression. How might wounds that have been endured far too long be witnessed and validated? What must be allowed to emerge before it can be released? And how do we embrace the painful passage that is our collective Mother/s Odyssey, in order to facilitate healing and social evolution? The myths and stories of the grieving mother archetype gesture toward the possibilities.

Ensouling - Mary

Mary, the mother of Christ is the epitome of the grieving mother. Her Mother/s Odyssey is one of the most recognizable, since she was present throughout her son's torture and death.

Unlike Anticlea, Mary is able to integrate the experiences of her Mother/s Odyssey, embodying them, thereby evolving into an icon of compassion. This is what ensouls her image—in essence, breathing life into it—as multitudes of individuals who suffer flock to depictions of the Blessed Mother (or Marian icons) seeking comfort and inspiration.

Mary's grief passage was initiated by her son's personal journey; like Demeter and Anticlea, she was engaged in a tandem descent. However, Mary poses a bit of a conundrum. In direct contrast to the visceral agony and annihilation illustrated by Ereshkigal, Inanna, Demeter, and Anticlea, the Holy Mother has become an archetype of tranquility and acceptance. How can this be? Where is her outrage? Where is the savage sorrow so familiar to those who have experienced profound grief?

Contemplating the placid face of Mary, one might think some supernatural ability to bear the unbearable must have been bestowed upon her. However, one image of the Blessed Mother known as *Our Lady of Sorrows* holds the key to her transformation. While there are depictions of a tearful and grief-stricken Mary, she is most often portrayed with a calm, benevolent gaze; her image generally seems to be scrubbed clean of the brutality of grief. *Our Lady of Sorrows* is unique in that there are seven swords embedded in Mary's chest. Those swords are a remnant of the violent truth of the Mother/s Odyssey.[24]

In Catholic and Greek Orthodox traditions, the swords symbolize specific wounds that Mary endured. First, the joy of new motherhood was muted by a prophecy about the impending grief she would endure. Secondly, she was forced into exile to protect her son. Third, Jesus went missing, only to be found in the temple. The fourth sword marked the final hours of her son's life, as he stumbled under the burden of his cross; the fifth represented the agony of witnessing his crucifixion. The sixth wound Mary bears mirrors the spear in Jesus' side; and finally, preparing her son's body for burial plunges the seventh sword into her chest. Thus, seven swords mark seven mortal wounds to Mary's broken heart.[25]

Our Lady of Sorrows evokes the excruciating heartache of the Mother/s Odyssey—when one is powerless to prevent the suffering of someone they love, when letting go of the desire to make things right is the only option, and when reluctant acceptance of unfathomable pain is required. Based on my experience with profound grief in June of 2018, I was skeptical about the serenity that accompanied images of the Blessed Mother—I was troubled by her lack of emotion, but intrigued at the same time. *Our Lady of Sorrows* revealed undeniable truths about the Mother/s Odyssey and how grief could be integrated into one's existence.[26] Mary had become an archetype of the grieving mother not because of her stoic ability to witness her son's torture and death; it was because she embodied transformation—those swords were living proof.

The enduring image of *Our Lady of Sorrows* promises that our grief passages need not destroy us. Instead, the traumas encountered along the way, when fully integrated, lead to transformation. Traditionally, Mary's grief has been subsumed into the story of Christ's torture, death, and resurrection. Though some religious circles acknowledge her grief passage, she seems a bit-player in the saga of her son's life. However, the longevity of the Blessed Mother, the popularity of Marian icons and imagery around the globe, and the love and devotion placed upon her tell a different story. Mary is not defined by the trauma of her wounds; she has integrated them into her heart, as it were. As a result, she is one who can provide compassion and comfort to those who suffer. Her ability to surrender to what was not in her control was the seed that bore the fruit of tranquility. Moreover, her wounds symbolize an empathic ensoulment; they have taken on a life of their own, which is why Mary's eternal presence is so deeply rooted in the collective psyche. *Our Lady of Sorrows* reminds us that the Mother/s Odyssey is a transformative process; and our deepest wounds can be our deepest source of wisdom.

Final Thoughts

Here, I have gathered together four mythic women whose stories speak directly to the Mother/s Odyssey. The wisdom they offer is a testament to the resiliency of myth and its healing potential. These four examples have wildly different expressions of grief, and yet they also have much in common. There is an elegant symmetry between the four women presented here and the circle of women I worked with in the beginning of my research on the archetype of the grieving mother. In that sacred collaboration we began to identify patterns of enduring, emerging, embracing, and ensouling that were inscribed on our hearts.

The beauty of the archetype of the grieving mother is that she resonates with a multitude of expressions of grief, not just for women, and not just for mothers. Julia Kristeva reminds us: "Today motherhood is imbued with what has survived as religious feeling."[27] Perhaps, this is why this Mother/s Odyssey archetype is so powerful and necessary for us today.

It has the substance and authority to guide us through a monumental time of grief. "Courageous mothers are considered the cornerstone of today's civilization, a civilization which [sic] has lost its points of reference," says Kristeva; and a "reflection on maternal passion" might just hold the keys to our survival, because, while "maternal passion generally concerns mothers [it] remains the prototype of the love relation."[28] Unless we reconcile that "love relation" within ourselves, with one another, and with the world, we may be unable to move beyond our collective trauma in order to realize our transformation.

We are facing cataclysmic changes in our world today on every level: personal, social, economic, and environmental. These changes have catapulted the entire planet into a Mother/s Odyssey. In order to manifest healing—as a people, and as a global community—we will be required to utilize all our resources and ingenuity. However, the most essential and difficult part of this process is confronting collective grief. This can be done only if we learn how to identify, validate, and integrate our individual experiences with grief. We do this by actively engaging in the Mother/s Odyssey, embracing the process with compassion for ourselves and others, and embodying our own transformation. This is a key to the collective evolution of humanity.

Bibliography

Avedano, Angelina. *Living Grief: A Mother/s Odyssey of Surrender, Renewal, and Mad Joy*. Sacramento, CA: Mandorla Books, 2021.

— "Rage, Ravages, and Rapture: Applying Goddess Wisdom to the Grieving Mother."

Association for the Study of Women and Mythology. Boston, MA, Panel proposal, 2016.

Campbell, Joseph. *The Hero with a Thousand Faces*. Novato, CA: New World Library, 2008.

Estés, Clarissa Pinkola. *Women Who Run with the Wolves*. New York: Ballantine Books, 1997.

Hamilton, Edith. *Mythology: Timeless Tales of Gods and Heroes*. New York: Warner Books, 1942.

Holweck, Frederik. "Feasts of the Seven Sorrows of the Blessed Virgin," *The Catholic Encyclopedia*. New York: Robert Appleton Company, 1912. https://www.newadvent.org/cathen/14151b.htm.

Homer, *Hymn to Demeter*, trans. Gregory Nagy. Cambridge, MA: Center for Hellenic Studies, Harvard University. 2018. https://chs.harvard.edu/CHS/article/display/5292.

— *The Odyssey of Homer*. Translated by Richmond Lattimore. New York: Harper Perennial Modern Classics, 2007. https://issuu.com/bouvard6/docs/homer_s_odyssey__lattimore_.

Hyginus, Fabulae from The Myths of Hyginus, translated and edited by Mary Grant. University of Kansas Publications in Humanistic Studies, no. 243. https://topostext.org/people/5370.

Kristeva, Julia. "Motherhood Today," *Revue Française de Psychosomatique*, vol. no 40, no. 2, 2011, 43-51. http://www.kristeva.fr/motherhood.html.

Mark, Joshua J. "Inanna's Descent: A Sumerian Tale of Injustice." World History Encyclopedia. Last modified February 23, 2011.

Schüssler Fiorenza, Elisabeth. "Reclaiming Our Power of Memory: A Keynote Address." *Wo/men of the Word*. Women in Church Leadership, 2005. futurechurch.org. https://www.futurechurch.org/women-in-church-leadership/women-and-word/women-of-word.

Wolkstein Diane, and Kramer, Samuel Noah. *Inanna, Queen of Heaven and Earth: Her*

Stories and Hymns from Sumer. New York: Harper Perennial, 1983.

Endnotes

1 My deepest respect and gratitude to Dr. Jaffa Frank, Dr. Stephanie Zachjowski, and Kayden McInnis for their vulnerability, honesty, and commitment to our collaboration, which allowed me to explore this work.

2 Angelina Avedano. "Rage, Ravages, and Rapture: Applying Goddess Wisdom to the Grieving Mother." (Panel proposal. *Association for the Study of Women and Mythology*, Boston: 2016). I first introduced this controversial idea in the 2016 essay/presentation. I use the term "shamanic" with utmost respect for the Indigenous traditions from which it emerges and wish simply to indicate the transformative potential in the work. In other words, an individual is utterly deconstructed in the process of their vocation (or avocation), and thereby discovers a deeper level of awareness and commitment to bringing knowledge and healing into the world. This process of disintegration and reconstitution mirrors the path of the shaman.

3 Elisabeth Schüssler Fiorenza. "Reclaiming Our Power of Memory: A Keynote Address." (Wo/men of the Word. Women in Church Leadership. futurechurch. org. 2005). https://www.futurechurch.org/women-in-church-leadership/women-and-word/women-of-word

4 Ibid.

5 Ibid.

6 Let the phrase "racial/ethnic" represent all exclusionary/discriminatory beliefs and practices.

7 A pseudonym for my son is used throughout this work.

8 Angelina Avedano. *Living Grief: A Mother/s Odyssey of Surrender, Renewal, and Mad Joy.* (Sacramento, CA: Mandorla Books. 2021).

9 Aaron Bernstein. "Coronavirus, Climate Change, and the Environment: A Conversation on COVID-19 with Dr. Aaron Bernstein, Director of Harvard Chan C-CHANGE." (Coronavirus and Climate Change. C-CHANGE Center for Climate, Health, and the Global Environment. Harvard T.H. Chan School of Public Health. 2019).

10 Ibid.

11 Ibid.

12 Joseph Campbell. *The Hero with a Thousand Faces.* (Novato: CA, New World Library 2008), 23. My concept of the Mother/s Odyssey is influenced in part by Campbell's "hero's journey," wherein he describes: "A hero ventures forth from the world of common day into a region of supernatural wonder: fabulous forces are there encountered and a decisive victory is won: the hero comes back [. . .] with the power to bestow boons on his fellow man" (23). However, the Mother/s Odyssey has distinct differences that are explicitly defined in this article.

13 This idea is later developed as the "tandem descent," a concept I use to describe how the Mother/s Odyssey is often related to the inability to protect, or the loss of the beloved; and/or it parallels the hero's journey of the beloved. In other words, the Mother/s Odyssey is many times instigated by the journey (or rite of passage) of the loved one.

14 Diane Wolkstein and Samuel Noah Kramer. *Inanna, Queen of Heaven and Earth: Her Stories and Hymns from Sumer,* (New York: Harper Perennial, 1983),158-162. My retelling of the descent of Inanna is derived from the Wolkstein/Kramer translation.

15 Joshua J. Mark. "Inanna's Descent: A Sumerian Tale of Injustice." (World History Encyclopedia. Last modified February 23, 2011). https://www.worldhistory.org/article/215/inannas-descent-a-sumerian-tale-of-injustice/. Mark points out that Inanna is responsible for the death of Gulgalanna, the Bull of Heaven, who is the husband of Ereshkigal. The tale of the battle that takes Gulgalanna's life is referred to in another Sumerian myth, The Epic of Gilgamesh.

16 Avedano, *Living Grief,* 36-38. This is an abbreviated summary, which is more thoroughly detailed in my book.

17 Ibid, 37.

18 Ibid, 135.

19 Edith Hamilton. "Demeter (Ceres)," in *Mythology: Timeless Tales of Gods and Heroes*, (New York: Warner Books, 1942), 50-55. My retelling is loosely based on Hamilton's version.

20 Clarissa Pinkola Estés. "Baubo the Belly Goddess," *Women Who Run with the Wolves*, (New York: Ballantine Books, 1997). 364-7.

21 Ibid.

22 *The Odyssey of Homer*. Richard Lattimore, trans. (New York: Harper Perennial Modern Classics, 2007). https://issuu.com/bouvard6/docs/homer_s_odyssey__lattimore_. This version is primarily used as a foundation for discussions on the relationship between Anticlea and Odysseus.

23 Hyginus, Fabulae from The Myths of Hyginus, translated and edited by Mary Grant. (University of Kansas Publications in Humanistic Studies, no. 243). https://topostext.org/people/5370.

24 Avedano. *Living Grief,* 110-112. This brief description is elaborated on further in *Living Grief.*

25 Frederik Holweck. "Feasts of the Seven Sorrows of the Blessed Virgin," *The Catholic Encyclopedia*, (New York: Robert Appleton Company, 1912). https://www.newadvent.org/cathen/14151b.htm.

26 Avedano, *Living Grief,* 40-50.

27 Julia Kristeva. "Motherhood Today" (*Revue Française de Psychosomatique*, vol. no 40, no. 2, 2011) 43-51. http://www.kristeva.fr/motherhood.html.

28 Ibid.

THE MOTHER OF THE BUDDHAS

KAREN NELSON VILLANUEVA

In Tibetan Buddhism, the impcrtance of the mother cannot be overemphasized. In this philosophy, all sentient beings have been another's mother because we experience countless rebirths in many realms. For most of us, our mother is our first source of love and compassion; even if she did not give this to some of us, she did give life. In this paper, I discuss how the mother is envisioned in Tibetan Buddhism as love and compassion through her mythology, a debtor to be repaid, the embodiment of wisdom, the mother of all the Buddhas and Bodhisattvas, and, through emptiness, as the mother of us all.

In Tibetan mythology, there was once a mother who was so worried about her favorite child, her daughter Yeshe, that she could not eat or sleep. Yeshe had a virulent disease, and her mother did not want her to suffer. This is known as compassion. In the Theravada tradition of Buddhism, this type of compassion—the desire for beings to be free from suffering—is also found. However, the desire to *save* beings from their suffering is *only* found in the Mahayana path. This compassion, demonstrated by the mother who wishes her daughter to be free from suffering and the love that wishes her daughter happiness, serves as an example of how humans are encouraged to feel about one another; however, extending such compassion toward many beings is a difficult task.[1]

The origin of compassion is empathy. It is from our own suffering that we can understand and thus empathize with the suffering of others. It is because the mother has known pain that she does not want her daughter to hurt. Without care or love, this emotion connotes sympathy. Care demands respect for another being and an appreciation for their place on the earth,[2] while love is "a force of attraction so strong that it makes you cherish sentient beings and hold them dear."[3] Speaking to an estimated 700 nuns and monks at a gathering near Lhasa, Tibet in 1921, the renowned teacher Kyabje Pabongkha Rinpoche stated, "Love through the force of attraction is the sum of three things: understanding that all sentient beings are your mother, remembering their kindness, and wishing to repay their kindness."[4]

Over the next twenty-four days, Pabongkha Rinpoche discussed in detail the causes for recognizing and repaying the kindness of the mother according to the great seventh-century Indian scholar of Madhyamaka philosophy, Chandrakirti, in his *seven-fold instruction*. The first cause is defined as understanding "that all sentient beings were once the ultimate form of friend or relative—your mother."[5] The second cause is remembering the kindness of the mother at the beginning, middle, and the end. In the beginning, she carried her child, her daughter, in her body for nine months. In the middle, she, or some being who acted as mother, cared for her daughter and fed her. In the end, Pabongkha claims, "she did the best she could within her power and knowledge for [her child's] welfare."[6] The third cause is to repay the kindness of the mother through introducing her to the Buddhist path—this is the sure way to end suffering in this life at least in these circumstances...[7] The fourth cause is the love that comes from attraction like the love the mother had for her daughter Yeshe. The challenge of this life is to love others as a mother loves her favorite child.[8] The fifth cause is the great compassion that is not just sympathetic, but actually wants to save others from suffering. Chandrakirti wrote, "Love is the seed for a magnificent crop.... [L]ike water, love makes that crop grow, and much later it ripens into the thing most desired...."[9] The sixth cause is known as altruism because ideally a mother did not bring her daughter into this world solely for her own benefit. This leads to the seventh and final cause, developing *bodhicitta*. As defined by Pabongkha Rinpoche, "Development of *bodhicitta* is desiring full enlightenment to benefit others."[10] This is dealt with when discussing the Bodhisattva ideal, a concept unique to Mahayana Buddhism where enlightenment is sought in order to benefit other sentient beings.[11]

Bodhisattvas are known as the children of the Buddha(s). This ideal of the Bodhisattva that aspires to be a Buddha is often depicted as a bird. Born to fly to the heights of enlightenment, the right side is the masculine and its strength is compassion, while the left side is the feminine and its strength is wisdom. In this vision of enlightenment, wisdom and compassion are bound together as the wings of a bird, male and female working together. Arising at around the same time as the Mediterranean Sophia,[12] the feminine wing of wisdom is known as the goddess Prajnaparamita, and this is translated as the perfection, *"paramita,"* of wisdom, or *"prajna."* She is not only a deity, but also sacred words (text), the *Perfection of Wisdom in 8,000 Lines*. First composed in South India around 100 BCE, the text was amended over the next seven hundred years;[13] thus, versions comprised of 16,000 and 32,000 lines also exist.

As Joanna Macy states in *World as Lover, World as Self*, the *Perfection of Wisdom* text defined Mahayana Buddhism and takes the Bodhisattva out of the realm of Shakyamuni Buddha's previous incarnations and reinstates it as an ideal for all women and men to achieve.[14] In the *Perfection of Wisdom* text, Prajnaparamita is labeled "Mother of the Tathagatas (those who see things as they are)," "Mother of the Sugatas (those who have gone to bliss)," "Mother of the Bodhisattvas (those who seek enlightenment for the benefit of all sentient beings),"[15] "Instructress of the Tathagatas in this world," and "Genetrix and Nurse of the Six Perfections,"[16] so she is clearly female and a mother deity. Her wisdom is the wisdom of the Tathagatas, those who see things as they are, free of ignorance. In her essential reference work entitled *The Buddhist Goddesses of India*, Buddhist scholar Miranda Shaw calls her "the supreme teacher and eternal font of revelation."[17] As Macy explains, "This wisdom, then, [as represented by the goddess Prajnaparamita] is not the kind one can think oneself into; it is a way of seeing."[18] However, unlike the creator gods found in many cultures, Buddhist scholar Rita Gross notes, "[S]he is not a saviour to whom one can appeal at all, but a vision of the goal."[19]

Prajnaparamita's children are known as the fearless ones, Bodhisattvas, and her path of the six perfections, or *paramitas*—generosity, morality, patience, diligence, meditation, and wisdom—are the ways to overcome fear. Unfortunately, she cannot remove fear for us; we must do the work ourselves. "Her reassurance is symbolized by the *abhaya mudra*, the fear-not gesture."[20] Also, as a Bodhisattva, one is not perfect but rather perfect*ing*, and this is illuminated by the translation of her mantra: *GATE PARAGATE PARASAMGATE BODHI SVAHA!* "Gone, gone, everyone gone, gone to the other side, to enlightenment! Rejoice!"[21]

The wisdom of seeing things as they are is the complex concept known as "emptiness." In contemporary times, in the typical, or conventional, worldview, beings see themselves as independent and separate from one another, when in reality—according to the concept of emptiness—all beings are interdependent with one another and completely reliant upon one another for existence. This is also known as "co-dependent arising," or "dependent arising," that is, *"pratityasamutpada."* Within this matrix or web of existence called emptiness, there is ultimately one mother, Prajnaparamita, the mother of all sentient beings, and she is symbolized by the call of the bell so frequently heard in Buddhist ritual.

To return to the myth of the mother and her daughter, Yeshe: The disease was too great for her daughter to overcome and she died. The mother made the best life she could for her other children and lived a long life. In her next existence, she was reborn as the daughter and Yeshe was her mother. Having known and demonstrated real love and compassion in her last life, the mother-now-daughter was that much closer to attaining enlightenment because what one does matters, and to be a mother who loves her children matters most of all. However, one does not have to give birth when incarnate to love others with empathy, care, and compassion. Ultimately, this is the message of Buddhism—to love one another as a mother loves her favorite child.

References

Conze, Edward. *The Perfection of Wisdom in Eight Thousand Lines and Its Verse Summary*. Wheel Series 1. San Francisco: Four Seasons Foundation, 1995.

Gross, Rita M. *Buddhism after Patriarchy: A Feminist History, Analysis, and Reconstruction of Buddhism*. Albany: State University of New York Press, 1993.

Macy, Joanna. *World As Lover, World As Self.* Berkeley, CA: Parallax Press, 1991.

Pabongka Rinpoche. *Liberation in the Palm of Your Hand: A Concise Discourse on the Path to Enlightenment*. Edited by Trijang Rinpoche. Translated by Michael Richards. Boston: Wisdom Publications, 1997.

Shaw, Miranda. *Buddhist Goddesses of India*. Princeton, NJ: Princeton University Press, 2006.

Yeshe, Thubten (Lama). "An Explanation of the Shunyata Mantra and a Meditation on Emptiness." Edited by Nicholas Ribush. *Mandala* (January/March 2009): 12–14.

Endnotes

1 Pabongka Rinpoche, *Liberation in the Palm of Your Hand: A Concise Discourse on the Path to Enlightenment*, ed. Trijang Rinpoche, trans. Michael Richards (Boston: Wisdom Publicat:ons, 1997), 583.

2 Personal notes from Gelek Rinpoche's dharma talk, Milpitas Community Center, Milpitas, CA, October 30, 2011.

3 Rinpoche, *Liberation in the Palm of Your Hand*, 583.

4 Ibid., 572.

5 Ibid., 577.

6 Ibid., 579.

7 Ibid.

8 Ibid., 581.

9 Ibid., 585.

10 Ibid.

11 Joanna Macy, *World As Lover, World As Self* (Berkeley, CA: Parallax Press, 1991), 106.

12 Edward Conze, *The Perfection of Wisdom in Eight Thousand Lines and Its Verse Summary*, Wheel Series 1 (San Francisco: Four Seasons Foundation, 1995), back cover.

13 Ibid.

14 *World As Lover*, 109.

15 Conze, *The Perfection of Wisdom*.

16 Ibid.

17 Miranda Shaw, *Buddhist Goddesses of India* (Princeton, NJ: Princeton University Press, 2006), 166.

18 Macy, *World As Lover*, 108.

19 Rita M. Gross, *Buddhism after Patriarchy: A Feminist History, Analysis, and Reconstruction of Buddhism* (Albany: State University of New York Press, 1993), 76.

20 Macy, *World As Lover*, 110.

21 (Lama) Thubten Yeshe, "An Explanation of the Shunyata Mantra and a Meditation on Emptiness," ed. Nicholas Ribush, *Mandala* (January/March 2009): 12–14.

SECTION 4

CONTEMPORARY ENGAGEMENT: CRITIQUE AND RECLAMATION

Fig. 12. **The Goddess** Dandelion. Ink jet print, Ceardai Demelza, 2019.

THE GODDESS DANDELION:
FIRST OF THE WEED WOMEN

CEARDAI DEMELZA

So, why a weed woman?

The dandelion plant is often considered a weed in modern Western society, even though many cultures have been consuming it for thousands of years. In recent years, the scientific community in the West has rediscovered this plant and its many health and nutritional benefits.[1] In addition, the flowers are valuable food for bees. Dandelions often appear in lawns, which contain no health or environmental benefits; in fact, the watering, feeding, and mowing of lawns is detrimental to the environment and to human, animal, and insect health. Nevertheless, to conform to social mores, people continue to participate in weeding the dandelion out and nurturing the lawn. The well-clipped lawn has become a symbol of status, perceived as more important than creature health and the environment. I have drawn the correlation between women and weeds because women are devalued in the same way. To be a woman who is no longer a commodity is comparable to being a weed.

I visually explore ideas around the correlation between the commodification and exploitation of women and of the environment. I create new worlds and characters who are the antithesis of current conditions, which serves to highlight the issues of a patriarchal capitalist system.[2] Western European history and mythology are dominated by stories that reinforce the patriarchy and male superiority. At the same time these stories diminish the roles of women and anyone else from a "minority" group as defined by powerful men. The stories extol the virtues of a capitalist society where

Fig. 13. The Goddess Dandelion. Ink jet print, Ceardai Demelza, 2019.

men dominate over the rest of nature, including all non-human creatures.[3] These stories are so entrenched in our psyches that often people do not even realize the impact they have on our values and actions, particularly toward women, animals, and the natural world.[4]

A soothing balm to this toxic perspective can be found in the knowledge that, prior to patriarchy, Western European cultures were often matriarchal and followed nature-based religions that honored, and even worshipped, goddesses rather than a single male sky god. In these cultures the goddess could be found in every aspect of nature. Vestiges of the stories from these cultures provide insight into how people lived without war and in harmony with nature. These stories, often thousands of years old with only remnants of writings and tangible artefacts remaining, sadly can never be fully restored and understood. I believe that there is much room for new stories for our own time and our challenges, and with new interconnections to be forged. This gives me a sense of agency and hope and also pays homage to what has been lost and can never be reclaimed.

References

Dumont, Marion., and Devi, Gayatri. Introduction. In *Myths Shattered and Restored: Proceedings of the Association for the Study of Women and Mythology*, vol. 1, edited by Dumont and Devi, 1-6. Women and Myth Press, 2016.

Robbins Dexter, Miriam. Foreword. In *Myths Shattered and Restored: Proceedings of the Association for the Study of Women and Mythology*, vol. 1, edited by Dumont and Devi, vii. Women and Myth Press, 2016.

Mies, Maria, and Vandana Shiva. *Ecofeminism*. London: Zed Books, 2014.

Wirngo, Fonyuy, Lambert, Max, and Jeppesen, Per. The Physiological Effects of Dandelion (*Taraxacum Officinale*) in Type 2 Diabetes. *Review of Diabetic Studies* 13, nos. 2–3 (2016): 113–31.

Endnotes

1 Fonyuy Wirngo, Max Lambert, and Per Jeppesen, "The Physiological Effects of Dandelion (*Taraxacum Officinale*) in Type 2 Diabetes," *Review of Diabetic Studies* 13, nos. 2–3 (2016): 113–31.

2 Maria Mies and Vandana Shiva, *Ecofeminism* (London: Zed Books, 2014).

3 Miriam Robbins Dexter, Foreword, in *Myths Shattered and Restored: Proceedings of the Association for the Study of Women and Mythology*, vol. 1, eds. Dumont and Devi, vii (Women and Myth Press, 2016).

4 Marion Dumont and Gayatri Devi, Introduction, in *Myths Shattered and Restored: Proceedings of the Association for the Study of Women and Mythology*, vol. 1, eds. Dumont and Devi, 1-6 (Women and Myth Press, 2016).

DECONSTRUCTING PATRIARCHAL MOTHERHOOD

MARIAM IRENE TAZI-PREVE

Motherhood is debated constantly during discussions on combining family and career, and on abortion or fertility. Although suffering caused by mothers is often mentioned, the hardships of motherhood are rarely a priority. During the Covid crisis, single mothers were/are locked up in small living spaces with their child or children, and in extreme cases, twenty-four hours a day for months on end, working from home as a one-woman office (often as precariats—vulnerable individuals with inadequate resources). Many of these very small businesses were founded because women need to plan their lives around their children. This kind of situation can have disastrous consequences. Before the pandemic most mothers were supported by female networks, starting with their own mothers, who were no longer permitted to help when elders were placed under quasi house arrest.

In government and other public fora, much is said about the health conditions during Covid and immediate effects on the economy. So-called "women's issues" are downplayed or ignored, while proclamations made by politicians, health-care professionals, and economists sound like mansplaining.

When talking about suffering originating in families, mothers are typically the first on the list. No one says that it is downright scandalous and negligent for a society to lament the falling birth rate and demand more children, while simultaneously accepting no responsibility for children, making them individual mothers' problems. Intervention often occurs only when violence occurs, such as mothers harming their children or (step)fathers who abuse children. Even if a (step)father is present, two adults are often inadequate to the task of providing adequate care for a young child twenty-four hours a day.

In Europe, motherhood has become a buzzword for combining family and career. This is motivated by sinking birth rates: in Southern and Eastern Europe the birth rate (fertility) is below population replacement levels and continues to decline. In German-speaking countries, the average is 1.4 (Austria) and 1.5 (Germany) children per woman, resulting in enormous pressure to create policies that raise birth rates and thus raise the gross national product.

The way women and families are portrayed in political debate suggests, even by some feminists—for example, by Sheryl Sandberg[1]—that women can have everything, namely juggling children and career. But in reality we have a completely exhausted and overwhelmed generation of women, who are condemned to failure as they struggle to live up to these impossible expectations.[2]

Legislation completely regulates private life, although the state is supposed to refrain from interfering in people's private affairs. In reality the entire "private sphere" is regulated by laws governing marriage, family, and health; abortion is perhaps the most obvious example.

At the beginning of my research on motherhood—as a young mother in my twenties—I realized that something was deeply wrong. Soon I became convinced that problems inherent within the concept of motherhood are based on a mechanistic approach toward women's procreative potential—I was particularly disturbed by the quantification of offspring (two per woman), the mechanical way of delivering a child, and reproductive technology's callous means of physically replacing mothers.

My analysis began with my own seemingly private experiences raising my child. During the course of many years working on this subject, it became clear that my approach must be multidisciplinary in order to grasp the philosophy or theory undergirding the issues. Until the 1990s, motherhood was not considered a topic of interest in political science. At that time I began conducting studies grounded in sociology as well as political science,[3] and studied the historical and psychological research on family, motherhood, and fatherhood.[4]

My goal is an interdisciplinary, systemic analysis of motherhood from the perspective of a critique on power. And in contrast to the dominant postmodern approach to gender in women's studies,[5] my approach begins with criticism of the patriarchy.

The lack of adequate answers in feminist and political theory led to development of the critical theory of patriarchy, *Kritische Patriarchatstheorie* (KTP), of the Innsbruck School,[6] which continued work on early developments in the feminist theory of the late 1970s to further cultivate and systematize them. The goal was to create a systemic meta-theory that facilitates an understanding of civilizations in all dimensions. The use of these analytical tools has revealed that politics and economics are engaged in ongoing destruction of nature and humanity itself in favor of a presumably improved new (artificial) creation. Controlling motherhood is an important part of the patriarchal project. KPT also explains where the delusional idea for a so-called "modern and progressive" world comes from, in which "progress" can only be achieved through shock and destruction,[7] that is, through violence.

Definition of Terms

When defining terms, precision is necessary in order to prevent misunderstanding and confusion. According to older definitions,[8] patriarchy was analyzed from a sociological and historical perspective as a system of dominance comprising all structures and institutions. Alternative terms were also widely used in feminist political science such as masculinist or androcentric.[9]

Since the inception of gender theory in the 1990s, a systemic concept of power has been rejected and female identity has been called into question. The focus has been directed toward concepts such as diversity and intersectionality, which require oppression to be differentiated. But the loss of the "woman" category has rendered radical critique impossible. This development undermines the united political advancement of women. In economic realities, this avenue also enables the incorporation of endeavors that use class, race, gender, sexual orientation, and so on to promote corporate agendas. For example, corporations have started to introduce new strategies grounded in the understanding that applying "diversity" would increase profits; for instance, employing more women or non-white people would create new markets.

The European Union is applying "gender politics" (which could also be called the application of liberal feminism) to neo-liberal goals, calling it "gender mainstreaming." In reality this means that the foundational concept of the European Union, which is understood to be nothing more than the realization of a neoliberal agenda, should never be questioned, yet at the same time accepted as progressive.

In this contribution a systemic concept of patriarchy is used, understood as a meta-principle that goes well beyond the dominance of men over women or as a principle according to which the society has been specifically gender structured. It is a mode of operation that characterizes our entire civilization—family, society, politics, and economy. The characteristics of a patriarchal civilization follow:

- Patriarchy declares itself to be original to the society, asserting that no other advanced cultures preceded it (e.g., Hellenic Greece denied the existence of Minoan culture).

- Matriarchal achievements are usurped (e.g., agriculture, production of household wares).

  - Ruling is exercised through hierarchical classification and domination, such as in political and corporatist institutions.

  - The "divide and conquer" principle prevents cooperation, such as playing women against each other—mothers versus childless women, good versus bad mothers, and egg donors versus surrogate mothers.

- Denying responsibility for life, such as human "collateral damage" in war.

- Dominance of an economy that exploits people and nature is considered legitimate; examples are, respectively, working conditions that resemble slavery, and the depletion of resources.

- The acceptance of violence, especially toward the bodies of women and children, such as when rape and sexual molestation are rarely sanctioned.

- Principles are turned on their head (inversion concept): war is considered good, while peace activists are denounced, in effect, as social justice "warriors."

- Natural reproduction by a mother and by nature are seen as value-less (i.e., no value added). Actual creations are the outcomes of intellectual and technological "regeneration" (e.g., surrogate mothers, artificial worlds).

Patriarchy far exceeds the individual "battles of the sexes" within nuclear families; it is a collective system of power that sees itself as the predominant way of thinking. All people are subjected to it, even men, who can also be run over by the wheels of patriarchy. This is evident when men object to the presumed ideal of the male provider and prioritize their private relationships; that is, when they behave like matriarchal men. Patriarchal women, on the other hand, master the game of power equally well or better than men.

What do I mean by matrilineality? Many currently existing matriarchal cultures spanning the entire globe have been well researched. They exist in southern China—the Mosuo,[10] and on the Indonesian island of Sumatra—the Minangkabau.[11] They are on the Indian subcontinent—such as the Khasi,[12] in Africa, and among the Indigenous peoples of the Americas.

For the most part I am referring to the work of Heide Göttner-Abendroth,[13] who has outlined models of the social organization of matrilineal societies. The basic principle is orientation on mothers' lineage, centering around the clan mother. In matrilineal families, mothers, mothers' siblings, and children live together or in proximity to each other. The mother's name is bestowed on each coming generation. The distinctive quality of matrilineality is that relationships are defined through the mother, not by marriage.

This concept of motherhood is fundamentally different from the Western concept, which was turned upside down and completely redefined. All women of a family take part in mothering. Erotic partnerships and marriage are not part of this concept of family, but are considered as extremely personal matters for both women and men. Usually a husband does not move into the household of his wife and vice versa. Marriages are generally less of a commitment than Western-culture marriages with all of their legal consequences. So-called visiting marriages are common. The emotional and economic support for children and adults comes through the mother's lineage. The lack of emotional and economic dependence on a spouse (or natural father is a fundamental principle. A mother's brother fulfills the functions of fatherhood, meaning that he is the social father to the children of his sisters.

Some matriarchal societies display all of these basic characteristics. Many more are transforming, being successively undermined by surrounding patriarchal societies on several levels: economic (renunciation of common property), religious (missions and conversions), and political (imposed marriage laws).

Characteristics of Patriarchal Motherhood

One of the most obvious detrimental consequences of living in current patriarchal societies in the context of raising children—even to non-feminists—is persistent economic disparity.[14] In German-speaking countries, such conditions are related to the relatively large proportion of women working part-time. Also, regulations regarding maternity leave cause German and Austrian mothers to leave their place of employment for much longer than women in other European countries or the USA.[15] On the other hand, European social-welfare policies compensate for at least part of their lost earnings.

Family policies in Austria and Germany focus on combining family and career,[16] reforming child-care subsidies, and increasing the number of child-care facilities.[17] For decades ideological questions have revolved around the image of motherhood and "how much mother does a child need,"[18] and what kind of child-care outside the home—without a mother—can children be expected to bear. Therefore, the political and economic structure of the (father) state is dependent on a moral imperative for women to be responsible for both child rearing and work.

The European welfare state functions as a substitute for actual fathers, who are often absent, in that it tries to improve the situation. Women can turn to the government if the father doesn't pay support or if child-care is needed. Usually women negotiate with the state, who acts as a mother and claims to care for its citizens. On the other hand, mothers are regularly suspected of abusing financial support. These policies also serve to maintain the gender role status quo—for example, special tax rates for families with dependents in Germany (*"Familiensplitting"*).

Ideologically, motherhood is understood to be an institution, which has been supervised and regulated by pedagogy, medicine, psychology, and law.

For example, regulations and recommendations on breastfeeding have been constantly changing based on the state of research or popular opinion of the time. A few years ago, breastfeeding was considered to be dangerous because mother's milk was thought to be contaminated with dioxins; today prolonged breastfeeding is highly encouraged.

Mother blaming is characteristic of patriarchal motherhood. Mothers (especially mothers of sons) are held responsible for criminality and weak academic performance, which occur more often in male children. Mothers are also held responsible (of course) for daughters' eating disorders. Psychoanalysis promotes the image of a terrifying mother. Patients usually lie on an analyst's couch symbolically alongside their mothers. In psychotherapy practice, suffering under the mother is given priority, while the suffering that mothers endure is ignored.

Women go to tremendous lengths to avoid accusations of being "bad mothers." The concept of "bad father" effectively doesn't exist. This implies the paradox that the mother is to be constantly present and bear all responsibility for the child while carrying out the impossible task of caring for a child twenty-four hours a day for many years in addition to providing for both her own and the children's financial and personal needs.

Conversely, it is argued that a mother's constant presence is psychologically detrimental; symbiosis with the mother must be dissolved unconditionally to allow development of individuality to take its "proper" course. This primarily concerns male children, who are expected to commit "matricide"[19] and then turn to their father. The Freudian model of triangulation claims that the family unity of father-mother-child is a constellation dictated by nature.[20] Feminist psychoanalysts[21] have since put a lot of work into questioning Freud's male-centered perspective and focusing on the identity development of female children. Nevertheless, Freud's patriarchal concept of family continues to be reinforced by scholars and politicians.

Motherhood as a threesome means that the male partner acts as an emotional surrogate for the female partner. In most cases this dependency is also economic. The ideology of romantic love prioritizes loyalty to one's partner. Matrilineality, including relationships to daughters and also to sons, is purposefully destroyed and replaced by husbands.

Separation from one's children is carried out very early in the West; in the USA teenagers are often sent away to distant colleges. This leads to early marriage or partnerships, which are a widespread and socially acceptable norm. Returning to one's mother—even temporarily—is considered to be emotionally infantile and/or career failure.

The isolation of mothers in nuclear families is the result of promoting the separation of mothers and children on all levels. So-called individualization occurs because women are not only cut off from their own mothers' lineage and other women geographically, but also mentally, because this way of life seems to be normal. Instead of sharing work with others, mothers perform their day-to-day tasks in "solitary confinement,"[22] according to detailed instructions concerning how she should accomplish motherhood. There is a lack of understanding of both the existence (from current to ancient societies) and value of social interconnectedness and shared responsibility for raising children. Christian institutions believe that the "individuality" and "materialism" of our times have caused the "deterioration of the family." Once again the mother is blamed for seeking "her own advantage if she is employed"[23] and/or has only one child. Like a boomerang every attempt a woman makes to keep her children while also developing an independent life circles back to strike her.

What is perfidious for a mother living in the patriarchy is the way she is continuously overworked, not only when she's single, but also if she is living in a relationship. Statistics prove time and time again that working mothers are usually subjected to an imbalance of child-care and household work.[24] Studies conducted during the Covid crisis[25] show that the unequal division of household chores has hardly changed. Even when home office work and child care could have been shared equally by fathers and mothers, that is not how it works out. Studies demonstrate the opposite, that women neglect their own work as well as their personal needs, while men remain "at work."

> Moms are also more likely to leave their jobs during the pandemic because they feel pressure to be a "good mom." ... It's not the same for dads. Even in the most egalitarian households[,] ... women typically do the bulk of the domestic labor: When something isn't working at home— if there's a pandemic, say, and the kids are bouncing off the walls—women are more likely to feel they need to be the ones to fix it.[26]

In addition, the ideology persists that women living in relationships are much better off than women who don't live with their child's father. Single mothers with a good social network often experience much more support from their own mothers and sisters as well as other mothers than mothers living in a nuclear family with a partner. Single mothers are marginalized in the USA and Europe and are considered to be potential abusers of government welfare services. Pushed to the fringes of society by the propagated family ideal, they are suspected of being "incapable" of maintaining relationships and of "denying" their children a "father figure."

The development of genetic engineering has finally brought about the elimination of mothers by removing them from the mothering process, except for the woman who provides the egg; the surrogate mother who gestates the fetus; and the "social mother(s)"—male "mothers"—who raise the child Consequently, there is no biological mother nor a social mother. Surrogate motherhood is legal in only a few countries—the USA, Ukraine, India, Thailand, and Mexico.[27] This technology is used systematically by male homosexual couples to "create a child." Separating the gestating mother from the egg donor ensures that there is no longer any biological bond between mother and child, and thus no need to fear that she will refuse to give up the child after birth. What remains is the biological father and the social father. The mother has been eliminated.

The relationship among conception, pregnancy, and birth has been definitively fractured, as male physicians in the 1980s presented themselves as the fathers of the first test-tube baby because they conceived a child outside the womb. Experiments on cloning animals are being conducted and scientists are racing to be the first to clone a human being. However, it is not yet possible to replace the human female uterus. Surrogate motherhood has become a business. "Parents" are charged enormous amounts of money when they hire surrogacy agencies.[28]

These developments are allegedly concepts of liberation—children for infertile women, women can "outsource" pregnancy, and gay couples can become the sole parents. The legal aspects are still lagging behind technological innovations: when a child "produced" in the USA immigrates to Europe, identification of the mother is still required. But here, too, technology is creating realities to which institutions will be forced to conform.

The characteristic of patriarchal motherhood is the mother being replaced by the father. On physical and technological levels, this process is being realized through reproductive technology. I discuss later how the replacement of mothers by fathers also extends to legal and theoretical levels.

The Modern Mother Trap

Motherhood allegedly has little value; "the real world" is "outside" the home, in politics and in the work world. But what does "the real world" mean? Its criteria are almost the opposite of what we consider to be nurturing in a relationship: competition, hierarchy, approval, and rewards occurring exclusively through the market/money system (commodification). Obviously, the "most natural" should not be valued.

The Covid crisis has revealed all of this in the extremes: almost one million women left the USA work force because the situation became unbearable and they valued their children more than their economic independence.[29] While governments compensated businesses that remained closed during the various lockdowns, mothers received nothing.

I call the situation of mothers today the "modern mother trap"[30] because women who depend on the wages they earn have three options, none of which are desirable:

- One is being a dependent housewife, which requires a husband who will support his wife her entire life. In light of the divorce rates of over 50 percent in Europe and the USA, this way of life is unrealistic for mothers.

- The second option is for her to work part-time and not be able to support herself. This option also requires either a breadwinner or dependency on social welfare from the state.

- The third option is to take on all responsibility for a full-time job, child-care, and housework. Few women are able to hire helpers or rely on help from relatives or their social network. Most try to square the circle. This generation is massively overworked; nonetheless they have been convinced that every woman can and should be able to do it.

This situation requires that women recognize that the only solution to the question of motherhood offered by such system is choosing among several unacceptable alternatives. Politically labeled "freedom of choice," for most mothers it is a trap. Critical analysis of the patriarchal system sheds light on the contradiction: instead of the postulated equality for women in general, individual freedom is granted only to childless women. This must be interpreted as a consequence of the ideological orientation of the state.

Economic Background

Historically, the housewife phenomenon was first created in an economic system that defined the work of creating and maintaining the social fabric of the family as non-work and thus excluded it from the gross national product. The sexist foundation of economics persists until today.

The persistent wage gap between men and women is explained by this phenomenon, which in Austria, for example, is about 20 percent,[31] even as wage-earners, women's work has been "housewified."[32] The labor market has proven to be heavily gender segregated in Europe and the USA. Most employed women are in service or caretaker fields, comparable to a housewife: secretary and assistant, as helpers providing education, health-care services, and social work—all typically less valued and compensated than typical male professions. During the pandemic, this work was indispensable to the functioning of society. In Europe employees in these fields received high praise as pillars of their community. In Austria they were placated with coupons for meals as a way to avoid giving them raises.

Moreover, the European idea of the welfare state, which was established at the end of the nineteenth century, has undergone dramatic changes in the past forty years through privatization of services that had previously been provided by the state. Included here are education, child care, transportation, and subsidized housing.[33]

The character of work also changed dramatically by "deregulation." Previous business organizational structures were replaced by corporations that fundamentally reject any responsibility for their employees and are hostile to unions. Workplace safety laws have been successively dismantled since the 1970s and real wages have been falling dramatically for years, while investment income has been rising sharply. Insecurity has been dubbed freedom, "flexibility" refers only to workers who work according the whims of their employers, ready to start and stop working at any time. The loss of full-time employment opportunities has led to large numbers of part-time and precarious workers. This affects men as well as women and could be referred to as "housewififying the First World." Erosion of the middle class, underway for the last forty years, continues. Following centuries of exploitation in many world regions,, the citizens of former colonial powers are now being conquered inside their own countries.

Thus the question of women's independence can be formulated as follows: Limited earning opportunities make the prospect of financial independence improbable. Women in positions of leadership are statistically almost non-existent. Dependence on the labor market is becoming increasingly precarious for women, so that women remain dependent on better-earning husbands or government welfare services. For these reasons, the feminist slogan—"women's liberation through work"—must be reconsidered. This type of liberation is available only to a tiny elite.

Historical Background

Patriarchal motherhood can be explained only in the context of its historical development. Greek travel writers (such as Herdot) documented the existence of matriarchies[34] at that time in Europe, the Near East, and North Africa. The Hellenic Greeks supplanted the world view of these pre-patriarchal civilizations[35] by reinterpreting their myths,[36] denying matriarchal achievements, and relying on abstractions instead of gaining insights through empirical observation.

The Republic contains Plato's artificial design for reproduction in a place separated from public areas designated for raising children. This was the first time that public life, the state, and military, and the area of reproduction were separated. From that point on, the birth of ideas was valued more than the birth of children. In warrior societies, the bond between mother and child had to be relaxed or utterly broken; otherwise, mothers would not send their sons off to battle. According to Plutarch, Sparta forbade mothers from mourning their children.

Roman law was significant in the patriarchal development of Europe. It formed the basis for the entire modern European legal system, including family law that was practiced until the 1970s. Laws derived from ancient Rome determined male succession, family names, and hegemony. Matrilineality was replaced with a legal system that legitimized only the father as the determinative parent. Ancient Roman legal texts document awareness that the role didn't have to be fulfilled by the biological father.

This created the artificial division of legitimate heirs, children born in marriage, and illegitimate descendants, devoid of rights.

Important vertices for the creation of patriarchal motherhood were determined for the first time since medieval Europe when the true nature of women was not solely defined by theological authorities, but by political theoreticians.[37] Mother and child were declared to be a natural unit and the complement of the individual male citizen. It is no contradiction that this symbiosis of male children would not be tolerated for long. A son was soon expected to turn from his mother toward his father, who symbolizes "real life." The Enlightenment created the citizen and the "mother" citizen who was excluded from public life. Here it was determined that motherhood is an obligation owed to (the father) state while regulations were created dictating how she was to go about fulfilling her duty.

Until the late 20th century, giving birth outside of marriage was a crime. Motherhood was legitimized only through marriage. From the late medieval age into the twentieth century, there are numerous accounts of women who committed suicide out of a desperate attempt to spare themselves and their unborn children life-long sanctions.

The vilification of motherhood was accompanied by a population explosion in Europe, especially between 1450 and 1700, when the population grew from 50 to 115 million inhabitants.[38] The context of this outcome is witch hunting. Victims of witch hunters were mostly women with medical knowledge about childbirth, contraception, and abortion. Their elimination led to an extremely high birth rate as well as to a large number of children being cast out—many died in orphanages. This phenomenon was cited by Badinter (1981) as proof of the lack of maternal instinct. One could more readily conclude that the large number of children contributed to the destruction or weakening of the mother–child relationship.

A variant of mother-hysteria occurred during National Socialism in Germany and Austria. The Aryan mother cult spawned the so-called "Lebensborn" (spring of life), where German children were conceived and born. Women were awarded gold, silver, and bronze Crosses of Honor for bearing many children.

Apparently contradictory developments in which mothers are praised and honored on the one hand and denigrated on the other, only seem to be contradictions. This division is a result of centuries of isolating women and thus mothers in sundry ways for centuries; once mothers were fragmented, they could then be dominated.

The Matrilineal Concept of Motherhood

Let's take a look at the matrilineal concept of motherhood, that is, caring for each other within the bond of family. This is practiced today in existing matriarchies and can serve as a model for non-discriminatory family structures. The fundamental difference compared to patriarchal motherhood is that there is a sense of belonging that does not come about through marriage, but through the relationship to one's mother. A woman's descendants and her brothers live in the same house or nearby. This allows people to feel rooted to a particular place because they live on and cultivate the land that they own communally. Connection is created and strengthened through communal celebrations. Most existing matriarchies are subsistence societies, which create everything they need, where paid employment is unknown. The Mosuo (China), the Minangkabau of Sumatra (Indonesia), and the Khasi (India) are among the most well-known of these societies. Most of these societies are gradually losing their unique way of life and economy through the corrosive influence of surrounding market economies.

The family system is experienced as an organic body "that is incomplete if the whole family system isn't intact."[39] The community is focused on "how we take care of each other without destroying the land." Motherhood is not a concept of individual responsibility, but a collective obligation performed by all women. The principle of caring includes male family members, the mother's brothers, who are social fathers to the children. Erotic partnership is held to be very personal and has nothing to do with family responsibility and economic support.

The crucial difference

What is the difference between the kind of motherhood described here and motherhood in the patriarchy? In contrast to patriarchal families, the principles of caring and community ensure that the needs of all children and adults are met. There can be no children traumatized by divorce because they grow up in a family based on matrilineal logic. There is also no neurotic bonding solely to one parent because many people share equal responsibility for child-care.

There is no economic nor emotional dependency on a spouse. The surrogate is unnecessary. Family is experienced as a safe place for both adults and children.[40]

In addition, the male role is not defined hierarchically, but rather is defined more practically than patriarchal fatherhood—as mother-brother, who consults with the family as the social father to his sisters' children and as a man who uses his physical strength and other skills and talents to protect the clan.

Living in an atmosphere of interdependence, solidarity, and responsibility is the counterpart to "divide and conquer," and comes from the fact that caring is a fundamental principle and the priority for all social interaction.

References

Ahnert, Lieselotte. *Wieviel Mutter braucht ein Kind? Bindung–Bildung–Betreuung: öffentlich und privat*. Heidelberg: Spektrum Akademischer Verlag, 2010.

Armstrong, Jeannette. "Indigenous Knowledge and Gift Giving: Living in Community." In *Women and the Gift Economy: A Radically Different Worldview Is Possible*, edited by Genevieve Vaughan, 41–49. Toronto: Inanna Publications, 2007.

Badinter, Elisabeth. *Mother Love: Myth and Reality: Motherhood in Modern History*. New York: Macmillan, 1981.

Beauvoir, Simone de. *The Second Sex.* New York: Vintage, [1949] 1989.

Danshilacuo, Hengde, and He Mei, "Mosuo Family Structure." In *Societies in Peace: Matriarchies Past, Present, and Future*, edited by Heide Göttner-Abendroth, 248–55. Toronto: Inanna Publications, 2009.

Freud, Siegmund. *Band 1: Elemente der Psychoanalyse*. Werkausgabe in zwei Bänden. Edited by Anna Freud and Ilse Grubrich-Simitis. Frankfurt am Main: Fischer, 1978.

Genth, Renate. *Über Maschinisierung und Mimesis. Erfindungsgeist und mimetische Begabung im Widerstreit und ihre Bedeutung für das Mensch-Maschine-Verhältnis*. Beiträge zur Dissidenz no. 10. Frankfurt am Main et al.: Peter Lang, 2002.

Göttner-Abendroth, Heide. *Matriarchal Societies: Indigenous Cultures across the Globe*. Frankfurt am Main et al.: Peter Lang, 2012.

Grose, Jessica. "America's Mothers Are in Crisis: Is Anyone Listening to Them?" *The New York Times*, February 4, 2021. www.nytimes.com/2021/02/04/parenting/working-moms-mental-health-coronavirus.html

Heinsohn, Gunnar, Rudolf Knieper, and Otto Steiger. *Menschenproduktion: Allgemeine Bevölkerungslehre der Neuzeit*. Berlin: Suhrkamp, 1979.

Jung, Carl Gustav. *Heros und Mutterarchetyp. Symbole der Wandlung.* Grundwerk Bd. 8, Olten-Freiburg: Walter-Verlag, [1946] 1987.

Kitchener, Caroline. "'I had to choose being a mother'. With no child care or summer camps, women are being edged out of the workforce." *The Lily*, May 5, 2020. www.thelily.com/i-had-to-choose-being-a-mother-with-no-child-care-or-summer-camps-women-are-being-edged-out-of-the-workforce/

Klein, Naomi. *The Shock Doctrine*. London: Penguin, 2007.

Klepp, Doris. *Lebenssituation und subjektive Lebensqualität von Frauen mit Kindern im Alter von 0–6 Jahren: Eine psychologische empirische Studie zur Mutterschaft*. Wien: Unveröffentlichte Diplomarbeit, 2003.

Kreisky, Eva. "Das ewig Männerbündische? Zur Standardform von Staat und Politik." In *Wozu Politikwissenschaft? Über das Neue in der Politik*, edited by Claus Leggewie, 101–208. Darmstadt: Wissenschaftliche Buchgesellschaft, 1994.

Lerner, Gerda. *The Creation of Patriarchy*. Oxford: Oxford University Press, 1988.

Lewin, Tamar. "Coming to US for Baby, and Womb to Carry It." *New York Times*, July 6, 2014: 1/12/13.

Moeller-Gambaroff, Marina. "Im Strudel der Regression." *Kursbuch* 61 (1980).

Mukhim, Patricia. "Khasi Matrilineal Society: Challenges in the Twenty-first Century." In *Societies in Peace: Matriarchies Past, Present, Future*, edited by Heide Göttner-Abendroth, 193–204. Toronto: Inanna Publications, 2009.

Plato. The *Republic*. London: Penguin, 2007.

Preve, Margit. *Amazonen. Ein Beitrag zur vergleichenden 'Mythen'-Forschung*. Innsbruck: Diplomarbeit, 1993.

Projektgruppe "Zivilisationspolitik." *Aufbruch aus dem Patriarchat—Wege in eine neue Zivilisation?* Frankfurt am Main et al.: Peter Lang, 2009.

Ranke-Graves, Robert von. *The Greek Myth*s. London: Penguin, 1992.

Reeves Sunday, Peggy. "Matriarchal Values and World Peace: The Case of the Minangkabau." In *Societies of Peace: Matriarchies Past, Present, and Future*, edited by Heide Göttner-Abendroth, 217–22. Toronto: Inanna Publications, 2009.

Rich, Adrienne. *Of Woman Born: Motherhood as Experience and Institution*. New York: Norton, 1976.

Rille-Pfeiffer, Christiane, and Olaf Kapella, eds. *Kinderbetreuungsgeld: Evaluierung einer familienpolitischen Maßnahme*. Innsbruck-Wien-Bozen: StudienVerlag, 2007.

Rousseau, Jean-Jacques. *Emile, or On Education.* New York: Basic Books, 1979.

Sandberg, Sheryl. *Lean In.* New York: Knopf Doubleday Publishing Group, 2013.

Sauer, Birgit, Elke Biester, and Barbara Holland-Cunz, eds. *Demokratie oder Androkratie? Theorie und Praxis demokratischer Herrschaft in der feministischen Debatte.* Frankfurt am Main-New York: Campus Verlag, 1994.

Statistics Austria (STATA), June 28, 2021. www.statistik.at/web_de/statistiken/menschen_und_gesellschaft/soziales/gender-statistik/index.html

Stromberg, Lisen. "The Not-So-New Mother: Finding Balance." *New York Times,* July 6, 2014: 7.

Tazi-Preve, Mariam Irene. *Der Mord an der Mutter. Das gewaltsame Brechen der Macht der Mutter als konstitutives Merkmal des Patriarchats.* Diplomarbeit Universität Innsbruck, 1992.

Tazi-Preve, Mariam Irene. "Presentation of Research Projects in the Fields of 'Gender, Family and Work'," in *Workshop 1: Gender Relations, Family and Work,* edited by Network for Integrated European Population Studies (NIEPS), 189–97. Zahradky, Czechia: Solicited Papers and Country Reports, 2000.

Tazi-Preve, Mariam Irene. "Die Vereinbarkeitslüge: Von der Unvereinbarkeit der Ansprüche von Staat, Familie und Arbeitswelt aus system- und geschlechtskritischer Sicht." In *Familienpolitik–Nationale und internationale Perspektiven,* edited by Mariam Irene Tazi-Preve, 57–84. Opladen: Verlag Barbara Budrich, 2009.

Tazi-Preve, Mariam Irene. *Motherhood in Patriarchy: Animosity toward Mothers in Politics and Feminist Theory—Proposals for Change.* Opladen-Farmington Hills: Barbara Budrich Verlag, 2013.

Tazi-Preve, Mariam Irene. *Das Versagen der Kleinfamilie: Kapitalismus, Liebe und der Staat.* Opladen-Farmington Hills: Barbara Budrich Verlag, 2018.

Walby, Sylvia. *Theorizing Patriarchy.* Oxford: Basil Blackwell, 1990.

Werlhof, Claudia. "Capitalist Patriarchy and the Negation of Matriarchy: The Struggle for a 'Deep' Alternative." In *Women and the Gift Economy: A Radically Different Worldview Is Possible,* edited by Genevieve Vaughan, 139–53. Toronto: Inanna Publications, 2009.

Werlhof, Claudia. "Ausflug in die Kritische Patriarchatstheorie: Die moderne Zivilisation und ihre fünf Basisverhaltnisse–aus der Perspektive der Alchemiethese." *Bumerang; Zeitschrift für Patriarchatskritik* (2015): 9–52. wwwfipaz.at/bumerang/

Werlhof, Claudia, Maria Mies, and Veronika Bennholdt-Thomsen. *Frauen, die letzte Kolonie,* Reinbek bei Hamburg: Rowohlt, 1983.

Wörer, Simone. "Gaben-Los? Grundrisse einer patriarchatskritischen Theorie der Gabe." *Kann es eine "neue Erde" geben? Zur "Kritischen Patriarchatstheorie" und der Praxis einer postpatriarchalen Zivilisation*, edited by Projektgruppe "Zivilisationspolitik," 179–201. Frankfurt am Main et al.: Peter Lang, 2011.

Zucco, Aline, and Yvonne Lott. *Stand der Gleichstellung: Ein Jahr mit Corona*, report no. 64 (Düsseldorf: Wirtschafts- und Sozialwissenschaftliches Institut, March 2021).

Endnotes

1 Sheryl Sandberg, *Lean In* (New York: Knopf Doubleday Publishing Group, 2013).

2 Lisen Stromberg, "The Not-So-New Mother: Finding Balance," *New York Times*, July 6, 2014: 7.

3 Mariam Irene Tazi-Preve, *Der Mord an der Mutter: Das gewaltsame Brechen der Macht der Mutter als konstitutives Merkmal des Patriarchats* (Diplomarbeit Universität Innsbruck, 1992); "Presentation of Research Projects in the Fields of 'Gender, Family and Work'," in *Workshop 1. Gender Relations, Family and Work*, ed. Network for Integrated European Population Studies (NIEPS), 189–97 (Zahradky, Czechia: Solicited Papers and Country Reports, 2000); "Die Vereinbarkeitslüge: Von der Unvereinbarkeit der Ansprüche von Staat, Familie und Arbeitswelt aus system- und geschlechtskritischer Sicht," In *Familienpolitik–Nationale und internationale Perspektiven*, ed. Mariam Irene Tazi-Preve, 57–84 (Opladen: Verlag Barbara Budrich, 2009); *Motherhood in Patriarchy: Animosity toward Mothers in Politics and Feminist Theory— Proposals for Change* (Opladen-Farmington Hills: Barbara Budrich Verlag, 2013); *Das Versagen der Kleinfamilie: Kapitalismus, Liebe und der Staat* (Opladen-Farmington Hills: Barbara Budrich Verlag, 2018).

4 For example, Christiane Rille-Pfeiffer and Olaf Kapella, eds., *Kinderbetreuungsgeld: Evaluierung einer familienpolitischen Maßnahme* (Innsbruck-Wien-Bozen: StudienVerlag, 2007); and Doris Klepp, *Lebenssituation und subjektive Lebensqualität von Frauen mit Kindern im Alter von 0–6 Jahren: Eine psychologische empirische Studie zur Mutterschaft* (Wien: Unveröffentlichte Diplomarbeit, 2003).

5 In this school of thought, gender is seen as a socially constructed category.

6 New theories and concepts of patriarchy are being developed at the Institute for Political Science at the University of Innsbruck, primarily by Claudia Werlhof ["Capitalist Patriarchy and the Negation of Matriarchy: The Struggle for a 'Deep' Alternative," in *Women and the Gift Economy: A Radically Different Worldview Is Possible*, ed. Genevieve Vaughan, 139–53 (Toronto:

Inanna Publications, 2009), and "Ausflug in die Kritische Patriarchatstheorie: Die moderne Zivilisation und ihre fünf Basisverhaltnisse–aus der Perspektive der Alchemiethese," *Bumerang; Zeitschrift für Patriarchatskritik* (2015): 9–52, wwwfipaz.at/bumerang/, among others]; Renate Genth, *Über Maschinisierung und Mimesis. Erfindungsgeist und mimetische Begabung im Widerstreit und ihre Bedeutung für das Mensch-Maschine-Verhältnis*, Beiträge zur Dissidenz no. 10 (Frankfurt am Main et al.: Peter Lang, 2002); Simone Wörer, "Gaben-Los? Grundrisse einer patriarchatskritischen Theorie der Gabe," *Kann es eine "neue Erde" geben? Zur "Kritischen Patriarchatstheorie" und der Praxis einer postpatriarchalen Zivilisation*, ed. Projektgruppe "Zivilisationspolitik," 179–201 (Frankfurt am Main et al.: Peter Lang, 2011); Ursula Schreiber and Mathias Baumann of Projektgruppe "Zivilisationspolitik," 2009); and Tazi-Preve, *Der Mord an der Mutter* and *Motherhood in Patriarchy*, among other works.

7 Naomi Klein, *The Shock Doctrine* (London: Penguin, 2007).

8 See Sylvia Walby, *Theorizing Patriarchy* (Oxford: Basil Blackwell, 1990), and Gerda Lerner, *The Creation of Patriarchy* (Oxford: Oxford University Press, 1988).

9 See Eva Kreisky, "Das ewig Männerbündische? Zur Standardform von Staat und Politik," in *Wozu Politikwissenschaft? Über das Neue in der Politik*, ed. Claus Leggewie, 101–208 (Darmstadt: Wissenschaftliche Buchgesellschaft, 1994); and Birgit Sauer, Elke Biester, and Barbara Holland-Cunz, eds., *Demokratie oder Androkratie? Theorie und Praxis demokratischer Herrschaft in der feministischen Debatte* (Frankfurt am Main-New York: Campus Verlag, 1994).

10 Hengde Danshilacuo and He Mei, "Mosuo Family Structure," in *Societies in Peace: Matriarchies Past, Present, and Future*, ed. Heide Göttner-Abendroth, 248–55 (Toronto: Inanna Publications, 2009).

11 Peggy Reeves Sunday, "Matriarchal Values and World Peace: The Case of the Minangkabau," in *Societies of Peace: Matriarchies Past, Present and Future*, ed. Heide Göttner-Abendroth, 217–22 (Toronto: Inanna Publications, 2009).

12 Patricia Mukhim, "Khasi Matrilineal Society: Challenges in the Twenty-first Century," in *Societies in Peace: Matriarchies Past, Present, Future*, ed. Heide Göttner-Abendroth, 193–204 (Toronto: Inanna Publications, 2009).

13 Heide Göttner-Abendroth, *Matriarchal Societies: Indigenous Cultures across the Globe* (Frankfurt am Main et al.: Peter Lang, 2012).

14 Among other aspects, such as part-time work and lower starting salary.

15 Certain political campaigns aim to include fathers, which are "double-edged" from a feminist standpoint. Fathers should be encouraged to take paternal leave and to play an active role in raising children. However, a movement dedicated to fathers' rights continues to grow and has actively and successfully lobbied governments to implement joint custody of children even when the mother never

had a relationship with the child's father.

16 Work–life balance has been introduced as a strategy for businesses, generally understood as programs designed to facilitate employees' efforts to coordinate responsibilities of work and family. In Austria and Germany these types of businesses can be certified.

17 Included are financial benefits as well as programs promoted by the government. Concrete political measures pursued by Austrian family policies include direct and indirect financial transfers, such as parental leave and family allowances, tax deductions for child benefits, provision of childcare facilities, insurance coverage for dependents, and retirement benefits for childcare and retirement compensation for childcare. There are also labor laws such as a prohibition on firing women on maternity leave, reforming child-care subsidies, and increasing the number of child-care facilities.

18 Lieselotte Ahnert, *Wieviel Mutter braucht ein Kind? Bindung–Bildung–Betreuung: öffentlich und privat* (Heidelberg: Spektrum Akademischer Verlag, 2010).

19 Carl Gustav Jung, *Heros und Mutterarchetyp. Symbole der Wandlung*, Grundwerk Bd. 8 (Olten-Freiburg: Walter-Verlag, [1946] 1987).

20 Sigmund Freud, *Band 1: Elemente der Psychoanalyse*, Werkausgabe in zwei Bänden, ed. Anna Freud and Ilse Grubrich-Simitis (Frankfurt am Main: Fischer, 1978).

21 For instance, Marina Moeller-Gambaroff, "Im Strudel der Regression," *Kursbuch* 61 (1980).

22 Adrienne Rich, *Of Woman Born: Motherhood as Experience and Institution* (New York: Norton, 1976).

23 Declaration by the "Familiensynode" at the Conference of Bishops, November 2015, Rome, Italy.

24 Tazi-Preve, "Presentation of Research."

25 For instance, Aline Zucco and Yvonne Lott, *Stand der Gleichstellung. Ein Jahr mit Corona*, report no. 64 (Düsseldorf: Wirtschafts- und Sozialwissenschaftliches Institut, 2021).

26 Caroline Kitchener, "'I had to choose being a mother'. With no child care or summer camps, women are being edged out of the workforce," *The Lily*, May 5, 2020. www.thelily.com/i-had-to-choose-being-a-mother-with-no-child-care-or-summer-camps-women-are-being-edged-out-of-the-workforce/

27 In most countries of the world, surrogate motherhood is (still) defined as the exploitation of female reproductive capacity (e.g., Germany and Austria).

28 Such agencies bring together the fertility clinic, the lawyers, and finally the egg and surrogate donor.

29 Jessica Grose, "America's Mothers Are in Crisis: Is Anyone Listening to Them?" *The New York Times*, February 4, 2021. www.nytimes.com/2021/02/04/parenting/working-moms-mental-health-coronavirus.html

30 In *The Second Sex* (New York: Vintage, [1949] 1989), Simone de Beauvoir was already talking about the "mother trap" of the 1950s, meaning the complete exclusion of women from public life through motherhood.

31 Statistics Austria (STATA), June 28, 2021. www.statistik.at/web_de/statistiken/menschen_und_gesellschaft/soziales/gender-statistik/index.html

32 Claudia Werlhof, Maria Mies, and Veronika Bennholdt-Thomsen, *Frauen, die letzte Kolonie* (Reinbek bei Hamburg: Rowohlt, 1983).

33 Austrian universities were traditionally free of charge until the "Universities of Appied Sciences" were founded which are not only fee-paying colleges but also favour market-oriented programmes.

34 Margit Preve, *Amazonen: Ein Beitrag zur vergleichenden 'Mythen'-Forschung* (Innsbruck: Diplomarbeit, 1993).

35 Göttner-Abendroth, *Matriarchal Societies*.

36 Robert von Ranke-Graves, *The Greek Myths* (London: Penguin, 1992).

37 For example, Jean-Jacques Rousseau, *Emile, or On Education* (New York: Basic Books, [1762] 1979).

38 Gunnar Heinsohn, Rudolf Knieper, and Otto Steiger, *Menschenproduktion: Allgemeine Bevölkerungslehre der Neuzeit* (Berlin: Suhrkamp, 1979).

39 Jeannette Armstrong, "Indigenous Knowledge and Gift Giving: Living in Community," in *Women and the Gift Economy: A Radically Different Worldview Is Possible*, ed. Genevieve Vaughan, 41–49 (Toronto: Inanna Publications, 2007).

40 Tazi-Preve, *Das Versagen der Kleinfamilie*.

SAN JUAN BAUTISTA, CALIFORNIA: RECLAIMING "TRUTH IN HISTORY" THROUGH THE ARTS

JENNIFER COLBY

Women's engagement in community art processes can provide a space for reclaiming Indigenous knowledge and relationality with Mother Earth. Matrifocal and gender balanced, the symbols that emerge in community artmaking reveal relationship with the land, reciprocity with nature, and honoring elders and ancestors. Having a matrifocal orientation means resisting androcentric norms by putting women's perspectives in the center as a first step toward undermining patriarchy.[1] To undo layers of a patriarchal, heteronormative, settler colonial mindset, one requires a deep examination of "truth in history,"[2] the truths that do not appear in history books about Indigenous peoples and people of color surviving racist oppression. The erasure of this history can be countered with contemporary women boldly claiming community space to reframe the narrative.

In 2019 a collective of Indigenous, Latina, African American, and Anglo women used artmaking to bring to life Indigenous narratives in a California mission town. San Juan Bautista is the site of one of the 21 Franciscan missions, major tourist attractions on the California coast. The mission and city of San Juan Bautista privilege the colonial narrative in their interpretation of history. By painting 40-foot mandalas on the street, the collective, with sponsorship from the city, was able to reclaim colonized space and narrate an Earth-based vision of an ecofeminist past and future. This paper explores the mandala's context, artistic process, symbolism, and the deeper intent of reviving ceremony, from the perspective of members of the collective, including the author.

My personal connection to San Juan Bautista began in 1992 when I co-founded Galeria Tonantzin, a gallery of women's contemporary art. Named with the Nahuatl (Aztec) word for Our Lady of Guadalupe, for twenty-one years the gallery was a center for art exhibits and multicultural feminist spirituality discussions during yearly conferences. Co-conspiring with Latina artists, Chicana feminists, and Indigenous women, I became a supportive ally to people of color through the gallery, community activism, and my teaching critical race and cultural equity education theory at the local university. I was elected to the local school board, and served on the strategic planning committee for the city. This committee became the mechanism for bringing the mandalas as temporary community art to memorialize and activate an Indigenous narrative in San Juan Bautista.

San Juan Bautista is called "The City of History," a phrase that reflects pride in the mission and the historic district that have been preserved in part as they stood in 1869. Tourists learn from the mission and state park docent talks and through the downtown self-guided walking tour. An in-depth presentation of Indigenous history is lacking in these presentations. Local residents Mandisa Snodey, Kanyon Sayers Rood, and others joined in envisioning a "cultural walking tour" that could permanently share the Indigenous history left out of the local narratives. The mandala project served as a process to inspire that reality.

For thousands of years, the Amah Mutsun (Ohlone) peoples have continuously inhabited the central coast of California. Mutsun is the language spoken by the people of Popelouchum, the name for the area surrounding present-day San Juan Bautista. Today, the message of descendants is, "We are still here." Mutsun descendants are reclaiming their language and ceremonies and working to preserve sacred lands.[3] The official history of California often posits that California Indians were eradicated. The Gold Rush promoted a bounty for killing Indians, and many were slaughtered. The "truth in history" not told is that many California Indians went into hiding, mostly by identifying as Mexican, to save their lives. In recent years individuals are reclaiming their heritage and the truth in California Indian genealogy is revealing a strong presence.

The history of San Juan Bautista is narrated in parades and by tour guides as beginning with the founding of the mission by Father Lasuen in 1797, a few years after the death of Father Serra. The purpose of founding 21 missions in California was to transform the native peoples into Spanish citizens and Catholics. The Amah Mutsun (Ohlone) were conscripted into building the Santa Cruz and San Juan Bautista missions. Facing harsh treatment, many escaped and took refuge in a canyon to the south of Hollister, the site of present-day Indian Canyon.[4]

The Spanish settlement, followed by Mexican rule, disrupted the balance of nature in California. Cattle decimated the grasses and traditional food sources. Diseases spread among the Indigenous populations. By 1850 the population had plummeted, especially in the coastal areas near the missions. In San Juan Bautista, the influx of Anglo settlers included the Breen family of the Donner party fame. The city was incorporated in 1869, at the height of the Wild West stagecoach days. Because of many factors, the city never grew beyond the population of that period, and the main street is frozen in time, lined with historic buildings. Docents who tell the history of the Spanish and Anglo settlers often leave out the early Mexican settlers and the continuous presence of the Amah Mutsun.

The City of San Juan Bautista planned a year-long 150th-anniversary celebration for 2019 focused on the colonial settler narrative. The creation of four mandalas in San Juan Bautista during the sequential year arose from the desire to provide an alternative narrative of the erased Indigenous history and the need for private ceremony and public-community art. The intention of the mandala was to make a space for the community to share upon, a sacred ground for ceremony, music, and storytelling. Kanyon Sayers Rood and Mandisa Snodey first conceived of a cultural walking tour and the mandala project as an outgrowth of their Community and Culture group, which focused on processes of decolonization, "truth in history," and restoring cultural knowledge and ceremony. A collective of women (including myself) joined them and approached the city requesting support for a community art project that would pave the way for a permanent means of representing the Californian Indian narrative.

The artist River Sauvageau, originally from Quebec, Canada, and a friend of local Indigenous elders, was invited to mentor the community art project. A mandala (Sanskrit for circle) is an art-historical image used by various traditions to represent the universe, thereby creating a sense of connection with a greater whole. Mandalas in many cultures serve the purpose of centering an individual or community on a given narrative in order to encourage introspection and, ultimately, an awareness of one's place and purpose in the world.[5] The purpose of this art form is to engage

Fig. 14. Spring Mandala in front of Mission San Juan Bautista, photo by author, 2019.

in a meditative process of centering within the geometric forms within the circle of the mandala. Traditionally, mandalas, like the Tibetan sand paintings, are not long-lasting, though much effort goes into creating their beauty. The creation of mandalas has captured the imagination of many contemporary artists who create small mandalas as a daily practice. Larger-scale mandalas, often made of natural materials, relate to land art and earth work sensibilities and are also impermanent.

River Sauvageau developed a unique approach to mandala creation over 28 years in Ojai, California. In Southern California's Ojai Valley, River's mandalas began as guerrilla art projects painted on the street the night before Ojai Day. The mandalas were painted to honor the Chumash, Indigenous people of the valley, using imagery from the pictographs found in local caves. The mandalas were so well received that later they were sponsored by the city. After 3 years, the local Chumash elders asked the artists not to use the symbols from their pictographs for street art; those symbols were not meant to be walked upon. The artists shifted their approach while continuing to honor Indigeneity. The approach that River Sauvageau developed is inclusive of an Indigenous worldview without appropriating specific symbols of the cave art. The design for the mandala evolves with the local design team and, on the day of painting, continues to evolve with community input.

While painting the mandala with washable tempera paint on the street, everyone is equal, regardless of social or economic standing or age. As

River Sauvageau says, it is the great equalizer, as each person who participates must "get down to earth." The brilliant colors fill the circle and last for public viewing in the street until the next rain. With the imagery, balance in nature is honored. The collaborative process of the design and painting process taps into a collective knowledge of Earth-based practices, and matrifocal and Indigenous knowledge.

The collective of women who organized the mandalas included the leaders of the Culture and Community group, the advocates in the strategic planning committee who planned the closure of the street with the city, the design team, and women artists who came to collaborate and facilitate sections of the mandala in San Juan Bautista on painting day. Painting in the mandala was open to all ages, genders, and abilities. The leaders' intention was to link mandala making with ceremonies for the four seasons. The spring mandala was allied with the spring equinox and the theme was "planting seeds." The summer mandala was created at the summer solstice, the theme being "the flowering," and the autumn mandala was close to the fall equinox, with "the harvest" theme. The winter mandala was painted on canvas and completed by the winter solstice. To bring Indigenous sensibilities into the historical narrative, the seasons are followed and reflect the year's cycles. In River Sauvageau's words, "[T]his relates to all peoples, the Indigenous peoples and the various waves of settlers to San Juan Bautista. In this way, we are bringing focus on the Indigenous narrative, and we are inclusive; this is community. The mandala represents the circle of life and includes all life."[6]

For the spring mandala in front of the San Juan Bautista mission on 2nd Street, the design team—comprised of Mandisa Snodey, Ramona Hill of Credo Studio, River Sauvageau, and myself—sought to honor the ways Indigenous people identify with the land, the cycles of the moon, and the seasons. The overall design was a four-petaled flower with a gray-layered undulating border around the center, which represented the trunk of the pepper tree, considered by Mutsun elders to be the village center. At the very center of the spring mandala, we depicted four cotyledons, cracked-open seeds with their first sprouts, looking like a flower. Each petal was bisected by a leafy branch of the pepper tree, which hung down. Waterways and mountains were depicted in between the petals, with the skies above. The four petals were oriented in the four directions, with the north being the top and the moon represented in its phases.

Representing the original peoples of the land in the west of the mandala was the oak tree and acorns, the main source of nourishment for the local Mutsun. The corn in the east honored the Mexican people of the corn who later settled in the land (Nahua/Aztec). Next to the oak in the other half of the west petal was a field of spring flowers, while the other half of the east petal had colorful abstract figures with stars and meteors. Under the moon were depicted hummingbirds, symbols important to the Mutsun people, while the south petal represented the roots of the tree with animals that live in and on the ground.

Input on the mandala design included knowledge gained in conversations with Kanyon Sayers Rood of Indian Canyon about symbols—the oak tree, acorns, and hummingbirds of the Mutsun—of the local land's peoples. Activist Kanyon Sayers Rood, Mutsun and Chumash, offered land acknowledgments in the Ohlone territory. She participated in the days of mandala painting. Kanyon's mother, Anne Marie Sayers, has been the guardian of federally recognized Indian land at Indian Canyon, the place that historically California Indian peoples went to escape the mission system. Sayers has opened the land of Indian Canyon as a Living Indian Heritage Area, making it available to all Indigenous people in need of land for ceremony.

> Indian Canyon receives upward of 6,000 visitors a year from around the world, including Aborigines from Australia, Maori from New Zealand, and Indigenous peoples from South America and Alaska. Another couple thousand annual visitors are students of Indian history from local colleges and universities. And each year Indian Canyon holds major ceremonial events for local Native Americans, including the California Indian Bear Dance and a storytelling gathering.[7]

At Indian Canyon, the telling of stories and supporting of ceremony is crucial to re-claiming history, ceremony, and a complex Indigenous worldview.

Anne Marie Sayers and her daughter Kanyon exemplify the leadership of women in the Indigenous community. On the days of mandala painting, women and men elders of the community were recognized in ceremony. Descendants of the Amah Mustun tribe's "matriarch" were present. Ascencion Solorsano de Cervantes (1855–1930) became a repository for

Fig. 15. Painting the Weather and Pollinators. Photo by author, 2019.

tribal history, learning stories and passing on traditions and tribal lore to the next generation. Her leadership in the first three decades of the twentieth century coincided with a time when tribal members were finally able to practice their culture publicly. J.P. Harrington interviewed Ascension before her death, providing some of the documentation for the revival of the Mutsun language today. Since 1930 women and men have served as tribal leaders.[8]

Another local Indigenous perspective included in the 2019 street mandalas was the people of the corn (Mexico). Mexican peoples of mixed Indigenous, European, and African inheritance entered California with the De Anza expedition in 1775–1776. Their presence during the Spanish mission period influenced farming practices. By the Mexican period, large ranchos dominated the countryside. For many generations, Mexican families were established in California, and the Guadalupe de Hidalgo treaty established the border. With succeeding generations of migration, San Juan Bautista became a community comprised mainly of Chicano and Mexican American families. Many families identify with Indigenous Aztec and Mayan symbols, including corn, and participate in the local theatre company El Teatro Campesino, the farmworkers' theatre.[9]

In the stalks of growing corn painted in the spring mandala, the artist Patricia Rodriguez depicted Our Lady of Guadalupe, a potent symbol of Mexican identity. Guadalupe's function in women's art and the ways contemporary women artists reinterpret these mythologies, claim space, and understand issues of appropriation and the complex processes of decolonialization is a complex topic I explored in my dissertation.[10] The centrality of the Guadalupe image to the largely Mexican American population of San Juan Bautista is celebrated with her presence in the mandala. The symbols arising naturally from the artists and community members are offered in a public sacred space in the mandala painting to express ways of connecting to the earth and to the seasons of life.

Guadalupe represents the mother of all, the great cosmic mother—she is pregnant with the future and stands beyond time as the woman of revelations. She is also seen as submissive, like the biblical Mary who acquiesced to her role. This Marian aspect served the needs of Mexican machismo, and was challenged by Chicana feminists who found in her roots the Indigenous mother. Chicana artists have recalled pre-colonial Mexican goddesses and strong matrilineal lines of passing down spiritual practices from mothers and grandmothers. The Chicana's questioning of how the Guadalupe image was used to subdue women led to a re-imaging of the powerful sacred female from an Indigenous culture of reciprocity and balance of male and female. The Catholic overlay on the Indigenous Tonantzin, mother of all, left room for the Mexican people to sustain threads of their Indigenous spiritual practices within Catholicism.

The image of Guadalupe entered Alta California with the members of the De Anza expedition in 1776, along with Franciscan priests. Unlike the Indians of Central Mexico, who embraced Guadalupe in a syncretic religiosity, I believe the majority of the California Indians were not attracted to Guadalupe as an image of remembrance of the Earth mother. The Franciscans presented her as a version of the Immaculate Conception, along with other Marian images, including the Mother of Sorrows, one who may have gathered the grief of the Indigenous people. California Indian spirituality was/is not based as the Mexican Indigenous spirituality is/was on god/goddess imagery. The concept of Mother Earth is not anthropomorphic. Therefore, my speculation is that except for a few instances in Southern California, there are no documented connections made with a mother goddess figure.[11] Rather than continue native spirituality through syncretic practices within Catholicism, California Indians sought to escape the missions. Many were baptized, but few were confirmed. The California mission padres forbade syncretic practices of traditional ceremony and dance. In comparison, the Mexican Indigenous experience included a continuation of traditional ceremony, with Catholic overlays and mixing of races—"mestizos" were born of rape and conquest, the mixing of Spaniards and Mexican Indigenous peoples.

The spring mandala brought together the Indigenous Mutsun and Indigenous Mexican symbolism into a unified circle, planting the seed for common understanding and a retelling of "truth in history," a herstory if you will. Herstory, defined as "history considered or presented from a feminist viewpoint or with special attention to the experience of women,"[12] is a term used by many women artists. Chicana feminist theory, along with Black feminist theory, provides tools of analysis such as intersectionality to describe women of color in herstory.

Chicana artist Patricia Rodriquez was a member of the San Francisco-based Mujeres Muralistas, the women muralists of the 1970s, who although not always embraced by white feminist art historians, saw themselves as both telling the truths of Mexican culture and forging a feminist identity. Telling the herstory of her painting life, Patricia recalls working collectively with women to create public art. As a community-based artist, Patricia Rodriquez had the tools to lead a section of the spring mandala, and to incorporate the children and adults who participated in the painting. Her decision to include Guadalupe in the corn reflects her agency and understanding of her people.

The second mandala was created for the summer solstice. The design process took place with a group of children aged eight to thirteen and youth leaders at Credo Studio summer camp, led by Ramona Hill, a woman of color and performing artist. The summer mandala was placed in front of the city library. It became the starting point for the ceremonial run from the city to Indian Canyon during storytelling week. In a reflective discussion a year after the mandala painting, the design team probed the imagery that evolved for this mandala. River Sauvageau remarked, "When you do the work with a lot of spirit and a lot of intention, there are other associations that are being made that you don't really see until the work is complete. So for me, what was really, really meaningful, was how [the mandala] was truly a piece that we all worked on together—we had multiple generations."[13]

The contribution by a 74-year-old woman who recalled the story of the mountain lion footprint in the adobe floor (inside the mission) transformed the mandala section depicting the mission bell tower into a work where nature and culture merged with recognition of the animal who left paw prints on the mission's floor. In another section, River Sauvageau noted synchronicity in the design: "We have the day and nighttime pollinators, which is a very permaculture-oriented view of things. This was pretty well designed, but there was a lot of room for extemporaneous additions, which makes it more open and available to whoever shows up. Which is really part of the magic."[14] We also reflected on the mandala section with the scene of the Pajaro River with the hawk flying over the Gavilan range. The iconography connects to previous work on the watershed restoration. After a salmon was painted, a little boy arrived and painted salmon egg nests in the river.

The themes of the summer mandala included seeking shade in the Mutsun hut (*ruk*) under the redwoods, a day at the beach, the weather cycles, and the chickens. The imagery of the sun rays tied the mandala sections together, and a ring of black-and-white basketry held the circle. The themes explored by the mandala artists, and planned by the youth of San Juan Bautista embrace ecofeminist and multigenerational sensibilities. Ecofeminist artists have been active since the early 1970s. Here Gloria Feman Orenstein describes the new millennial ecofeminist artists as:

> ...being concerned with listening to and understanding the
> language of nature, and in engaging in a healing relation-
> ship and dialogue with nature, speaking to nature in its
> own language—be that the language of the water, the soil,
> the air, the trees, the waste recycling processes, or any
> other process of life maintenance and ecological balance.

Fig. 16. Autumn Mandala with Hummingbird, photo by author, 2019.

> In what ways can the artist collaborate with Gaia to create
> a visual experience that enhances the Earth's regeneration
> that purifies the pollution of a given site, or that increases
> our human understanding of our positionality within the
> Earth's body, making us conscious that we are the Earth,
> and that anything we do to Gaia, we do to ourselves?[15]

Increasing human understanding of our positionality within the Earth's body is achieved through the mandala project and discussions and interactions surrounding the creation process (with non-toxic, non-permanent paint). Knowledge of ecology arises from the youth and adults listening to nature and Indigenous ways of thinking. It is ecological and feminist, drawing from herstory and the lineage of wisdom passed down from women elders. The act of painting within a circle on the Earth creates a dialog with nature and a space for reclaiming knowledge of Earth ways. Kanyon Sayers Rood shared traditional knowledge of plants with the youth at the camp. She has confronted colonial concepts that drive organizations involved with ecological restoration, challenging them to learn from Indigenous knowledge, including controlled burning. The foundation created by the local

Amah Mutsun tribe is focused on recovery of native-informed ecological knowledge in partnership with local universities and state and national parks in their homeland.

> The Amah Mutsun Land Trust (AMLT) returns our tribe to our ancestral lands and restores our role as environmental stewards. Due to our difficult history and generations of physical, mental, and political abuses, our land steward-ship practices were disrupted, and much of our culture was lost. AMLT serves not only in the re-learning of our history and restoration of Indigenous management practices, it also serves as a vehicle for healing. By restoring our traditional ecological knowledge and revitalizing our relationship to Mother Earth, we also restore balance and harmony to the lands of our ancestors.[16]

The third mandala represented the autumn harvest. All themes were about human contributions to life in San Juan Bautista: Agriculture, weaving, fishing, the bakery, and the blacksmith, all elements of human culture based in nature. River Sauvageau noted, "[I]n this mandala we have in the outer circle the mature manifestation and in the inner circle, we have the elements. So we have a tree and the acorns,"[17] the weaver and the sheep, the bakery and the wheat, the blacksmith and the fire, all gathered in a symbolic basket woven around the circle.

The design team for this project included students from California State University, Monterey Bay (CSUMB) who attended my class, "Arts in the School and Community," for undergraduate, pre-service teachers. I often engage CSUMB students in community art projects. We met with River over Zoom to explore the themes for the mandala. I assigned the following research projects to teams of students: Mutsun history, San Juan Bautista attractions, and local ecology. We used community mapping techniques to understand San Juan Bautista's assets. I also set up an exchange of art and letters between elementary-school children and the college students. I offered a series of art experiences at San Juan School that produced images that the college students could focus on to understand what was important to the children of San Juan Bautista.

The morning ceremony for the autumn mandala took place in the Mutsun Native Garden, restored by the Amah Mutsun Land Trust, a place where the representation of Mutsun life is found in San Juan Bautista.[18] On that day the honoring of elders and ancestors contrasted with dedication of the monument for the 150th anniversary created by a colonial settler, white men's fraternal order, whose members brought a disturbing display into the historical parade. A parade banner for the Mustun proclaiming "We are Still Here" and the mandala were the only signs of an alternative non-colonial history during the celebration.

The fourth mandala was a very different project. Rather than face the winter weather to paint outdoors on the street, we planned to paint inside on a canvas that would be revealed during a community event on the morning of the winter solstice. For almost 20 years, Indigenous communities have been gathering in front of the mission to celebrate the winter solstice. Elder Laynee Reyna, the mission church priest and local archaeologist, Ruben Mendoza, made the public aware of the solar alignment each year on the morning of the winter solstice.[19] Recently, hundreds of people come each year to watch the sunlight move up the adobe stones to then strike the altar. The revealing of the winter mandala on December 21, 2019 was the culmination of our year of painting mandalas.

The winter mandala, painted with acrylic on canvas by many collaborators, consisted of four sections and recaptured themes of the first three mandalas. Winter was represented by the storyteller, an image that showed up in the autumn mandala. Ramona Hill observed that the four sections in the winter mandala could also represent progressions in human history or personal history—childhood, youth, work, and storytelling in old age.[20] In the winter or old-age section of the mandala, the storyteller had books flowing out of her lap that transformed into representations of theatre, the storytelling of El Teatro Campesino. The white drama masks and symbols depicted ancestral bones in her hair. The storyteller, grandmother, represents the matrifocal reciprocity of the generations in San Juan Bautista.

Community engagement in mandala painting throughout 2019 was the public face of the deeper work of restoring ceremony and Indigenous protocols and recognizing the elders and histories of the community. During each of the mandala painting days, a private ceremony occurred. Mandisa Snodey recalled the importance of that process as follows:

Fig. 17. Reveal of Winter Solstice Mandala, photo by author, 2019.

The goal was to bring ceremony four times a year, with no "selling" of spirituality. We would offer a closed, private portion and an open portion through the mandala. For the closed portion we danced at sunrise and honored our elders.

The first step in decolonization is to reclaim personal narrative, tell your own story, and family stories. Claim it as part of San Juan's history. In facing the colonial system, if you grew up here you have to remove yourself to find true connections to ancestors, step out of the system. To re-integrate, to live here again, the youth had to address parents and fight who they think you are, now that you are outside the system. The parents are afraid to recognize what they have not confronted in their own youth. Youth[s] woke [sic] up, want to be recognized. Youth[s] carry forward,

> reclaim their humanity. It is a political fight; [it is] ... diffi-
> cult to reform the system—we need a new system.
>
> We offer the public part because we are humane. My
> practice is a natural unification of my three blood lines
> (Indigenous, African American, European).
>
> In [the historical] perspective, if we did ceremony openly in
> town it [was] ... called witchcraft, called evil by Christians.
> Our ancestors lost lives for praying the way we pray, so
> we do it veiled, private. It was considered illegal till 1978.
>
> We have to protect and support the private ceremony
> while re-establishing public ceremony, the sacred process.
> Because we are humane, we package it for the public (in
> the mandala).
>
> The descendants of a prominent Mutsun ancestor came in
> the spring and back in the fall. They saw the mandala on
> social media and came to celebrate, asking who is having
> ceremony on our land? The mandala created a beacon,
> opened a portal and the two men came walking in (feeling
> welcomed in the city where they had [previously] not felt
> safe to return).[21]

Mandisa Snodey's clarity grounded the mandala process. I asked her
how to respond to people of European descent who might be spiritual seekers with a desire to connect to the private ceremony. She responded that
it is not safe because "they may still project their colonial energy. Pray in
[your own] community, challenge your privilege."[22]

Kanyon Sayers Rood has also voiced a nuanced perspective on protecting the sacred ceremony.

> I recognize that all of our community has been deeply
> impacted by colonization. I have said and will continue
> to say that I truly believe that when non-Indigenous peo-
> ple gravitate to Indigenous spirituality and ceremony, that
> it is something deep within themselves, where their own
> ancestors are calling them home.

> The problem with that is: If [a] community is raised in a
> capitalistic, materialistic, disposable society, that is negli-
> gent of its sense of accountability to the sacred, then they
> do not engage in decision making that is of right relation-
> ship.... [Thus,] ... they capitalize, exploit, and consume ...
> in their effort to reconnect.[23]

The parallel processes of private ceremony and public creation of the mandala invited everyone to participate, to honor the spirituality and earth-based symbols alive in the community through artmaking, while protecting the private ceremony and supporting youth and elders with loving energy. The complexities of collaboration required attention to issues of appropriation. I believe that the mandala process and resulting imagery in San Juan Bautista is an example of an ecofeminist, matrifocal, and decolonizing art form that respectfully brought Indigenous knowledge into the public sphere with the energies of the concurrent ceremonies. Reclaiming connections with nature and images of Mother Earth, Guadalupe, and the storyteller through a collaborative process that engaged community members offered an alternative narrative for San Juan Bautista.

Although the year of mandala painting provided an intervention, the official history continues to be told from the colonized perspective in the "City of History." We have a long way to go to transform the narrative, and in that process, the voices of Indigenous women and women of color need to be recognized. I am grateful for the courage of multicultural voices, Indigenous women, bold elders, and youth who are ready for "truth in history," a herstory reclaiming narratives and reclaiming colonized spaces with the visual arts process of mandala creation.

References

Amah Mutsun Land Trust. "Gardens." https://www.amahmutsunlandtrust.org/the-mutsun-gardens. Date of access March 21, 2021.

Amah Mustun Tribal Band. "History Section." http://amahmutsun.org/history. Date of access March 21, 2021.

Buchalter, Susan. *Mandala Symbolism and Techniques: Innovative Approaches for Professionals*. Jessica Kingsley Publishers, 2012.

Clough, Charles W. *San Juan Bautista: The Town, the Mission & the Park*. Quill

Driver Books, 1996.

Colby, Jennifer. "Sacred Female Images and Identity at the Crossroads: Guadalupe/Tonantzin." In *Working Papers*. Monterey, CA: Center for Conflict Studies, Middlebury Institute of International Studies, 2015.

Colby, Jennifer. "Transforming Tonantzin/Guadalupe: Cultural and Spiritual Identity Politics in Latina and Euro-American Women's Art in San Juan Bautista, California." Ph.D. diss. California Institute of Integral Studies, 2001.

Colby, Jennifer. "Transforming Tonantzin/Guadalupe: Women's Art and Dialogue in Central California." *Femspec* 19, no. 1 (2019).

Cordero, Jonathan. "Concluding Thoughts: On Decolonizing the Study of Mission Art." *Latin American and Latinx Visual Culture* 2, no. 3 (2020): 109–11.

El Teatro Campesino. Luis Valdez, director. San Juan Bautista, CA. https://elteatrocampesino.com Date of access March 21, 2021.

Faia, Michele. *Art in My Heart: The Power of Watercolor Mandala Making.* 2015. https://www.michelefaia.com/books/

Hannibal, Mary Ellen. "Rekindling the Old Ways, the Amah Mutsun and Recovery of Traditional Ecological Knowledge." *Bay Nature* (2016): 29–35.

Hart, E. Richard. "Federal Recognition of Native American Tribes: The Case of California's Amah Mutsun." *Western Legal History* 16 (2003).

Lopez, Valentin. "The Amah Mutsun Tribal Band: Reflections on Collaborative Archaeology." *California Archaeology* 5, no. 2 (2013): 221–23.

Mark, Joshua J. Ancient Mandalas. *World History Encyclopedia*. Retrieved from https://www.ancient.eu/mandala/ Date of access March 21, 2021.

Mendoza, Rubén. *Solstice Chronicles*. http://solsticechronicles.org/#!/ Date of access March 21, 2021.

Orenstein, Gloria Feman. "The Greening of Gaia: Ecofeminist Artists Revisit the Garden." *Ethics and the Environment* 8, no. 1 (2003): 103–11.

Public Sphere Project. "Definition of Matrifocal Orientation." https://www.public-sphereproject.org/content/matrifocal-orientation Date of access March 21, 2021.

Rizzo, Martin. "If They Do Not Fulfill What They Have Promised, I Will Accuse Them": Locating Indigenous Women and Their Influence in the California Missions. *Western Historical Quarterly* 51, no. 3 (2020): 291–313.

Rodriguez, Carolyn Terese. "(Re)Writing California Native American Representations: Amah Mutsun Sovereignty and Educational Experiences of Tribal Elders." Master's thesis, University of California, Los Angeles, 2020.

Tucci, Giuseppe. *The Theory and Practice of the Mandala*. Courier Corporation, 2001.

Warner, Natasha, Quirina Luna, and Lynnika Butler. "Ethics and Revitalization of Dormant Languages: The Mutsun Language." *Language Documentation & Conservation* 1, no. 1 (2007): 58–76.

Endnotes

1 Public Sphere Project definition of matrifocal orientation, https://www.public-sphereproject.org/content/matrifocal-orientation

2 Term used by Kanyon Sayers Rood.

3 See history section in Amah Mustun website, http://amahmutsun.org/history

4 For information on Indian Canyon, Hollister, CA, see website: https://indian-canyonlife.org/

5 Joshua J. Mark, "Ancient Mandalas." *World History Encyclopedia*. Retrieved from https://www.ancient.eu/mandala/

6 Personal conversations with River Sauvageau in December 2019 and March 2021.

7 Indian Canyon website.

8 Amah Mutsun website.

9 El Teatro Campesino, Luis Valdez, director, San Juan Bautista, CA, https://elteatrocampesino.com/

10 Jennifer Colby, "Transforming Tonantzin/Guadalupe: Cultural and Spiritual Identity Politics in Latina and Euro-American Women's Art in San Juan Bautista, California" (PhD diss., California Institute of Integral Studies, 2001).

11 Jennifer Colby, "Sacred Female Images and Identity at the Crossroads: Guadalupe/Tonantzin," in *Working Papers* (Monterey, CA: Center for Conflict Studies, MIIS, 2015).

12 Definition of "herstory" from https://www.merriam-webster.com/dictionary/herstory

13 Personal conversations with River Sauvageau and Ramona Hill, March 2021.

14 Ibid.

15 Gloria Feman Orenstein, "The Greening of Gaia: Ecofeminist Artists Revisit the Garden," *Ethics and the Environment* 8, no. 1 (2003): 103–11.

16 Amah Mutsun Land Trust, https://www.amahmutsunlandtrust.org/

17 Personal conversations with Sauvageau and Hill.

18 Amah Mutsun, "Garden," https://www.amahmutsunlandtrust.org/the-mutsun-gardens

19 Ruben Mendoza, "Solstice Chronicles," http://solsticechronicles.org/#!/about

20 Personal conversations with Sauvageau and Hill.

21 Personal conversations with Mandisa Snodey, March 2021.

22 Ibid.

23 Kanyon Sayers Rood, Facebook, February 2021 (used with permission).

AFTERWORD

DR. VANDANA SHIVA

Mothering: Reimagining the Economy
as the Art of Giving, The Art of Living

We think of the economy as the market and money. Life disappears, nature's creativity and women's creativity disappear.

Economy, *Oikonomia,* according to Aristotle is the Art of Living, not money making. Money making is *Chrematistics.*

> The Art of Living is the Art of Giving.
> This is the economy of Mothering.

The essays in this volume *MATERNAL THINKING: Gifts, Mothers' Bodies, and Earth* edited by Sid, Mary Jo, Denise, and Simone are a gift by the contributors to the world to create another future, beyond the destructiveness and anti-life ideology of capitalist patriarchy, beyond the myopia of anthropocentrism that assumes humans are superior to other beings, and its associated human privilege, including the privileging of rich White men over all women, all people of colour, and non-industrial, non-capitalist, Indigenous cultures. The illusions of separation and superiority have created the multiple emergencies of our times. To respond to these emergencies we need another imagination, another thinking, that this volume offers us.

Together the contributors weave another human story—the story of mothering as the basis of care and basis of life and sustenance.

Mother Earth Mothers us, her soil, plants, animals, insects, microbes mother us by creating and regenerating the infrastructure of life. When we care for Mother Earth, we too become mothers.

Mothering is a gift economy based on love, care, compassions, oneness. The gift economy is the truly free economy.

As Genevieve Vaughan writes in her essay in this volume:

> The human free economy is aligned with the "economy" of Nature, which is also free. Only human property and the market are artificial and dysfunctional.

In Indigenous cultures, land is Mother Earth, Terra Madre, Pachamama, Vasundhara.

In colonial economics, Land is not Mother Earth, it is merely property to extract rents from.

Adam Smith is called the father of modern economics. His wealth of nations describes colonial commerce as the "economy."

Even though Adam Smith was writing during the violent appropriation of the lands of the peasantry through "Enclosures of the Commons," there is no mention of land as commons or the 3,380 bills that had to be passed by British parliament to rob the peasants of their land. Private property in land is made timeless in Smith's fictions of how wealth is created. Collection of rents from land is central to his extractives paradigm.

Smith defines the rich Indigenous cultures of both America and India into primitiveness, he defines the rich textile industry of India, which supplied the world a "trifling manufacture," which are destined to supply the small wants of a small number of people." [1] This when Indian textiles were being sold globally, and the East India Company was created to appropriate the wealth of India, her rich textiles and spices. Truly free and sovereign trade became forced trade. In typical doublespeak, forced colonial extractivism was renamed "free trade."

According to Genevieve Vaughan, "*Free* is at most a gimmick used to sell more commodities"

Through this fiction, Smith hides the colonial extraction and destruction of our textile industry, he presents the loss of skills and autonomy of artisanal production by the violence colonialism as "inferior skills" even though the muslins woven by Indian weavers continued to be of higher quality than industrial production. A false history thus lays the foundation of the dyseconomy of colonial commerce and capitalist patriarchy as the source of the wealth of Nations.

Smith's economic model based on extraction through colonial commerce has no place for nature, no mention of the wealth of the lands that were being colonized for their wealth is based on the false assumption of scarcity.

"The context of scarcity created by the market makes gift-giving difficult. Not only gender roles but the lack of access to independent sources of the gifts of Nature and the community penalize anyone who does not do monetized work and especially those who are responsible for the lives of their children. *It is isolation in the context of exchange that makes the free labor of motherers difficult and sometimes self-sacrificial, not the gift economy itself.*" *(Gen Vaughan this volume.)*

> Scarcity creates completion and conflict.
> Giving creates abundance and peace.

For Smith, competition is the 'desire that comes with us from the womb, and never leaves us, until we go into the grave.'

What comes from the womb is the gift of unconditional giving and care, of love and life as Genevieve Vaughan has written in "Women and the Gift Economy." [2]

As Ronnie Lessem and Alexander Schieffer indicate, "*if the fathers of capitalist theory had chosen a mother rather than a single bourgeois male as the smallest economic unit for their theoretical constructions, they would not have been able to formulate the axiom of the selfish nature of human beings in the way they did.*" [3]

> Life is a Gift from Mother Earth, from the air we breathe to the food
> we eat. Thanksgiving is our gratitude.

All Indigenous cultures thank the earth through their ceremonies. Native Americans celebrate Thanksgiving. In India our thanksgiving and harvest festivals are as diverse as our cultural diversity. Makar Sankranti, Baisakhi, Nuakha, Nabanna, Gudi Padwa, Onam, Pongal Vishu, Bhogali Bihu are harvest festivals celebrated across India.

> Living Economies nourish life through giving.
> Living economies are gift economies based on the ethics of St. Francis
> that "it is in giving that we receive."
> Giving is based on the "law of return," of recycling.
> The Law of Return is the law of gratitude.

As Genevieve Vaughan writes in "Women and the Gift Economy"

> It is also important to recreate the connections which have
> been severed, between the gift economy, women and the
> economies of Indigenous peoples, and to bring forward the
> gift paradigm as an approach, which can help to liberate us
> from the world view of the market that is destroying life
> on our beautiful planet.[4]

Living economies are circular economies that are aware of and maintain nature's cycles by giving back to the earth Life's flows of regeneration work in cycles, not in linear extraction. When the carbon cycle, nitrogen and mineral cycles, the water cycle, the energy cycle work in harmony, nature's economy is robust and resilient. When we give back to nature to heal her cycles while meeting our needs, we create abundance and true wealth.

In the circular economy we give back to society. Wealth is shared. Wealth circulates. In circular economies wealth does not concentrate in a few hands.

In real economies, plants grow, soil organisms grow, children grow in well being and happiness.

The circular economy replenishes nature and society. It creates enoughness and wellbeing for all. In the care of the Earth and society, diversity of meaningful and creative work is possible. It is based on nature's law of return. In nature, there is no waste, no pollution.

When economies are circular, every living being, every place, is the center of the economy, and nature and society evolve and emerge from multiple self organized systems, like the trillions of cells in our body.

Circular economies as living economies are by their very nature biodiverse, spanning from the intimate and local, to the global and planetary.

The earth gives us food. When we give back part of her organic gifts to the soil, we act according to the law of return and create a circular economy of the nutrition cycle, we sustain the food web which is the web of life. When we give organic matter back to nature, as food for her soil organisms, she continues to give us food. The work in giving back is our work, our gratitude, our oneness. Giving us food is nature's gift through the working of her complex living systems—through her soil food web, her biodiversity, her water, the sun, the air.

The Earth gives us seeds. Our ancestors have CoCreated with her to multiply her diversity. When we save seeds, and sow a seed as a gift to the Earth, she reproduces and multiples the seed manifold. When we share seeds in the commons, seed sovereignty grows, food sovereignty grows.

The earth gives us water. When we act to conserve water, we are engaging in the oikonomia of giving and create the circular economy of the hydrological cycle, the water cycle. When we share water in the commons, we are creating economies of giving and sharing. The earth gives us seeds. When we save and share seeds, we create timeless economies of the continuity of life. We are participating in the cycle of life.

All ecological crises are the rupture of nature's cycles—of nutrition, of water, of life—and the transgression of what have been called planetary boundaries.

In the circular economy we give back to society. Wealth is shared. Wealth circulates. In circular economies wealth does not concentrate in a few hands. Wealth is not extracted, creating the polarization of the 1% and 99%.

In circular economies wealth is not extracted from nature and society in linear exploitation, allowing a handful of billionaires to become trillionaires and the new Landlords, Seed Lords, Food Lords, Life Lords. Extractive economies are extinction economies.

Circular economies replenish nature and society by giving back. They create meaning, dignity and wellbeing for all. In the care of the Earth and society, diversity of meaningful and creative work is possible. It is based on nature's law of return. In nature, there is no waste, no pollution, no scarcity, no extraction. Nature evolves through cycles of giving. This is the economy of permanence.

Giving creates economies of abundance. Taking without giving back is a recipe for scarcity, hunger, poverty, disease, expendability, extinction.

Scarcity is the consequence of violating the law of the commons and monopolising common goods & resources for greed through enclosures and privatisation. Scarcity is created when the law of return, of recycling, of giving, of participating in the cycle of mutual dependence is violated. Scarcity is created by pollution and the heavy and clumsy processes of attempting to substitute and displace nature's ecological cycles, systems, and technologies. Rivers, oceans, the poor drowning in plastic waste and pesticides is how the greed economy is an economy of scarcity creation.

Earth Care and giving to the earth creates abundance through Regeneration and maintenance of nature's ecological cycles of nutrients and water, which are nature's circular economies on which all life depends.

And they too give to us. What we need is received as a gift. Such gift economies and economies of care are the basis of nature's economy. They are the basis of all Indigenous economies. And they are the basis of new economies of care and solidarity that are emerging everywhere.

Extractivism has made us imagine that making profits is the economy. But it is the diseconomy of greed, which creates scarcity.

Gift economies create abundance. When we give back seed to the earth, she gives us multifold more. When we save seeds and share seeds we have abundance of seeds. When corporations monopolize seeds through patents and intellectual property rights, they create scarcity and seed famines. When they use new technologies to rob seed of its renewability and paper of regeneration, they create seed scarcity and poverty for farmers who are forced to buy seed every year.

When we give back organic matter to the soil as food for soil organisms, they allow plants to photosynthesize, more produce more food, more nutrition in the food. Returning organic matter to the soil is our gratitude to the earth, our giving back. And the earth gives in abundance. Food production can increase 500% by giving to the earth. Conserving biodiversity with love and care, we can grow enough nutrition for two times our population.

If we give back water to the soil, we have more water. If we have air to breathe, water to drink, food to eat, it's all a result of the gift economy. We know this but science is having to recognize it. All ecological relationships are about gifts. And giving creates a balance. It is not an accident that Indigenous cultures had abundance and were the original affluent societies. Colonized, industrialized, globalized economies have created scarcity misery and poverty, including in the richest land. Look at the food deserts in America, the land with the richest agribusiness corporations. The billionaires are talking about 99% people being useless in the future. This creates a sense of inevitability and hopelessness. But humanity can choose to create societies based on the gift economy. My reading is, when 99% of humanity is being told you're useless, disposable, dispensable people, the gift economy is where we create emerging economies for the wellbeing of all, especially those being told you do not have a right to live on this earth. Through giving as the Art of Living we can create systems which have a place for the last person, the last child, the tiniest of microbes. The gift economy is the answer to the extinction crisis and the expendability world view which assumes that 70-80% of the species can be pushed to extinction, and 99% of humanity can be rendered dispensable.

In my lifetime I have seen water scarcity being created by mining and pollution as in the case of the Coca Cola plant in Plachimada, Kerala. Hunger and malnutrition have been created by imposing food and agriculture systems for extracting superprofits, instead of taking care of the Earth and people.

Chasing the pseudo efficiency of the fossil age in which "More is Less" we were forced to replace the recycling of organic matter for soil fertility with artificial fertilizers which destroyed biodiversity, exhausted the soil and water, desertified the land, created dead zones in the ocean and contributed to Green House Gases and Climate Change, created hunger and poverty.

Industrialism, extractivism, and monocultures hide the true costs of industrial production systems that the earth and society are left to bear.

The heavy Resource and Energy footprint which has pushed ecosystems and communities to collapse is made invisible, the destruction of soil, water, biodiversity are left as externalities whose costs are born by other species and the poor. Pseudo efficiency creates scarcity The scarcity created by extracting more than ecological limits of nature allow is at the root of the ecological crises. Extractivism that robs people of resources and livelihoods, creates scarcity in society. It is at the root of the hunger, poverty, and dispossession crises.

Extractivism, which grew with colonialism and the fossil fuel age, has disrupted nature's ecological cycles, contributing to the ecological emergency, the crisis of desertification and the water crisis, as well as the crisis of hunger and poverty. Extractive economies assume and create scarcity. Greed created scarcity in nature is the ecological emergency. Taking the share of others is the social scarcity of poverty, hunger, the denial of the right to breathe, the right to water, the right to food, and the right to health.

As Genevieve Vaughan writes in this volume:

> "By framing mothering as economic, a mode of dis-
> tribution in contrast to market exchange, we can
> understand its commonality with the gift economies
> of Indigenous peoples."

To be truly green, not just a "greenwashed" greed economy of the market, economics needs to return to their roots in Mothering, which is the art of giving, the art of living.

Mothering shows us the way home to *oikos,* to *Gaia, to* Mother Earth.

References

Lessem, Ronnie and Alexander Schieffer, *Integral Economies*, Farnham, UK. Ashgate/Gower, 2010

Rasmussen, D. 2006, "Does 'Bettering Our Condition' Really Make Us Better Off?" Adam Smith on Progress and Happiness. American Political Science Review. 100(3): 309-318.

Smith, Adam. *An Inquiry into the Nature and Causes of the Wealth of Nations.* 6th edition. London. G.Bell and sons. 1887.

Genevieve Vaughan ed, *Women and the Gift Economy: A Radically Different World View is Possible*, Toronto: Inanna Publications, 2007.

Endnotes

1 Adam Smith, *An Inquiry into the Nature and Causes of the Wealth of Nations,* 6th edition. (London: G. Bell and sons, 1887). 110.

2 Genevieve Vaughan, ed, *Women and the Gift Economy: A Radically Different World View is Possible* (Toronto: Inanna Publications, 2007), 1

3 Ronnie Lessem and Alexander Schieffer, *Integral Economies* (Farnham, U. U.K: Ashgate/Gower, 2010).

4 Vaughan, ed., *Women and the Gift Economy: A Radically Different World View is Possible.*

ACKNOWLEDGMENTS

This volume would not have been born without the assistance of many people. We are thankful for the careful editing (and re-editing) of Barbara Kohl, and the cover-to-cover book design of Rebekkah Dreskin. We are grateful to Katie Hoffner and Bob Ruyle for permission to feature Lydia Ruyle's "Bee Goddess of Rhodes" banner for cover art. And we want to thank Anne Key for her wisdom and support in the production of this series.

We recognize that scholarship can include relevant imagery to help open all channels for learning. For this volume we want to thank Christina Biaggi for sharing the image of her sculpture "Raging Medusa," Raine Dawn Valentine for permission to include her work "Raining in the Dawn Woman of the Turtle Mountain Chippewa," Laura Shannon for her photos of Gournia, and the authors whose illustrations or photos accompanied their words. We also want to thank Walter Holt for assistance to reformat illustrations.

In order to realize the vision of this volume, we expanded our process to interview some contributors and scholars. In particular we want to thank Beverly Little Thunder for her supporting interview, Michelle Boyle for assistance with author interviews, and Lauren Mitten for interview transcription.

We are also grateful to all the women whose work appears here, for their noteworthy contributions that explore maternal thinking, sacred story, and reciprocity with nature.

CONTRIBUTOR BIOGRAPHICAL NOTES

Angela Avedano is a contemporary mythologist. Dr. Angelina Avedano explores grief, transformation, and the creative process. Cycles of life, death, and rebirth inform her approach to creativity, personal growth, and metamorphosis. Her recent book, *Living Grief: A Mother/s Odyssey of Surrender, Renewal, and Mad Joy* describes grief as a catalyst for transformation. Angelina launched Cyc*ADA* Personal Metamorphosis to help individuals realign with their transformative potential and offer support as they move through seasons of life. She is also a full-time Assistant Professor at Massasoit Community College in Massachusetts, teaching mythology, literature, and writing. Angelina earned a Master of Theological Studies from Harvard Divinity School, a Master of Arts in English from Boston College, and a PhD in Mythological Studies with emphasis in depth psychology from Pacifica Graduate Institute. Her articles, poems, and short stories appear in several publications. You may contact Angelina at dr.aavedano@gmail.com.

Carol P. Christ held a PhD from Yale and was author or co-author of eight ground-breaking books on women and religion, including *Goddess and God in the World, Rebirth of the Goddess, She Who Changes, Laughter of Aphrodite, Odyssey with the Goddess* (republished as *A Serpentine Path*), *Diving Deep and Surfacing, Weaving the Visions and Womanspirit Rising*. A leading feminist theologian and historian of religion, she was named one of the most influential voices in the Goddess movement. Carol led the Goddess Pilgrimage to Crete for over 20 years, was an expert on the archaeology, culture, and religion of ancient Crete, and a member of the Gournia archaeological study team. She received two National Endowment for the Humanities Fellowships, and taught at Columbia University, San Jose State, Pomona College, Harvard Divinity School, Claremont Graduate

School, and California Institute of Integral Studies. Carol passed away in Crete in July, 2021. Her work continues through her non-profit foundation, the Ariadne Institute for the Study of Myth and Ritual and the Goddess Pilgrimage to Crete (www.goddessariadne.org).

Dr. Jennifer Colby is a visual artist, community activist, curator, scholar, and faculty in the Liberal Studies Department, California State University, Monterey Bay. Author of *Arts in the School and Community: Visual Art, Music, Dance, and Drama* (2021) Kendall Hunt Publishing, she received her PhD in Humanities and Women's Spirituality from the California Institute of Integral Studies, San Francisco, a Masters in Studio Art from Fresno State University, and a Masters of Theology, Religion and the Arts from the Graduate Theological Union in Berkeley, CA. In 1992 she co-founded a women's art gallery, Galeria Tonantzin, in San Juan Bautista, CA and began an artistic and scholarly journey with the image of Guadalupe. Dr. Colby's creates social justice visual art installations to tell women's stories. She produced two California Council for the Humanities community watershed art projects and was named 2007 Champion of the Arts – Educator for Monterey County.

Ceardai Demelza is an Australian visual artist. In 2019 she gained a BFA with Honours from the Victorian College of the Arts. She creates new myths using an 'ecofeminist' approach and works across sculpture, photography and video to tell stories of the divine feminine and her healing powers. She has exhibited in numerous group shows including at the Ian Potter Museum of Art. Website: www.ceardaidemelza.com.au Email: ceardaidemelza@gmail.com Instagram: @cearda

Dilşa Deniz is a socio-cultural Kurdish anthropologist and presently is visiting scholar at Harvard University Divinity School. She was dismissed from her position in Turkey, in February 2016 after signing a peace petition. She worked extensively as an activist and organizer in women movement in Turkey. She holds PhD in Social Anthropology and published articles, book chapters as well as her monograph. Her research focuses on gender, the cultural, political, religious practices in relation to Kurdish Alevis, Alevi geography, myths of Alevism in Kurdish communities, particularly in the city of Dersim, an ancient urban center for Kurdish Alevism in Anatolia. She studies Alevism as an old independent Iranian (land of

Arian) religion and thus refuse to be illustrated as a sect of Islam. She is presently researching on Shaymaran, as the Mother Goddess of Kurdistan and decolonization of this Kurdish myth at Harvard University.

Lushanya Echeverria, EdD, is a spiritual leader, teacher, storyteller, writer, and motivational speaker. She specializes in Indigenous storytelling to address childhood onset trauma, psychological effects of trauma stewardship, and women's leadership development. Dr. Echeverria is a graduate of Mary Lou Fulton's Teacher College at Arizona State University, and a field researcher specializing in organizational development to cultivate cultures of connection using Indigenous practice and pedagogy. Dr. Echeverria is the director of educational programming for Kunsi Keya Tamakoce, a spiritual retreat center sharing the practices, beliefs, and ceremonies of her Lakota heritage. Her spiritual upbringing is in her Lakota heritage and matriarchal-focused ceremonies, including central and south American traditions.

Jaffa Frank is an archetypal mythologist, teacher, writer, and licensed therapist. Dr. Jaffa Frank engages experience, body, and story archetypal to discern the underling significance and deep beauty alive within creation. She cultivates a mythic, embodied, relational understanding of transformation and healing that engages the creative imagination and collective wisdom of myth to mediate meaning-making and build resilience. Dr. Frank holds a PhD from Pacifica Graduate Institute in Interdisciplinary Mythological Studies and Depth Psychology and an MA in Counseling with emphasis in Grief and Trauma from Southwestern College. She has expertise in dreamwork, active imagination, mindfulness, thanatology, shamanic and wilderness-based healing, and interpersonal neurobiology. Dr. Frank teaches courses in altruism and the psychology of consciousness and is a founding faculty member/curriculum developer for the PhD in Visionary Practice and Regenerative Leadership at Southwestern College. Her book, *Eyes of the Gorgon: Endometriosis, Mythic Embodiment, and Freedom*, is available on Amazon. Contact: jvfrank8@gmail.com or jaffavfrankphd.weebly.com

Heide Goettner-Abendroth has published on philosophy of science, and extensively on matriarchal society and culture, and, through her lifelong research on matriarchal societies, has become a founder of Modern

Matriarchal Studies. Her magnum opus: *Matriarchal Societies. Studies on Indigenous Cultures across the Globe,* (New York 2013, Peter Lang) defines scientifically this new field of knowledge and provides a world tour of examples of contemporary matriarchal cultures. In 1986, she founded the "International ACADEMY HAGIA for Matriarchal Studies" in Germany, and since then has been its director. She guided three World Congresses on Matriarchal Studies: 2003 in Luxembourg, 2005 in Texas, USA, and 2011 in Switzerland. In 2012, she received the Saga Award for Contributions to Women's History and Culture from The Association for the Study of Women & Mythology. She has been twice nominated for the Nobel Peace Prize, in 2005 by a Swiss initiative, 2007 by a Finnish initiative (www.goettner-abendroth.de; www.hagia.de).

Hannah Irish, MA, is a doctoral student at Pacifica Graduate Institute in the Mythological Studies program. Her dissertation explores Jesus as an embodied ecofeminist. She holds a BA in both English and theater, and an MA in mythological studies with an emphasis in depth psychology. As well as a student, she is a freelance editor, and is also slowly building a business as a personal development coach. Additionally, she is on the board of directors for Fernweh Collective, a cultural education non-profit. Hannah is passionate about storytelling, feminism, social justice, interfaith spirituality, and re-mythologizing Christianity to better serve the twenty-first-century American Psyche. She loves hiking, coffee, the Oregon coast, wine, reading, sharing good food and stories with friends and family, and traveling whenever possible.

Lisa Ransom Lubarr is coordinator for the Max Planck-Harvard Research Center for the Archaeoscience of the Ancient Mediterranean. She is a classically trained artist, with an MFA in Painting (Boston University) and a BA in Fine Arts (Amherst College). She has spent the last decade researching the religions and symbols of the ancient world for a historical novel which she is also illustrating; her focus has been on female philosophers and theurgists spanning from Egypt to Greece and beyond. She is also creating a series of mythologically-inspired paintings: visual metaphors for our highest possibilities as women. Her further studies include female librarians and scholars of 10th century Al-Andalus and the medieval Islamic world. She is currently pursuing a master's degree in religion, centered on archaic traditions and the divine feminine. Her current research includes the relationship in the ancient Mediterranean of women, flowers, and the afterlife.

Karen Nelson Villanueva, PhD, MPA is a practicing Tibetan Vajyarana Buddhist and a member of the Tse Chen Ling Center for Tibetan Buddhist Studies. Additionally, Karen has wide-ranging experience as a hospice and hospital chaplain. She has a PhD in Philosophy and Religion specializing in Women's Spirituality from the California Institute for Integral Studies, a Master's degree in Culture and Spirituality from Holy Names University, a Master of Public Administration specializing in Organizational Management from George Washington University, and a Bachelor of Arts degree in Psychology from the University of Michigan – Ann Arbor. Karen's interests include the use of mantra as a healing modality to overcome fear, writing, academic conferences, and international travel.

Vandana Shiva Besides being a physicist, ecologist, activist, editor and author of numerous books, Dr. Vandana Shiva is a tireless defender of the environment. She is the founder of Navdanya, a movement for biodiversity conservation and farmers' rights. She is also the founder and director of the Research Foundation for Science, Technology and Natural Resource Policy. Intellectual property rights, biotechnology, bioethics and genetic engineering are among many fields where she has contributed intellectually and through activist campaigns. She fights for changes in the practice and paradigms of agriculture and food: "I don't want to live in a world where five giant companies control our health and our food."

Mariam Irene Tazi-Preve was born in Innsbruck, Austria. I am teaching at the University of Central Florida; before that at the University of New Orleans and University of Vienna. My own biography and the birth of my son led me to research the subject of motherhood, which would determine my entire body of scientific work. Thus my areas of research are: Politics and Reproduction, Political/Feminist Theory, Theory of Civilization, the European Welfare State. I am the author, coauthor, editor of several books and numerous scientific articles. Among them are *Motherhood in Patriarchy* (2013) and *Fathers Aside* (2007). In 2015 I co-launched Boomerang, Journal of Critique on Patriarchy (Austria, USA). My recent book *The End of the Nuclear Family. Capitalism, Love and the State* currently in German and Italian (in 2022 in English) was released in 2017 (2nd ed 2018) and received much public attention. My website is: https://www.mariamtazi-preve.com/english/

Lynne Thomas is a proud Biripi (White pointer shark)/Umbarra (Black duck) Yuin woman and a Yuin-Biripi-Maleema custodian living on the South Coast of New South Wales, Australia. Lynne has represented Aboriginal children in the local schools as an Aboriginal Education Officer working to develop Aboriginal perspectives into the school's curriculum while working with students and families from the community. She has held government has roles of a Field Officer, Female Aboriginal Cultural Heritage Officer, Discovery Ranger, threatened species Officer in Koalas and Potoroo recovery programs, and firefighter. Lynne's mother greatly influenced her thinking, and for Lynne a deep respect for the environment is an important process of her responsibilities through teaching. Lynne re-teaches significant places of knowledge, such as the sacred mountains of Gulaga (Mother), and shares knowledge through guided walks into other Aboriginal sites re-enforcing cultural heritage, and sustainability. Her educational teachings in the outdoors, respecting Mother earth, were taught to her by her father Guboo Ted Thomas Yuin Tribal Elder, 1909 - 2003, her mother Anne Thomas, and woman Elders of the past.

Genevieve Vaughan (b.1939) has lived between Texas and Italy most of her life. She has three daughters and two grandchildren. Genevieve founded the all-women multicultural Foundation for a Compassionate Society 1988 – 2005 in Austin, Texas, the International Feminists for a Gift Economy network 2001-ongoing and the Temple of Sekhmet in Cactus Springs Nevada (1992-ongoing). She is the author of *For-Giving*(1997*), Homo Donans* (2008*), The Gift in the Heart of Language*(2015) and the editor of *Il Dono/ the Gift* (2004), *Women and the Gift Economy(*2007), and *The Maternal Roots of the Gift Economy* (2018). An Issue of the *Canadian Women's Studies Journal*: Vol. 34, *Feminist Gift Economy: A Maternalist Alternative to Patriarchy and Capitalism* appeared in 2020 and a festschrift - a book of articles by her colleagues *Mothering, Gift and Revolution: Honoring Genevieve Vaughan's Life Work* was published in 2021. Throughout 2021 and ongoing the International Feminists for a Gift Economy have been holding free biweekly salons presenting various aspects of the maternal gift economy in daily life, in activism and in conscious practice. Register for these and see the archive at www.maternalgifteconomymovement.org. See also www.gift-economy.com.

ASWM Proceedings Editor Biographical Notes

Editors, as well as authors, bring their perspectives into the work that they do. Our locations have shaped our choices and our framing as we worked on this volume. Below are short biographical statements of the four women who worked to put this book together.

Simone Clunie is an artist and independent scholar with research interests in feminism, the visual arts, goddess scholarship and popular culture.

Denise Mitten, PhD, globally recognized for her innovative scholarship in environmental and adventure pedagogy, ethics, and gender, advocates and writes about caring and compassionate leadership. Professor Mitten (emerita) highlights social, emotional, and spiritual safety in group dynamics, first working with women recovering from abuse in the early 1980s. A widely experienced international adventure guide, from SCUBA to mountaineering (Swiss Alps, Himalayas, and USA, including Denali), Professor Mitten has developed outdoor programs to strengthen bonding between parents/caregivers and children, a leadership program for women felons, and an award-winning leadership training and apprenticing program for women, opening the door to outdoor leadership to many women. A recent book is *Health and natural landscapes: Concepts and applications,* Cabi Press. Much of her theoretical grounding was influenced by being a mother to her adult child, Lauren.

Mary Jo Neitz is Professor Emerita at the University of Missouri in Columbia. She is a founding member of the MU Department of Women's and Gender Studies and holds a PhD in sociology from the University of Chicago. She taught feminist theories and methodologies to graduate and undergraduate students. She studies religious practices and experiences in a variety of settings, primarily in the US. She currently serves as the United States representative on the governing council of the International Society for the Sociology of Religion. She serves on the Board of the Association for the Study of Women and Mythology. She lives with two young cats in beautiful Boone County, just a few miles from the Missouri River, and she celebrates native plants inside and outside of her gardens.

Sid Reger, EdD, received her doctorate in adult education from Indiana University. She is an artist, educator, and independent scholar whose passions are prehistoric arts, matrifocal cultures, and mythology of and for women. Growing up in the West Virginia hills inspired her lifelong interests in archaeology, Appalachian culture, and ecological justice. Now semi-retired, she still teaches widely, relating these topics to women's spiritual journeys. She is co-founder, with the late Patricia Monaghan, of the Association for the Study of Women and Mythology, and currently serves as its president. She lives in western Pennsylvania with two sentient felines.